JANUSZ TOMASIK

THERAPY OF SCHIZOPHRENIA ON THE SPIRITUAL WAY

Warsaw 2022

Book edited by the own sources of the author

On the front page
drawing «Schizophrenia» by Andrzej Zbigniew Rządkowski

Composition of the text
"Radon" Radosław Kierełowicz vel Kieryłowicz

ISBN 978-83-930467-3-7

CONTENTS

The billows swell, the winds are high,
Clouds overcast my wintry sky;
Out of the depths to thee I call,-
My fears are great, my strength is small.

O Lord, the pilot's part perform,
And guard and guide me through the storm,
Defend me from each threatening ill,
Control the waves, - say, "Peace, be still."

Amidst the roaring of the see
My soul still hangs her hope on thee;
Thy constant love, thy faithful care,
Is all that saves me from despair.

Dangers of every shape and name
Attend the followers of the Lamb,
Who leave the world's deceitful shore,
And leave it to return no more.

Thought tempest-toss'd and half a wreck,
My Saviour through the floods I seek;
Let neither winds nor stormy main
Force back my shatter'd bark again.

CHAPTER 1

INTRODUCTION

In the Holy Gospel according to Mark, there is a description of a man who lived behind the lake and was possessed by the devil - *This man lived in the tombs, and no one could bind him anymore, not even with a chain. For he had often been chained hand and foot, but he tore the chains apart and broke the irons on his feet. No one was strong enouht to subdue him. Night and day among the tombs and in the hills, he would cry out and cut himself with stones.* (Mark 5:3-5). (NIV) Matthew writes about the two possessed: *two demon-possessed man coming from the tombs met him. They were so violent that no one could pass that way.* (Matthew 8:28). (NIV)

This is a description of schizophrenia, a terrible illness, which is a symbol of the worst thing that can happen to a man in a spiritual and intellectual life.

The fact that this description can be found in the Holy Gospel shows (and I will try to prove this), that for sanity, beside a medical science, **the science of the theology of internal life is also necessary.** Schizophrenia is healed by way of unification with God – at the one of the following stages of it.

Stages of this unification are described by the theology of internal life. The aim of this theology is to lead a man to a union with God to spiritual perfection which results from the observation of commandments of God.

How the spirituality of the ill person looks against this background? The French translation of the phrase 'no man now could bind him' reads *personne ne pouvait lui maîtiser*, where the last word is derived from the word *maître* – a master, sovereign, teacher). It means that nobody could make the ill man acknowledge somebody as his master, sovereign, teacher – as the first and most important person in his life. **The healing will come when the ill person will admit such person in God.** Alas, the traits such as exuberant independence, savagery, as well as solitude and isolation are the characteristic spiritual symptoms of this illness.

This world seems not to be created for the person with schizophrenia. It paralyses them by a brutal struggle for survival and by a spiritual falseness which s/he can feel immediately. With their mental and spiritual delicacy and subtleness, and trying to lead their life in truth by observation of ideals, the future sufferer is very quickly thrown out on a margin of life. Immersed in their problems, s/he thinks that normal, current affairs are banal, strange, and do not concern them. S/he is as if absent, withdrawn.

But neither is s/he a man from other world. In this world s/he is imprisoned by a huge feeling, or by a blessing, which make it impossible to exit from it - this also makes the spiritual progress impossible. **The ill person is suspended between the two worlds.** S/he has not developed fully upper spiritual powers (will and intellect). Their will is hobbled, emotions dominate the intellect. Their lower spiritual powers are undeveloped and devastated. Memory is crippled and surcharged. Rigidity and lack of naturalness are visible in emotions. In interpersonal contacts – there is embarrassment. Body is also rigid. This is a reason why the movements are stiff and mechanical, often quick and violent.

With such limitations, it is difficult to function from the beginning and later it proves quite impossible.

Romanian poet Eminescu writes:

Of the hundreds of tall ships
sailing out of harbour,
how many will end as wrecks,
in the winds, in the waves?

Of all the birds migrating
in flight across the world
how many will drawn
in the waves, in the wind?

The great internal fervour, which the future ill person possesses in the beginning of their life, is quickly exhausted, simply shackled. S/he loses initiative, is not able to undertake any activity. The external difficulties overwhelm them. Slowly, s/he retires from life and becomes only a passive observer of it.

The demands which the future ill person imposes on themselves are extremely high. And, for different reasons s/he is not able to realise them, as a result, s/he starts to hate oneself. Saint Mark writes that the ill person ...*cut himself with stones* (Mark 5:5). (NIV)

This shows a tragic internal tear symbolised by a mountain and a grave. The mountain is the symbol of not fulfilled expectations, while the grave is the symbol of reality in which the schizophrenia sufferer lives.

Because of the **insatiability** the ill person will never express the words from Psalm 131:

My heart is not proud, Lord, my eyes are not haughty;
I do not concern myself with great matters or things too
wonderful for me.
But I have calmed and quieted myself,
I am like a weaned child with its mother; like a weaned child
I am content.

(NIV)

In the depth of spirituality s/he dreams of this, but mysterious power pushes them to activity. S/he is doomed to activity.

Additionally, a very strong spiritual injury which s/he received in the early beginning of their life doesn't allow them to integrate themselves. S/he resembles Odysseus, who against their own will sailed on exile and couldn't go back to their homeland, s/he couldn't find it even though s/he wanted it very much.

Besides the break after the original sin, which touched everybody, the ill person has their own internal break. S/he struggles not only with the world, but also with oneself, which is not a destiny of a healthy person. The disintegration goes even deeper, such a person closes in to a catastrophe, and very often is not conscious of it. **The unquietness**, which is a motor of their activity, which doesn't allow them to stop, to relax, to reflect, but leads them to a senseless whirl of activity is another characteristic symptom of the onset of this illness.

Generally, the feeling of falling short of the expectations towards life is expressed in the quotation from Scott-Fitzgerald – *Gatsby believed in the green light, the orgastic future that year by year recedes before us. It eluded us then, but that's no matter – tomorrow we will run faster, stretch out our arms farther...And one fine morning...*

Sometimes the future sufferer strives to overcome this deep disintegration by embarking upon a great endeavour.

However, as usually it does not succeed – as it cannot succeed – instead of affirmation of the self-worth – the bitterness of defeat appears which deepens the hate to oneself. The contents which have accumulated in the emotional memory for a long time lead to a moment when "something has finished", "something has gone," "Nothing is like before," "life has stopped," "has burned out".

O'Neill adds: *None of us can help the things life has done to us. They're done before you realize it, and once they're done they make you do other things until at last everything comes between you and what you'd like to be, and you've lost your true self forever.*[*]

And at this moment the illness explodes. From this moment, we can talk about schizophrenia – earlier it was only a schizoid trait. The machinery by which a man perceives the world fails. Because of this, a contact with the world is broken. Often, further functioning is not possible. It can be accompanied by the entrance of terrible spiritual pain to the consciousness which causes a quick and great exhaustion. All barriers of defence are broken and if such a man does not receive a quick help, s/he can take their life.

Why is light given to those in misery,
and life to the bitter of soul,
to those who long for death that does not come,
who search for it more than for hidden treasure, (Job 3: 20-21) (NIV)

---

[*] Eugene O'Neil play «Long day's journey into the night» from Complete plays published by © The Library of America

A person who survived this experience comes back to these events for many years. S/he is imprisoned by these events.

Emotions and feelings of the future ill person are usually great and violent. This results from the injury which had been suffered in this sphere.

The ill person who is often as if absent and withdrawn can provoke a violent attack not appropriate to the situation. S/he can't put the matters and problems in the proper perspective. S/he confuses fundamental matters with minor problems, and magnifies the latter. S/he wants to impose such values on others and s/he can be very arduous in this behaviour. It is very difficult to anticipate their reactions and therefore, s/he is very difficult to their superiors. In the long term s/he is not able to lead anybody nor to bring anybody up, because s/he lacks the global perspective. Their rhythms are heavily distorted, including the work and rest rhythms.

Evangelist Matthew writes that – *two demon-possessed man coming from the tombs met him. They were so violent that no one could pass that way.* (Matthew 8:28). (NIV)

Hence, the questions arise about the society from which they come from. What was the hierarchy of values, that these people had to go away and live among the graves? Was it possible to reach to the consciousness of this society other than by way of aggression? Now we are touching on the external, social factors of schizophrenia, to search for or to deny the truth in a community life.

The external events enter to the interior of the ill person, severely hurting them. **Their own "self" and the border dividing their own problems from the problems of other people have not been crystallised.** S/he feels strongly all outside problems as relating to them, as problems of their life. Therefore, the society and what happens within it have a great influence on the future ill person. The lack of the proper place in the society and disturbed emotional reception of the reality cause the aggressive reactions.

Simultaneously, s/he has a very deep desire to live in social harmony. But usually it ends up with a total surrender and social withdrawal.

The feelings of the ill person are often grand so they could compensate for spiritual wounds. S/he deludes themselves that such grand feelings exist also outside their consciousness and they will be a treatment for their deep injurie. Here the situation of the man is much worse. With the great need for feelings, the man will not ensure the woman a protection which is so important to her. He will not ensure it, as separated from the world, he hardly holds on to the surface of life. Therefore, men with a schizoid trait often remain alone throughout their lives.

In the case of women who more often find a partner (because they are a passive side), their problems will be connected mostly with the maternity. Women with a schizoid trait are afraid of whether they will handle the difficulties, whether they will be confident as mothers, whether they will give tenderness and affection to the child.

The attempt to live in truth is a trait of a person suffering from schizophrenia. The truth – without retouch, embellishments, mendacity. In the truth proclaimed with a naturalistic brutality, emphasizing even the negative elements. This trait results from a disposition for contemplation – the greatest gift possessed by the schizophrenia sufferer.

However, as a result of the illness, the schizophrenia sufferer moves around the vicious circle from which s/he cannot break. A mountain – a grave, day – night, anger at oneself – anger at other people – they are all border points between which s/he moves around – and outside of which s/he is not able to go out. S/he is trapped by a mysterious power which pushes them down deeper and deeper, isolating them – and does not let them go away from its orbit. And all this takes place in solitude, in a desert far away from society. This distance to other people can be very often a spiritual distance – it is symbolised by a desert – it can also take place in a crowd of people.

The injured heart and the ill emotionality cause also a specific relation with God and religion. The place of the most important relation – relation with God – is occupied by own problems of the ill person and problems of community life. The ill person doesn't see the correlation between the relation with God and their own problems. And because s/he doesn't see it (due to the spiritual injury), s/he doesn't try to change this relation, to improve it. God is perceived as somebody who treated them cruelly, who punishes them all the time, whom s/he ought to be afraid of, and who is dangerous – but distant.

As a result of the original injury, the ill person has problems with a truthful reflection of reality in their heart and intellect. For this reason, it was schizophrenics who were the authors of many heresies and divisions in the Roman Catholic Church.

There have also been great reformers whom a schizoid trait, obstinacy, (but acting for the good of the Church) helped to fulfil their vocation. There have also been ill people whom the explosion of illness radicalised lives and helped to make the right decisions which leaded them to sanctity.

CHAPTER 2

THE DEVIL*

In the beginning I will present the most important information about an apostate spirit which is the devil. This information will serve for further considerations.

The **devil is a spirit, a person.** As every spirit he has the intellect and the will. He does not have a sensuous cognition – what is sensuous he cognises by the intellect. By his will he is separated from God. Created by God together with the world as a good spirit, he rebelled against him. His will is a total reversal of the will of God. With such reversed will, he has stayed for the eternity – and he will not change this reversal of will. He can't change it, because he has the perfect cognition and he can't change what he has once confirmed to be the truth. **He has his will fixed in evil – and he will never reverse this.** By this reversed will, he rejects the arguments of God which are important for the salvation. He proposes other false values instead.

In the intellect – as to the supernatural cognition – he has totally false opinions. In the natural cognition he takes into consideration some facts, because he can't ignore or falsify them. In the devil's intellect there are many arguments against the Word of God. By this denial the devil is separating people from God, because a man unites with God by the spiritual powers of soul – by the will and cognition. The devil falsifies some of the arguments which are truth in God – not all arguments. His every theory has arguments against the Word of God. Therefore, all these theories can be name as the **anti-word.**

---

* Some information and the logical scheme of the chapter is derived from a logician, Lech Kucharzyk, MA.

In the place most important to the devil – in the summit of the spiritual, where the will and the intellect merge with his nature and where he should be open to God – the devil has a falsified image of the Holy Trinity.

There is no equivalence between God and the devil. God is a creator, the devil is a creature. God also absolutely dominates the devil in cognition. Despite the apostasy, God loves the devil, but his love does not reach the devil – he is closed to it. The devil cannot do anything to God, he only attacks God's beloved creature – a man.

As to the nature, the devil is a creature much more perfect than a man. As to the grace – he is not, because he has lost the grace. **In this world, in this life the devil is the cognitive enemy of man.** It is very important to him that a man will not know the truth. He tries to divert a man from the truth. Hence, the cognition of truth requires from a man to struggle with the devil and many purifications, because often the falseness is a first thought provided by the devil to a man. This is clearly visible in the cognition and its history.

We can cognize the existence of a devil by a power of natural intellect, but to see his complex constructions by which he deceives a man – it is necessary to have the light given by the Holy Ghost – which is given by the grace of God.

Because the devil is a spirit, and his intellect is not dressed in a matter, what he knows – he knows immediately. He has all the cognition at his disposal immediately, and thus he has a great advantage over a man.

A man has to go step by step to obtain knowledge, by reasoning. The devil has greater cognitive capabilities than a man. **However, the devil will not be able to penetrate the entire relationship between God and a man.** He is intellectually too weak. He observes it from outside and draws hypotheses. He knows the weak points of a man and the points where he can hurt a man, the sides from which he can attack and where he expects to succeed. **But the total insight to the spiritual heart of man has he not.** If for example he suggests that a living man is condemned right now and also after his death, he lies, as he can't know anything about this – he wants to deceive a man by instilling such theses in his consciousness.

This **relationship between a man and God is also veiled to other man.** Another man can attempt to get closer to it, but s/he will not cognize it until the end.

There is an old saying that the devil is like a chained dog which will bite when a man approaches him. Considering the matter in terms of the will – it is so. This chain is the spiritual falseness from which the devil can't liberate himself. The devil can't move to the side of truth, he can't move in the area of truth. This is his greatest limit. If a man listens to the theses which are in God, and when lives according to them – he will not move to the side of devil and he will not be in his area. The devil will try to attack such a man, but he will not break his will and he will not enter to such man's will.

In the case of schizophrenia, because of the so-called 'original injury', **the situation of a person is a little bit different** – I will explain it in the following chapters.

The devil is the enemy of God and the enemy of a man – he is a spiritual killer. He wants that a man be eternally condemned like he is. All his acts against a man will serve him to achieve this purpose.

The devil hates God and despises a man.

The aim of a man in this world is to struggle with the devil. **The devil is an ultimate source of the evil.** This source is neither God nor another man who can be only an indirect source. **If there were not spirits rebelling against God, there wouldn't exist the evil in the world.** The devil wants to destroy a man – he will use every opportunity to do this – **the devil will not reverse this hate.** The spirituality contains the struggle against the devil, not the competition with other people. It is not necessary to look for the devil, as he will find everybody who started his way to God. He will find him and he will try to disturb him. A man should know the rules of the spiritual struggle to effectively fight against the devil and to reach out to the truth which the devil tries to efficiently cover, to change, to block.

The devil doesn't know the mercy. If he wants to destroy somebody – he will do this. If he can take advantage of a certain situation – he will do it. In such a situation it is very easy to see his presence and his activity. Because of his will fixed in the evil – he has no dilemma as whether to do the evil or not – he just does it.

The devil gives in only to the force – the force of God or force of his saints.

The domination of devil over the world has been overcome by the passion, death and resurrection of Christ. It has already been made. The aim of a man is to conquer the devil in personal and social life on the model and with the help of Christ. It is only possible to do so with the grace.

The help of Mother of God is of a great importance in this struggle with the devil. A victory over him and taking his place by the immaculate creature of Mother of God situates her and her worshippers in the total opposition to the devil and his followers. Therefore, the Marian spiritual way is very effective in the struggle against the devil. Everybody who wants to start this struggle should undertake this Marian way. A person who has not chosen this way has practically no chance in effective struggle against the devil.

The devil is a cruel and tough enemy. If he succeeds in possessing a man, he can have a great power over him. Because of his higher nature, the devil can dominate not only a single man, but also a group of people or a group of countries.

The devil has the insight of what was in his cognitive range in the history of man. This insight does not penetrate the deepest cognitive and volitional motivations, because they relate to God and the devil cannot penetrate them. But he uses this insight for accusations. He often finds out the old sins, even from the childhood, to accuse a man. He knows the science of Church, but he will never accept it. He can juggle with the quotations from the Bible, but only to hit the opponent.

The devil accuses in all directions. Before God, he accuses a man. Before a man, he accuses God. He accuses a man before another man. As a result of his attacks, a man accuses himself. **The devil is a very perverse intriguer.** He divides, he breaks all possible relations. He divides to set up a fight. He is the reason for many wars and social miseries.

He has some hypotheses about the future of the world and about the future of a single man which may appear to be false, because the devil cannot perceive the deepest regions of human consciousness.

He cannot give happiness, because he doesn't have it. He lost it and he can't offer it to nobody.

In the world of devils there is a hierarchy. All apostate spirits hate themselves, but they keep together due to the hate of God.

God admits the activity of devil in personal and social life. The devil plays a part in God's plan against his own will. He forms the saints, who are the people who renounced him totally.

The science of devil provides some conclusions:

1. **There are people who serve the devil.** A man doesn't sin out of oneself – the source of evil is the devil. But a man is responsible for being tempted by the devil. Everybody who committed a mortal sin goes under the power of devil. Reversal of this situation is a confession or a perfect repentance. Division into those who have lost a grace and depend on the devil - and who are free of him – is clear and sharp. **A border point is a mortal sin.** People who serve the devil are very often free of many problems which are faced by people who struggle against him. They depend on the devil, they fulfil nearly all lusts which the devil provides them. Moreover, their "good acts" after a mortal sin have no value, because it would be a proof that somebody can do a good act without God and without reconciliation with Him. These people ar deceived, they think that they are do good. They also does not have a cognition that unifies them with God.

2. **The devil will act until the end of the world.** The apostasy will also exist until the end of the world. It can be pushed on the margin, but it will always exist. The dreams about the existence of the world without the evil and without the devil are utopian.

    The struggle against the devil is not the aim in itself. The devil is a real obstacle on the way to unification with God. He is a hostile power which appears when a man tries to unify with God. The devil tempts, the devil attacks, the devil introduces a false cognition. He touches the will and the intellect, emotions and feelings - and through them he also touches a human body. Hence, everyone who started the way to God must struggle with the devil. **Such are spiritual conditions of life in this world and they will not change.** There is no simple relationship between God and a man, but there is an attempt to disturb this relation by the devil.

3. **It is no possible to resolve a problem of schizophrenia without touching upon the problem of devil.** The ill person in the beginning of their life (or sometimes later) is attacked by the devil. I call this attack "the original injury". It happened against the will of a person, it broke all existing barriers, and took place when the barriers had not yet functioned. Against their will s/he was dragged into the area of devil's activity. It distorted the perspective – the devil and his acts will be more visible in their personal life and in the environment than the activity of God. To repeat to such man that God loves them will be not enough. Such person should be acquainted with the rules of the spiritual struggle which s/he will be forced to carry on during the major part of their life.

4. **Schizophrenia is the illness where the healing of its spiritual side can take only place in the religious way.** To see the activity of devil in your own life and to struggle with him – **a grace is necessary.** Furthermore, the suffering is so great and unbearable that without understanding the learning about the cross – the ill man is doomed to a total failure.

The way to God is also the way which can relieve you from the power of devil. If the ill person does not undertake it, s/he will never be fully healed. The full perspective requires to take under consideration your own person, other people, the devil and God. These relationships are totally destroyed or not developed during the illness. They may be restored with the help of God's grace in a man and by own effort of a man. Taking medicines, although they help with this illness, will not restore the correct relationships between people.

The truth liberates from schizophrenia. It is construed without spiritual errors by the Roman Catholic Church. Other churches have smaller or greater errors in their comprehension. Proportionally to the number of negated dogmas, the power of Holy Ghost is limited. Other churches do not have the theology of internal life on the sufficient level to resolve the problem of schizophrenia.

CHAPTER 3

THE ORIGINAL INJURY
AND A SCHIZOID TRAIT
AS A CONSEQUENCE OF IT

The original injury is, as named by me, a very strong movement of sensitivity of a spiritual nature which has touched so strongly the sphere of emotions and feelings and has been so permanently recorded in the emotional memory that very early in life by starting the spiritual disintegration it deformed and blocked the emotional development, and later influenced the will and intellect.

By the original injury, the evil spirit instilled himself in the emotions or feelings of a person to such an extent that **they have stopped to react freely.** After that, the so injured emotions and feelings have distorted the perceived reality and have limited the cognition. This all have caused the number of consequences, the most important of which is the lost balance between the will and emotions and feelings, which after years leads to the explosion of the illness.

Thus, the emotion which was instilled by the evil spirit in the whole system was the original injury. It is also important to underline its spiritual character, because this spiritual presence causes later the disintegration. Another problem is a question whether the evil spirit instilled himself permanently, or he has only left his mark which has resulted in consequences later.

An extremely strong emotion with a great spiritual element which was the original injury will cause in the future the **blocking of emotions and of the spiritual development.** The evil spirit by a violent attack instilled himself in the emotional memory. The future ill person was not able to remove this spirit from his memory, because he had no spiritual power to do it, he was not spiritually well developed, he did not know how to do it (and it is not possible to do it by own efforts).

After the original injury emotions and feelings will not be act freely. Their proper functions can be restored after a separation from the spirit, which caused the original injury. It is often a complicated task to be performed for many years.

The question arises about when the original injury has happened, as its first symptoms are visible in the age of 5-7 years. The answer in many publications is that it happens in the first weeks after the birth, in the early childhood.

The answer to this question is very difficult, because the moment when it happened can be recognised after years, when during the therapy one analyses the quality and nature of memory contents. This excessive accumulation of spiritual contents has its beginning.

There are certain duties towards the children ensuring the protection of their emotional and spiritual development. Prophet Ezekiel writes about a symbolic non-fulfilment of these duties. *On the day you were born your cord was not cut, nor were you washed with water to make you clean, nor were you rubbed with salt or wrapped in cloths. No one looked on you with pity or had compassion enough to do any of this things for you. Rather, you were thrown out into the open field, for on the day you were born you were despised.* (Ezekiel 16:4-5). (NIV)

The events which could cause the original injury are the absence of a mother (her presence is very important up to 3rd year of life), the rude or cruel behaviour of a mother or a father, the suicide of one of the parents, excitation of sexual organs of a child and other drastic situations.

In all these cases it is easy to see the evil spirit which acts through other people or events and it is easy to find these events in the history of life. However, there are many cases where the external event does not exist, or it is very difficult to find it, but the original injury had taken place.

In this book I will present the thesis that if a mother of the ill person has a schizoid trait, the original injury could have taken place in the mother's womb.

A lot of people suffering from schizophrenia have a peculiar re-lationship with their mother – the relationship of not fulfilled in mother's love and a lack of spiritual separation from a mother. If a mother possesses a schizoid trait, and a baby has a personality similar to the mother, the child can be spiritually injured by the mother. The baby can be injured only by staying near the mother's spirituality. If the baby has a personality of a healthy father, the evil spirit will be not able to do anything to him/her, as s/he will have no common points with her personality.

A person injured in the mother's womb will never be able to feel her closeness. The spirit will enter between this person and their mother. Such person will have a resentment towards their mother, even if the mother has taken good care in their raising. Regret, a feeling of non-fulfilment in mutual love, the aggression against the mother and a simultaneous feeling that the mother dominates. Such person will be so unified with their mother that the changes in the mental state of the mother will result in the changes in their own mental state – and the other way round. But their contact with the mother will only relate to a negative aspect. Such person will never notice the natural gifts which they inherited after their mother such as beauty, strength, intelligence, intellectual capac-ities. Such person will never be grateful to the mother for these gifts, and the permanent resentment can be a source of suffering for the mother through the rest of her life.

After the original injury, the person's **emotionality is damaged.** This has many consequences.
1. Damaged emotionality **makes cognition more difficult.** The in-jured person has problems with cognition and with the correct interpretation of reality. Emotionality should influence a sen-sual cognition, whereas the cognition should modify the emo-tionality. This mechanism does not exist in schizophrenia. The future sufferer does not acquire emotional experience. Many kinds of emotional behaviours could not form in him. What is more, he does not perceive correctly many emotions and he does not understand them. He is also not able to reflect on his own emotions.

2. Emotions of a person after the original injury **cannot develop to a full form of expression nor change it over time.** Because of their merging on the spiritual level, emotions have to process certain limited (partially or totally) reactions. A form of expression of emotions by the schizophrenia sufferer is limited and it does not change even during the extraordinary experiences.

   The future sufferer does not control his emotions. One can compare it to a operation of a car which passes all road obstacles at the same low gear. Later in his life one can observe the emotional hardness which he is not able to get rid of.

3. Emotions are to separate the reaction of person from the impulse. After the injury, because of the merging on the spiritual level, this separation does not work. As a result of this and progressing spiritual disintegration the future ill person **does not acquire the emotional distance** to the events which happen around them. Almost every event touches them directly. S/he feels trapped by the external events. S/he mainly perceives negative events and emotions.

4. There is **no change in the emotionality** of the future sufferer. For a moment this emotionality can be moved by the extreme stimuli, but **all comes back to the old autistic scheme.**

5. The original injury **has also blocked a spiritual development.** Because of this, **the sphere of spiritual problems is all the time the same.** The same problems are accompanied by the same emotions and the same manner of their expression.

The original injury touches also the sphere of **affection.** It has a spiritual nature – it is caused by a spirit. A spirit inflicts the injury in the affection which is impossible to be compensated in the future life. This injury **causes the isolation, paralyses by anxiety, pain and tensions – deforms innate love by giving it a nature of desire.** The need for innate love is over-exaggerated, it may not be satisfied, satiated. This spiritual injury in the beginning of adult life elevates the scope of spiritual problems and the sensuality is offered as therapy, resulting in the progressing internal disintegration. Apart from the fact that the feeling may be satisfied only to a limited degree, the injured person looks for this feeling in people who will not give it, even to a small degree. The spirit through the original injury significantly reduced the injured person's cognition. He also isolated such person is such a way that s/he does not see anybody beyond the person chosen. But even here he opened up the abyss not based on anything. It is not exclusiveness, which is a trait of true love, but idealistic, unreal isolation.

Affection is associated with anxiety. Affection causes more pain than joy. And the ill person withdraws from it because of great emotional spiritual tension. Romantic affection with the main thesis about liberation by innate love magnified to monstrous dimensions is an example of the affection after the original injury. Problems related to this kind of affection are shown well by the poems of Lermontov, Goethe. I will present the poem *A little violet stood upon the meadow* by Goethe as an example of affection after the original injury.

A little violet stood upon the meadow,
Lowly, humble, and unknown;
It was a dear little violet.
[There] came a young shepherdess
With a light step and a merry spirit
Along, along,
Along the meadow, and sang.

The beginning of the poem shows the image of oneself possessed by a person after the original injury. It is the image of a solitaire, isolated, not loved, and unknown personality. A shepherdess (the image of a loved person) occupies all space. The one who describes her has seen her once – and immediately has fallen in love in her. The first sight was enough to give his heart to her. He did it without getting to know her better, without longer emotional contact, by idealising her.

Ah! thinks the violet, if I only were
The most beautiful flower in nature,
Ah, only for a little while,
Until the darling had picked me

And pressed me to her bosom until I became faint,
Ah only, ah only
A quarter of an hour long!

The first reaction to such great affection which he was long-ing for is a sense of indignity and comparing yourself to someone much better – and placing yourself as the least important – and observing the next events from this position. This is a typical be-haviour, if he were perfect, he would be entitled to fulfil his own affection. Moreover, to fulfil this great affection, he will look for a sensual person, weaker in the spiritual cognition than he is. He will look for the affection in the place where he will not find it. Because of the original injury he partially abandoned the sensual dimension. He will not find and compensate in the nature some-thing which was by force extracted from the nature. This will only make his disintegration deeper.

Alas! but alas! the maiden came
And paid no heed to the little violet,
She trampled the poor violet.
It drooped and died and yet rejoiced:
And if I must die, yet I die
Through her, through her,
Yet [I die] at her feet.*

He was trampled, because he found himself outside the spiritual perception – he was not seen. Moreover, the person after the orig-inal injury pays a great emotional price for the contact: s/he gets ashamed, confused, nervous – or s/he is excessively bold. S/he dreams about living with somebody – but s/he is afraid of this. The affection causes them a great pain and tension. The greater the affection is, the greater fear, pain and tensions accompany them. As a result, the injured person very often gives up on this feeling, as its emotional cost is too high. Despite a great longing for affec-

---

* Goethe – poem *A little violet stood upon the meadow* translated from Ger-man to English by Sharon Krebs © 2015 by Sharon Krebs – source lieder. net website used by permission

tion, s/he finds some kind of peace, satisfaction in non-fulfilment of it, in withdrawal. A person after the original injury is unlikely to satisfy their affection.

Great wounds inflicted on the future sufferer in the childhood, and which are still inflicted cause certain expectations towards a person whom s/he gives their affection. S/he thinks that there will be somebody who will understand them, who will cure their injuries, who will liberate them from the internal entanglement with love, who will give sense to their life and who will defend them against the evil world. Moreover, this affection should last eternally and with the same huge intensity and with nearly ecstatic tension. And it should never change. In such an idealistic approach the union should be great and pure. Often people after the original injury say that they are alone, because they have not met a person who would love them with such enormous and exclusive love. They have not met them, because such people do not exist. There is only an injured, isolated, degenerated, great feeling which practically cannot be satisfied.

Such affection will cause pain, because the injured person by loving will at the same time touches their injuries. After the original injury this causes suffering. It will accompany the affection and additionally it will be recorded in the emotional memory.

The future sufferer very often will not know how to express such great affection – and s/he is afraid of it. S/he will wait until somebody will understand their intentions – s/he is afraid of a sentimental defeat. S/he will not propose, because s/he has a feeling that s/he will not fulfil the expectations of the other person. S/he has such a low self-esteem or even indignity that very often s/he withdraws from involvement. Often s/he hesitates to start a life together. Finally, s/he feels better with unfulfilled affection.

S/he will stay alone confined in the unfulfilled affection, surprised that the time to undertake a common life has passed. S/he will cultivate this unfulfilled affection, s/he will not permit to be deprived of it. This feeling will imprison them for a long time. It will stop their spiritual development. S/he will recognise a lack family as their biggest failure. S/he will start to feel resentment towards God that their life is so unsuccessful as compared to other people. The explosion of illness will put their dreams about great affection in the another perspective. O'Neill noticed this – *The man was dead and he has had to kill the thing he loved.*[**]

It is an extremely painful and difficult experience. The fundamental questions will return. Affection, which played the major role, will become less important.

The trait of a schizophrenic sentimentality, the result of the original injury is **the desire. It is not a result of the original sin, but of the original injury.** During the injury devil damages all or part of the centre of sentimentality, takes it under his possession. He also merges it with the spiritual heart where he is also partly present. **Overloaded emotional memory also causes great tensions.** The result of all of this is that in the person after the original injury **"I love" will be merged with "I desire" – against the will.**

How much of it will be "I love" and how much "I desire", it depends on the idealistic attitude. But this "I desire" will be present always. If it is only "I desire", all that I have written before about affection is not valid. Such attitude will be unhappiness for the ill person, a source of sins committed with somebody else or by oneself, by which such person is caught and kept by the evil spirit.

After the original sin the will has no influence on emotions and affection. They liberated from the power of will – and they are not subordinate to it. The external world influences them independently of the will. The existence of such double system after the original sin is kind of a fracture in a man.

Using a comparison of Saint Teresa, one can compare the will to the queen and emotions and affection to servants. Generally, the will and the emotions function independently, but also freely. However, after the original injury it is different. **Emotions and affection lose their spiritual freedom.** By contact with the evil spirit they become hobbled or possessed. After this influence of the external spiritual power leads to **the hobbling of the will. Emotions and affection start to determine the manner of perception**

[**] Eugene O'Neil play "Long day's journey into the night" from Complete plays published by © The Library of America

of the reality. The will which accepted or denied the reality – now has nothing to say. Emotions and affection determine the perception of reality, but they do not do it freely – they are sensitive to a spiritual presence which entered during the original injury. They are sensitive to his appearance from outside. They will not perceive freely the reality associated with this spirit. Moreover, the entire manner of perception (by the partly hobbled will), gives limited and partly false cognition which is difficult to be ordered. **It causes cognitive confusion and the false image of surrounding and of oneself.** This reversed and incomplete image of the reality will be recorded in the emotional memory and will deform later the cognition. As another effect of the original injury it will have a lot of major consequences.

The first one is the impossibility of the internal integration. The result of this gradual disintegration is almost total perturbation in life. Over time such person will not find their identity. S/he will not see the meaning of their life.

With the deepening disintegration, such person will be looking for the answers to fundamental questions. S/he must raise these questions and find the answers to them to give meaning to their life which is meaningless. Healthy people rarely raise such questions – or they avoid them. The answers to fundamental questions are not necessary for them.

As a result of the disintegration, the person after the original injury will focus only on his/her own internal problems.

Sometimes such person will try to overcome the disintegration by making great internal or external effort, but experiences which will accompany this effort will isolate such person even more.

The disintegration introduces **perfection, tendency to compete, to constantly compare yourself to other people, to activity.** It happens so, because the disintegration doesn't allow to leave the sphere of senses which is the lowest sphere of human life. As a result of disintegration a person will not be ready to undertake her vocation – to live in the family, to work, to a perform in public – such person will wait until s/he is perfect, s/he will wait for the ideal situations. Because of the disintegration s/he has problems in gaining life experience, and makes the same mistakes all the time. S/he is hesitant in their opinions. Such person will not divide the problems into principles and details – problems of minor and major importance. S/he will be chaotic in thinking and in the activity. Almost every effort of such person can be called "heroic," because it will require from him/her a maximal disposition – to almost exceed his/her emotional capacities.

Such person will try to overcome the disintegration – to prove to themselves and other people that s/he is not disintegrated. Very often all activities of such person are oriented at overcoming the disintegration, but not at leading a normal life. S/he will be always occupied by something, possessed by the idea – as if absent. S/he can practice extreme sports, look for the danger and to try to overcome it – to confirm their own value, and to cope with the anxiety resulting from the disintegration. Such person lacks self-esteem and spiritual identity, s/he must confirm it all the time in external situations. This inclination to confirm themselves, to prove themselves in every situation will be their characteristic trait. Also the inclination to great risk, to the "win or lose" perspective. She perceives regular life and its typical obligations as banal, boring – and s/he can ignore people who lead such life.

But s/he will notice that they have – despite trivial cognition – the sort of internal harmony which s/he lacks. S/he will also notice that even with their great efforts s/he is not able to cure this perplexity which is getting deeper and deeper.

A second result of the injury is **the multiple and anxious perception of the reality**. Every next injury, even much weaker, is perceived equally strong. Every mental burden will not be a training factor, but a destroying factor. Also every next injury will be added to the first and will accumulate in the emotional memory. With such perception, soon normal problems will grow to extraordinary dramas and greater difficulties to a catastrophe. Furthermore, there is no scale to express what happens. After the exhaustion of certain amount of burdens, such person doesn't acquire the immunity, but s/he falls into the illness.

The disintegration starts to instil **the anxiety and anxious perception in life.** The future ill has his/her emotional and spiritual development blocked, but encounters more and more difficult situation in his/her life. At first s/he will cope with them by engaging all physical and mental powers. Later – these situations will overcome him/her or s/he will cope with them with such great mental cost, that s/he will recognise them as a failure and s/he will see that it is impossible to handle them. S/he will focus on avoiding such situations but not on normal life. This will be also a characteristic trait of their behaviour.

By avoiding difficulties, s/he will subject his/her life to external situations. S/he will be absolutely convinced that s/he has no influence on their own life. If one adds to this a very strong perception of behaviour of other people – this all together will cause **the hate to the surrounding world.**

The hits of the devil through other people instil the **anxiety** into a disintegrated mentality. It appears relatively early and suddenly. A 12-19 year-old person starts to be afraid to stay alone at home, to go to a neighbouring street, to go to a sport field of a district club. S/he will start to be afraid, s/he will start to feel strange. In the places which s/he has known well, in which s/he has felt well before, in which s/he has not paid attention to their mood.

The next consequence of the injury is **that problems which concern such person and those which concern other people – s/he will take like his/her own.** It happens as a result of gradual merging with the spiritual reality which is a background to the surrounding. The problems of other people will cause pain, the ill person will worry about them. S/he will experience their problems deeply. S/he will be paralysed by the fact that somebody was attacked, stabbed or thrown out of the train. As a 12-year old child a person after the original injury will experience home problems such as lack of money, failures at work as adults. S/he will take on her shoulders others' problems and s/he will not be able to bear this burden.

Moreover, by this spiritual merge their perspective will be **to see only the evil.** By the hit of the devil, they will be partly united with the devil. They will only see his activity in the world which will be perceived as evil. It will be very difficult to step out of the perspective of seeing only the evil things. They will see evil everywhere. They will talk to everybody about it. They will be a harbinger of bad news. By complaining, permanent unhappiness and anxiety, they will discourage everyone to themselves. The consequences of such perspective will be also no faith in any activity or the lost will to live.

Other consequences of the original injury which can be seen later in life are **a failure to accept their own lives or hate to themselves.** Unsuccessful attempts to make the internal integration, great tensions present in such life will start **the discord between the image of themselves – the ideal one and the real one.**

The hate to themselves can result also from the ability to contemplate. **A person with such ability possess in themselves the perfect image of the reality** in which they live. And the perfect image of oneself too. It is the image unconsciously read from God. The image of social relations and environment in which such persons live as well as their own lives are compared to this ideal image.

The future schizophrenia sufferer strives to the image of oneself which is not real and not true. They should be a physical, intellectual and spiritual giant. Somebody who possesses all possible gifts of nature and grace. Only such a person could manage in the world surrounding such disintegrated personality. Therefore, they often devote their whole lives to make this perfect image of themselves come true.

The hate to oneself is instilled by the devil by the blows given through other people. In scoff, humiliation, mockery, verbal aggression are directed to people with disintegrated psychic, they will very quickly instil in them the hate to themselves.

This hate can have different forms. A person with such trait is cruel, tough, severe to oneself, s/he can humiliate themselves. They will permanently train, exercise themselves. They can also make these acts very regular and be proud of this. They can be overworked. Work exceeding one's limits can be the unconscious form of overburdening oneself. In the spirituality they often like hard ascetic exercises and great penance.

The acts of self-torture, taking place before the explosion of the illness can serve as the examples of hate to oneself.

The feeling of indignity is associated with hate to oneself. The person after the injury will put God or another person on a great pedestal – impossible to reach. But to oneself, such person feels the indignity. They will create a huge distance to another person and they will be not able to reduce this distance. Humiliating oneself, exaggerated complaisance to great expansiveness, exaggerated backing down, exaggerated emphasizing of the merits of others – these are also the symptoms of indignity.

Sometimes such person demands such attitude from other people and with such demands they can cause the scruples in other people.

The future ill doesn't want the evil world – s/he doesn't accept it. They introduce the image of the ideal world, and they live with this idealising image. The world of truth, beauty, goodness, nobility, the world of great ideals. But here they make some mistakes. They assume that they are good (or they want to be) – as opposite to other people who are evil.

They accept without reflection, in a faulty way, the assumption read from God. And this makes them proud and cause that they judge people and start to distance themselves from them. Because of the original injury they have difficulties starting the spiritual way. They perceive the ideals of truth and goodness and others only in their sensual aspect, therefore, they incomplete picture of them. As a result, they often fight ambitiously for matters not worthy of such great fight.

They look for the truth without God and without His grace – grace which would illuminate them, and which would build them up from inside. **They don't know that the cognition of truth is grace which they can receive from God and they don't know that they will not cognize the truth by their own intellectual forces.** They also don't know that the search for truth involves bearing the cross because the cognitive enemy of man – the devil tries to attack everybody who wants to get closer to the truth. Hence, without illumination and without reinforcement by Holy Ghost the life in truth is not possible. As a result, often after a great and noble beginning – the ill person attacked and ruined by the devil reminds of the smouldering ruins with the rests of ideals.

The feeling of the alienation – of desert on which the future ill person has found themselves against their own will – will accompany them for the rest of life. The great unfulfilled affection, inability to make any moral compromises, pushing out of many areas of life – the problems with oneself due to disintegration will cause that their way of life will be different from the ways of life of other people.

This will be another way. Solitaire, because such person does not have anyone to share this different experience with. The way full of despair, great difficulties, without the visible aim. The way of ridicule, mockery even by the closed ones. Sometimes, as a result of the disintegration the feeling that there is no other way appears, because every way leads to the catastrophe.

As a result of these experiences and a lack of understanding such person isolates themselves, they are pushed on a margin. They will be also spiritually too weak to defend themselves against the more or less false but strong perspective which exists around.

A person after the original injury and with an aptitude to contemplation over time starts to feel that s/he is a person different from others, that their life is more difficult and incomprehensible to others, that they have more obstacles which they deserve. This all creates **resentment toward God.** Shelley noticed this:

Monarch of Gods and Demons, and all Spirits
....regard this Earth
Made multitudinous with thy slaves, whom thou
Requitest for knee-worship, prayer, and praise,
And toil, and hecatombs of broken hearts,
With fear and self-contempt and barren hope.

Ah me! alas, pain, pain ever, for ever!
The crawling glaciers pierce me with the spears
Of their moon-freezing crystals, the bright chains
Eat with their burning cold into my bones.
Heaven's winged hound, polluting from thy lips
His beak in poison not his own, tears up
My heart; and shapeless sights come wandering by,
The ghastly people of the realm of dream,
Mocking me: and the Earthquake-fiends are charged
To wrench the rivets from my quivering wounds.

This resentment can be articulated (like in the poem of Shelley), or denied, but it exists. How great they are one can see in the spiritual way before the union of will, when they inhibit the perception of God's presence, when they create a barrier between God and a man, and it is necessary to eliminate them by active purifications.

In the scale of whole society it is difficult to avoid the cases of the original injury. It is also difficult to confirm that it happened and it have caused negative consequences, as this is visible only after a certain time. Which event have caused the original injury will be seen during the healing process. If it was a blow in the sphere of emotions or feelings, or it was only a great weakness which was used later by the devil. All these events are recorded deeply in the emotional memory. They will be called upon and healed by God. Then it will be possible to say which one has caused the original injury.

It is necessary to guide the disintegrated person well during their life. To minimise the results of disintegration, to avoid a dangerous crisis, and later on the way to God, to remove it to the end. To show a young person the way to God as the only one way of rescue. One must also recognise and overcome thousands of obstacles which a person after the original injury poses against people who will try to guide them in the life.

Unfortunately, the original injury is a kind of internal break, because of the instilling of the spirit in emotions and affection. It is a kind of disposition, which doesn't determine the occurrence of illness. However, it causes much weaker resistance to the influence of the environment, living the reality more internally, less possibilities of using natural gifts. Above all, however, it gives an untrue image of subjectively perceived world. This is a tragedy of a man who ...*was a many-sided mirror, which could distort to many a shape of error, this true fair world of things* (Shelley *Prometheus unbound*). To the original injury one can add **the conditions of life, family relations, spiritual attitude, attacks of devil, environment and society.** This all together determines whether the explosion of the illness happens or not.

CHAPTER 4

EMOTIONAL MEMORY. PICTURES – REASONS AND RESULTS OF THEIR CREATION

French poet Jules Lefèvre-Deumier writes about the emotional memory, what and how it stores: *You are asking what happens with the days which have passed and whether it is the heart of man that serves as their tomb. No, believe me, though it seems that everything dies, nothing really dies. The yesterday still lasts, only we do not see it. Our days which have passed are like the absent people who return but are not lost forever. They have hanged their pictures in our souls as in the sanctuary and when we sleep, when we dream, they often come to speak as in the past and blow the dust covering their portraits. The past still lives under the snow cover of the years. It is the living water that still runs under the shell of ice, the living water that coils like arrows of purple and gold, like bunches of wandering precious stones, like flowers that flee and do not fade, a thousand silent swimmers who are the memories.*

I name the picture to be the closed in time, unchanging contents once stored but still present in the consciousness and emotional memory many years after their real creation, motionless, but as if living their own spiritual life. They will not disappear by themselves and it is not possible to remove them. They are not subject to the process of forgetting. The passed time and problems are held in them.

The existence of pictures means that the ill person has stuck themselves in these remembered places and moments together with the pictures. There is a huge amount of these pictures – there can be hundred thousands of them. The ill person can recreate practically all their life from their memory, image after image.

The pictures have been created as a result of perception of reality made through the spirit which invaded during the original injury. **They are not a real perception of reality** which was different from those included in the image. **Pictures are the reality perceived through the spirit. The future schizophrenia sufferer is not separated from the spirit that invaded them – a lot of emotional experiences have their own spiritual tone.** The events from the past as if still lived in this tone – they live in this spirit.

The pictures show that there have occurred situations which have made such great impression that they have been recorded in the emotional memory. This record is a proof that the emotion was registered and is still kept in the nervous system. **The pictures express recorded parallel emotions and feelings as well as tensions which accompanied them and also a spirit which was present in them.**

In this book I **differentiate emotion from affection.** Emotion is for example anxiety, anger. Affection is something that is felt by people who have fallen in love. I differentiate them because of pictures stored in the emotional memory. **They have different influence on the blockade of limbic system and they are released by other techniques and at another stage.**

Why are these pictures so permanent? Why they cannot be forgotten or removed?

As I has written before these pictures are also composed of the spiritual factor and it was so permanently recorded. It is no possible to remove the image, because it is difficult to remove the spirit which accompanied the emotion and which was recorded together with it. Van Gogh in his letters repeats many times a critical sentence about him told by a certain person. The time stopped at this emotion and in this image. Emotions overloaded beyond the bounds of possibility are not able to perceive and register more – they are not able to perceive more events and pictures which accompanied them. In this subjective perception time has stopped – they are remembered for years – the person can't be liberated from them. Time has really stopped at these events to for such person.

Pictures prevent any spiritual progress, as they do not permit to leave the sphere of senses – they cause the prisoning entrapment in the sphere of senses. Parallel accumulated emotions accompanying the pictures also cause neurological blockades with many side effects such as sleep deprivation, rigidity of body, lack of concentration and vital powers. There is a relationship between accumulated emotions and pictures - when emotions disappear, associated tensions will also disappear. In the therapy this is an important indicator of the healing progress.

The image of the accumulated spirit in the emotional memory changes. Therefore, pictures in life before the illness also change. After difficult but joyful, full of light and hope scenes, the pictures full of pain and melancholy appear. It is visible in the paintings of painters with schizoid trait.

When the illness explodes, it means when the evil spirit invaded the spiritual heart, the ill person seemingly loses the majority of pictures. They will be still stored in the emotional memory, but because of the change of spiritual perspective, the ill person will not be able to find them. They will not be able to use them as before, they will not find support in them as before (even if they hurt them), they will not find their identity, due to a lack of them. It will be difficult for them to find themselves in the new situation.

The real world will burst in violently together with the injuring image perceived through the evil spirit. The painful image deprived of any spiritual colours. The schizophrenia sufferer has never before seen such world.

The explosion of the illness (it means the incident of psychosis) is strictly related to the amount of accumulated pictures. If there are no pictures accumulated for years in the emotional memory – there will be no schizophrenia.

What should be a normal way of an image associated with a certain event?

The image is created as the record of the event. It passes through the memory of the emotion or the affection. It means that it passes through the emotional memory where it stays or erodes over time. However, in the case of the future sufferer the image is created in the consciousness and **moves to the emotional memory**

where it stays – does not move to the deep memory. In order to be moved to the memory, the image must be devoid of the spiritual factor. In the case of the ill person this happens because of the original injury – because of the hypersensitiveness to the spiritual presence. **Such pictures stay in the emotional memory.** After years such memory is like a huge disorganised overloaded storage. Being aware of this, a natural consequence for therapy should be to make order in and liberate the emotional memory. **It means that the accumulated pictures should go further and complete their cycle.**

There is a very strong transmission of what is accumulated in the emotional memory to the body. Rigidity and deformation of body will be in many cases characteristic to this illness. Together with the healing this deformation and rigidity will disappear. The body will return to its previous shape.

How pictures and tensions associated with emotions and feelings affect the body throughout the life is a very interesting open question.

During active purifications **different techniques should be used to release pictures associated with emotions, and different to pictures associated with affection.**

Is it possible to purify the emotional memory?

It is possible, but not by oneself, because of the spiritual factor from which only God can liberate. It depends on Him to what degree and when He will make the purification. In people who want to unify with God, the greater part of the unification will take place at the stage of unification of will. Whereas after the blockade of emotional, sentimental and spiritual development (as during the illness), the emotional and sentimental factor, simultaneously with the activity of God should be purified by the man himself.

The pictures which are the result of the original injury close and imprison the ill person and they do not allow unifying with God. I will name later these purifications **as active purifications.** The liberate the emotional memory from pictures, they are essential to make spiritual progress. When they should be started and how to make them I will explain in one of following chapters.

To recapitulate, the emotional memory contains **the memory of emotions** and **affection**, and this is how they should be named correctly. It is an important difference, because **these memories are differently transmitted to the body, and one can be liberated from them by other techniques and at another spiritual stage.** Each of these memories creates **its own specific net of internal tensions and transmits it to the body.** Only precise liberation from the pictures **with a spiritual factor** and **from these tensions transmitted to the body** by active purifications can liberate the emotional memory and heal schizophrenia.

CHAPTER 5

FAMILY AND SOCIETY AS THE ENVIRONMENT OF THE SCHIZOPHRENIA SUFFERER

The aptitude for contemplation and disintegration after the original injury cause **that maternity may be beyond the possibilities of a woman with a schizoid trait.** Even the decision about conceiving a man who is to live in the unfriendly environment is very difficult for the future mother.

A woman with a schizoid trait as a mother makes many mistakes in the upbringing of her child which deepens the consequences of the original injury. These mistakes are **constant blaming, permanent discontent, coldness and inability to express feelings, emotional absence, lack of consistent rules in upbringing.**

The main reason for that is that the **mother is spiritually united** (but by the evil spirit it means by the negative aspect) **with a child.**

This union later results in **the spiritual dependence**. United people are not free. In the life of the growing child the question – what God wants from me? will be replaced by the question: what my mother will say? This dependence is bilateral. First the dependent parents destroy a child, and later after a certain point – the child is starting to destroy spiritually their parents.

It is very easy to ascertain whether the dependence has taken place during the active purifications. Positive changes in the ill child, for example after the expression of anger, will cause immediately changes in the emotionality of a mother or father (depending on with whom a child was united).

As a consequence of the union, there is constant blaming.

The basic trait of a mother with a schizoid trait is that **she constantly blames her child:** that s/he didn't make a bed, didn't polish the shoes, wash a plate, didn't switch off the light. If the child corrects this, next accusations appear: that s/he didn't take an umbrella although s/he has known that it would rain, that s/he didn't check the timetable and all family must stand at the bus stop etc. There are a lot of such accusations, even tens a day. If we multiply them by a number of days in a year, it will give an unbelievable number of them in total. The schizophrenia sufferer is a person blamed by the closest person whom s/he loves. **Accusations and permanent dissatisfaction** make the child convinced that everything s/he does, s/he does wrong. In the future s/he will apologise for almost every act and ask if s/he didn't hurt anybody.

These accusations will not end, only their negative influence can be reduced when the spiritual separation takes place.

The next trait of a mother is **her emotional absence.** She will not read the school essay of the child, she will not watch a film or play with them. She will not watch sport competitions in which her child takes part. She creates such extreme tensions for example when her child does not wash a spoon that later there is no scale to express real problems. Such mother is not able to create the atmosphere of home – an emotionally warm place where a child returns with pleasure and where they gain energy to fight with external difficulties. Often such child gets emotional rest at school, despite school stress associated with education.

Such mother also **doesn't allow a child to leave.** She doesn't like any changes. She is afraid for the child. She constantly worries about the child. Her child will not gain experience which is necessary for independent life. They will not gain it mostly due to the original injury and progressing disintegration, but in a part due to the overprotective mother. The mountain camps for 30-year-old schizophrenics and their mothers are full of funny situations – "be careful not to twist your leg", "not too fast as you get sweaty," "give me a hand, I will help you to step down" etc.

A mother with a schizoid trait **doesn't have consistent rules for the appraisal of the child's behaviour.** Once it will be unjust reproaches, another time undeserved praises. On the basis of mother's behaviour a child will not crystallise any hierarchy of values. The mother **by her behaviours also provokes moral dilemmas in her child.** A child doesn't know if s/he should be on the side of mother, whom s/he loves by a great insatiable feeling, and whom s/he should defend or it on the side of a person attacked by their mother. The mother with a schizoid trait doesn't see that **if she starts such conflicts – she spiritually attacks her own child.** She thinks about her child all the time, but in their presence she is emotionally cold and absent. Sometimes she loves her child with great affection, but she doesn't express it – she doesn't feel a necessity to express it or she doesn't know how to do it. She wants to raise a child perfectly. But she doesn't do this gently, but strictly, constantly criticizing her child.

In this way she tries to remove the disintegration which her child possesses and which she observes. But by constantly nagging her child, she imposes conditions on the unconditional love felt by the child. By her behaviour she seems to say that if you do this or that – I will love you. In the future the child will transmit such behaviour to their partner, but with awareness that s/he doesn't fulfil the expectations ands/he should deserve love. All mentioned problems are the consequences of the original injury of a child but the unconscious behaviours of a mother can add a great part to the injury.

A father with a schizoid trait is **very strict, sometimes cruel and violent.** He applies inadequately severe punishments. He reproaches, even beats him/her when the child is late or has not done their homework. He demands that all should be done exactly as he wishes – not otherwise. He destroys **emotionality and affection by trying to adapt them to his own emotionality and sentimentality. He wants to control everything** – there is no area of the child's life which is not controlled by the father. His child behaves well (of which he is proud), but s/he is terrorised, anxious and without initiative. **His paternity is a negation of the paternity of God** – paternity full of goodness, gentleness, patience – paternity which does not look out for mistakes. **In the spiritual problems of the child, such father is absent.** Emotional censorship deepens the disintegration. **He interferes even with the form of expression of emotions** which makes it practically impossible to express them.

Saint Paul writes: *Fathers, do not embitter your children, or they will become discouraged.* (Colossians 3:21). (NIV)

A father, as every man, is responsible for conveying ideas. With very strict treatment he can damage the emotional memory and spiritual heart of the child. It happens so, because the father due to the original injury doesn't reflect goodness, gentleness, tenderness of God. These traits should accompany conveying ideas. Apart from the fact that the evil father does not reflect the image of God, he injures the spiritual heart. After the original sin a heart of the child doesn't perceive the image of God, only later the grace of God will evoke this image. But the grace can face difficulties. **With the heart injured by the father, it is difficult to reflect the image of God or this image is distorted.**

Apart from the father, other people are also responsible for conveying of ideas. They can also injure the spiritual heart. These are priests, teachers, thinkers, philosophers, politicians who present the most important idea in the country. They are all responsible for the condition of spiritual heart and emotional memory of citizens. The person of the priest is very important, because a rude priest can add to the injuries deriving from original injury, and by this he distorts the image of God as the source of all paternity. Other people mentioned above can also do this, but to a lesser extent.

Spouses with a schizoid trait are emotionally cold or even frigid towards each other. They are not able to express positive feelings towards each other, for example the joy of return home of a spouse, or because of some family success. In the moments of failures they blame each other. They are brutal with these accusations, they present all possible arguments to attack the other person. In this way, they very quickly destroy the relationship between them, and they are not able to repair it. Because of the original injury, **their emotionality does not change.** They live in the atmosphere of permanent conflict, which is often hidden from the outside world, the atmosphere of hostility, rivalry or revenge, because of unfulfilled expectations.

There is no unity **in the schizophrenic family**. Members of this family are not able to work, rest, talk together. Each of them goes in their own direction. They are tired of themselves. They are not able to open to each other. Despite seemingly appropriateness in their home, there is no atmosphere of mutual friendliness, warmth, understanding, sincerity.

They are also closed towards to environment. They live their own, often selfish life. They don't reciprocate the invitation, they don't try to stay in touch with their environment.

The life in such family deepens the original injury. It creates conflicts between the life in truth and mutual love in the conscience.

To sum up, everyone in such a family (or almost everyone) are united by the apostate spirit which is reprinted in their memory. They are separated by this spirit, deprived of closeness, they are individualists – each of them tries to go their own way. They need affection, they admonish each other (because they have the perfect image of situations), and mutually they hurt each other (as a result of the union), they are not able to open themselves to each other.

If they do not start a therapy, nobody will liberate them from this condition. Often, only a death of one of them causes some changes – partial transformation in emotionality of the other members of family.

Elaborating a subject of **the participation in a social life**, to identify oneself with a society, one need to pose a question – why is it so difficult for a person with a schizoid trait? Why the schizophrenia sufferer is thrown out on a margin of the social life?

The structure of the society is created by **the pyramid of natural gifts.** The one who has greater gifts has a higher place in the pyramid. Climbing to the top of the pyramid is a natural social process. The higher place somebody takes, the better. One should bow to the stronger one, the weaker can be mocked. Natural gifts must be used to gain as much as possible, but not to serve with them. People participating in the pyramid are spiritually prisoned by the attachments, arrangements. They have strong natural wills and with them they push out others – the weaker ones. They are not interested in the problem of truth and searching for the truth. Attached to their natural gifts, they demand from others. There is only one top place and the rest must accept it. There is a great fight waged for this place. All titles in the pyramid are practically distributed.

Since cognition occurs in the spirit, it is even juxtaposed with the spirit – the people from the pyramid can know only as much as the spirit permits them, but it doesn't permit them a lot. **A turning point would be the reversal of the order – from the natural order to the supernatural one.** Because of the original sin not everyone will do this so the pyramid bigger or smaller, this or the other one will always exist.

The instilling of the spirit in the emotional memory and the hobbling of will after the original injury cause that a person is not only disintegrated, but also very united with the environment by this spirit. Every event from environment **is perceived by such person as the event concerning them.** The external world perceived in such a way will touch almost always touch them, but it will also injure, cause pain, impose a great spiritual burden, take hope away. A person with a schizoid trait is also **broken by social sins.**

As a result of the illness, **the person has lost their natural gifts**. They cannot use them. The consequence of destitution, which they went through, is that such a person loses the natural hierarchy of values. This **destitution** has also liberated them from the competition at the level of natural gifts. It also moved them away from people climbing up the pyramid.

This is a situation where the ill person is united through the spirit with the pyramid, in a negative aspect its existence touches them, and at the same time they are separated, because they do not want (due to destitution) and cannot (due to a loss of gifts) climb up this pyramid. And they remain torn between desires and capabilities.

The Gospel according to Mark (Mark 5:1-20) has a description of society. It could be characterised, but what is interesting is that the spirit with whom inhabitants lived in symbiosis (and who wanted Jesus to leave its borders) possessed one of them – prevented his normal life. It was probably the only person who resisted against this spirit in this society.

Another problems making it difficult to live in society are – **the subtlety in the will and the aspiration to live in truth.**

The subtlety and gentleness in the will are related with the aptitude for contemplation. The ill person recalls: *I got into the* *express train Cracow – Warsaw. I sat at my seat near the window. After a moment 3 older ladies came and one of them asked me if I could change the seat with her, because she likes to sit near the window. I agreed and I went out to the corridor. After a moment a young girl came with her boyfriend who didn't have a ticket and he sat at the seat which was to be mine after the change. Then the conductor came and sold him a ticket for this seat. Other passengers also came. The train started to go. Because it was cold they closed the doors to the corridor. I stayed in the corridor without a seat and I analysed with disbelief the situation which took place during 4-5 minutes.*

When they meet strong, sometimes even brutal personalities, subtle people with subtle wills are pushed out on a margin. There are many such situations in life. Such people don't want to hurt anybody, don't want to take somebody's place, do something at the cost of other person.

With such arrangement of the will and even entering to other wills or with giving them the place in their own will, the person with the schizoid trait cannot win any social competition. This arrangement causes the "illness of will" such as indecision, hesitations, withdrawal under little pressure, surrender. Later, according to the pendulum principle, this will cause that a person after the original injury can respond to brutal wills even greater brutality. And it happened so in this evangelic example.

The Church should be the alternative to the pyramid. *Christ's – Not so with you.* (Mark 10:43) (NIV) and *...seek first his kingdom and his righteousness* (Matthew 6:33) (NIV) reverse social relations. In the parable of the pounds (Luke 19:12-27) or of the talents (Matthew 25:14-30) the endowed people do not compare who of them received the most, everybody is responsible, with the help of grace, for multiplying their own aptitudes. In the church there are no unnecessary people. Everybody has their own place and their own vocation prepared by God. God gives them a place together with grace. Vocation is opposite to climbing up the pyramid. One should serve other people with gifts and graces. God not only liberates from natural aspirations, but also gives totally different perspective.

CHAPTER 6

FROM THE FIRST VISIBLE CHANGES TO THE EXPLOSION OF THE ILLNESS

Every recorded image changes the emotional memory and divides the spiritual heart – disintegrates and breaks. It is because there is spiritually alien content which does not allow for spiritual integration – it gradually detaches from the reality.

Autism and disintegration – spiritual detachment and internal break are the consequences of the original injury. What one can find in the emotional memory, in spiritual terms is reflected in the spiritual heart. The spiritual heart is a kind of lenses in which the emotions and affection reflect the spiritual light. **The spiritual heart divided and occupied by the evil spirit is a characteristic trait of the ill person.** Their own spiritual heart – the place where they can meet God, other people and themselves – is occupied and divided by somebody who threw them out of their own place.

Apart from that the spirit breaks and disintegrates, he **unifies with the spiritual reality which he represents, from which he originates. He unifies against the will of the person whose heart he divided.** This external reality occupied by the evil spirit starts to be present in the spiritual heart and the consciousness of the ill person. As this reality is dominated by the evil spirit, it causes pain and suffering from which one cannot be liberated.

Later, by the union with the spiritual heart, **the will** based on the spiritual heart **is hobbled**.

After the original injury a person emotionally (and spiritually) weakened, can plunge into the illness by **direct** or **indirect attacks of the evil spirit** or **by the perforation of the system.**

Attacks of the evil spirit do not result from the aptitude for contemplation. In contemplation there are people who experience it in a violent way and the majority of people who do not experience it so strongly. It is a mystery why on the spiritual way the devil torments some people like a dog tugging a rag, while others are spared this. This is not related to the level of spirituality – these bold attacks are a certain characteristic of their spirituality, a difficult one, present also in the schizophrenia.

Indirect attacks are performed through people. The devil has limited capabilities so he looks for collaborators among people and he finds them. In God there is no thesis to hit another person with irony, mockery, lie, vulgarity, but such acts are very common. People do them, from presidents, prime ministers, professors of universities, persons sacred to God and others from the bottom of social hierarchy. This results from their low level of spiritual development, but also from the activity of a spiritual person who engages their will to do such acts. There are very few subtle, tender people who in their wills have no intention of attacking others.

In such conditions, between of the activity of devil and his collaborators, the disintegrated person after the original injury lives.

Direct attacks are less frequent. In the beginning, they are very difficult to be recognised by the ill person. Such person does not know the reason for the periods of bad mood, they do not recognise their spiritual states as attacks of the evil spirit. They are not aware of them and not prepared for them. And they are also helpless against them. During the progress in the spirituality such person learns to diagnose these states and learn how to cope with them. They become aware of the attack by a sudden disturbance of a good mood, a sudden feeling of a tormenting presence, a feeling of a sudden despair. Outside, one can see a person, who a few minutes ago was full of joy, was smiling, was suddenly attacked and tormented by a strange invisible force. It can last for a couple of hours and this state passes as sudden as it began, leaving the surprised and spiritually exhausted person. This can be repeated everyday or every 2-3 day, it can disappear for a certain period. The ill person after a longer spiritual way is fully conscious of this all, but before active purifications of the emotional memory, they cannot to prevent these attacks – they are a passive observer of them.

These states cannot be explained medically, they can be explained well by spirituality. **After the healing, these indirect attacks and the attempts of direct attacks does not vanish.** The healing doesn't liberate from them. These attacks are a characteristic trait of spirituality of such people. But after the healing and internal integration these attacks will not make such great impression as before. A formerly ill person will know how to recognise them and how to cope with them.

The result of the original injury is also a phenomenon which I named as a **perforation of the system.** It means that **the spiritual influence is not registered by emotions, but still this influence is accumulated in the emotional memory.**

The spiritual action can be compared to radiation. Only being in the area of spirit presence causes that in a person after the original injury the accumulation in the emotional memory is quicker even if any evident external events were not registered by emotions or affection. For a healthy person such phenomenon doesn't exist. Emotions are conscious and only these to which they react are accumulated in the emotional memory.

The spiritual influence takes place in the scale of family, environment, the country, in the area of influence of the religion. A given country is under the influence of a given spirit. It is created by the religion, political tradition and in the present time this spirit is articulated by political leaders. Also people presenting publicly their opinions articulate this spirit. One can write the theses which such people present and compare them to the theses which are in God. The bigger the differences, the worse the conditions for mental health are, especially for people after the original injury, their memory will be quickly overloaded.

This perforation of the system causes so quick degradation of the ill person.

It should be also mentioned **that common life, common work, living together with a person possessed by the devil or a person being under the influence of the devil (which are numerous in**

society) may also cause the perforation of the system – one can get ill or worsen the state of the emotional memory.

Thus, the future sufferer after the original injury is a person emotionally and sentimentally weakened, exposed in a particular way to the activity of the evil spirit present in the environment. This arises some consequences.

The most important is **the total defencelessness** against the spirit dominating in the environment.

There are better and worse environments in the scale of the continent, country, region, city, town, district. This an important therapeutic indication. For quicker healing, together with starting the spiritual way one should change (if it is possible) the environment for more convenient for some time.

As the attacks of the evil spirit disintegrate as from the side of a person the same influence have **personal sins, especially against purity.**

Every act of the will against the commandment of love is a sin, if this act is committed voluntarily. After the original injury this voluntarism is limited. The sexual act should be a completion of affection, of mutual love. Practically, it also serves as a therapy of different tensions, emotional and sentimental injuries accumulated in the emotional memory. The sexuality shows the state of emotions and feelings. In the case of the future ill person the injuries in this area are so great and contradictory (because of the anger at other people, yourself, devil, God) that they cause great tensions which are difficult to be removed, which have a bearing on sexuality. If a person does not find a way to liberate themselves from the emotional and sentimental tensions (which arose against their will) and releases them through sexuality, it can be also the source of sins which inhibit the spiritual progress.

Also **aggressive attitudes** because of a very strong perception of the external world, if the ill person will not cut them by their will, this can be also a source of sin.

What characteristic changes happen after the first significant crisis, beginning **the regress in life and spirituality?**

The perception of reality becomes different. Such person thinks that something in her life had been definitively finished. Friends leave, they walk away as if forever, even if they live nearby and they shall never come back. Situations, even joyful ones are for the last time and shall never return.

Vocation given by God opens another reality, takes out from the environment, gives meaning, awakes to the life different than before.

But in the case of illness, **the unconscious going away in the direction of the evil spirit,** to his depth, to isolation take place. The future sufferer has an impression that other people are going away, but not them, that the situations pass forever, without return. Such person breaks down the relations with others, withdraws from the different sorts of engagements. This causes the surprise to the environment which was starting to accept such person, to open to them.

It happens, because the cognition (and later the life), is strictly associated with the spirit. The penetration of the spirit results in the exit from the real life. Exit from the life without the possibility of return. The return is blocked by the alien spiritual contents accumulated in the emotional memory which cannot be removed by such a person.

The attacks of the evil spirit are getting stronger. He acts with a great pressure through other people. When observing this situation from outside, his aim is clear. After a partial limitation of cognition, he wants by brutal attacks to ruin a weakened person. He does this by the whole sequence of hits given with the visible logic, but not known to the person attacked. The future ill perceives this very strongly.

These hits are given by the people from the family, environment, by stranger, but they complete in a logical system. **All people who do this are not conscious of their role in destroying another person.**

However, the mechanism of this is very simple. First, such person enters to the area of sin. Later, the evil spirit takes such person in a sort of partial possession and with this possessed part, over which such person doesn't have the spiritual reflection, attacks the other person. The devil can't do very much on his own, he has wrongly set will and false cognition, and he is dangerous only when he finds collaborators among people.

The hits given by the devil and the inscription of images causes a very strong, nearly psychotic perception of reality. Normal events which can seem spiritually neutral are perceived by the ill person as the attacks to their person. Such person will perceive positively practically only the situation full of evangelic love, but such situations does not happen often in life. As a result of spiritual sensitiveness, the person after the original injury and after the first crisis is so injured and spiritually weakened that even if there are no attacks, they feel brutally touched and attacked.

The future ill person with the blocked perception of reality moves to the side of the evil spirit, who has a great influence on their cognition. The evil spirit cannot give him the unified cognition, because he does not possesses it. The first symptoms of moving under the direction of the spirit is the radical narrowing of the cognitive horizon and the reduction of cognitive perspective. There is no cognitive unification, but increasing cognitive break. The future ill person starts to think by fragments, the lose the global perception and comprehension of reality. The evil spirit makes an impression of cognitive depth, but this illusion of depth causes greater and greater complications (which is logical because of the cognitive capabilities of the spirit), but does not give clear explanations.

The spirit draws the future sufferer to these complications and thinking about them, and he does not provide any solutions beyond the false confirmation in the imaginary wisdom and false illusion about deep cognition.

Simultaneously, **the ability to remember and the reduction of the capacity of memory occur.** There are long periods of tensions, nervousness, lower concentration, **the dissociation starts.**

The future ill person stops to react to what is going outside and they are not aware of this. They do not know who is the new parish priest, they will not notice a new housing estate being built. The upcoming springtime with blossoming trees will not make any impression.

However, such person is conscious that they are not themselves, they are not the same as before, deprived of the joy of life. They infect the environment with discontent. They want to go out of this state, but they cannot do this, even with great effort. Van Gogh writes to his brother;

"Don't imagine that I think myself perfect — or that I believe it isn't my fault that many people find me a disagreeable character. I'm often terribly and cantankerously melancholic, irritable — yearning for sympathy as if with a kind of hunger and thirst — I become indifferent, sharp, and sometimes even pour oil on the flames if I don't get sympathy. I don't enjoy company, and dealing with people, talking to them, is often painful and difficult for me. 3r:12 But do you know where a great deal if not all of this comes from? Simply from nervousness — I who am terribly sensitive, both physically and morally, only really acquired it in the years when I was deeply miserable. Ask a doctor and he'll immediately understand entirely how it couldn't be otherwise than that nights spent on the cold street or out of doors, the anxiety about coming by bread, constant tension because I didn't really have a job, sorrow with friends and family were at least ¾ of the cause of some of my peculiarities of temperament — and whether the fact that I sometimes have disagreeable moods or periods of depression couldn't be attributable to this?

But neither you nor anyone else who takes the trouble to think about it will, I hope, condemn me or find me unbearable because of that. I fight against it, but that doesn't alter my temperament. And even if I consequently have a bad side, well damn it, I have my good side as well, and can't they take that into consideration too?"*

These states are reinforced by the hits from the closest people: the mother, father, brother, teachers. They all don't understand what is going on with such attacked person. They are not aware that the devil uses them to attack. The future ill person cannot express their thoughts, problems, can't open themselves in such

---

* From letter 244 – To Theo van Gogh. The Hague, Thursday, 6 July 1882

a tragic moment to them. They stay with their own problems out of their perception limited by devil.

To recapitulate, the sensual way has finished, the spiritual way (in the Holy Ghost) has not started yet. It only went in the direction of the evil spirit. Isolation in society is only one of the first symptoms. One can observe: gradual isolation, inability to go beyond own growing problems, deeper distance to other people, weaker perception of reality, distraction, increasing problems with mental recovery, permanent mental and physical fatigue, long periods of irritability, nervousness, increasing problems with minor issues.

Moreover, one can feel a total lack of influence on their own life despite great effort to change it. Also hesitance in the opinions, tiredness of life and tiredness with constant problems, the feeling of being pushed on the way on which one can't stop, although it is senseless.

The future ill **is totally defenceless** against the brutal blows of the evil spirit, every blow touches them deeply, shakes the fundaments of existence. **The ill person doesn't know the reasons for their state**, because they don't understand the complicated spiritual mechanisms which influence them.

The original injury (in the spiritual sphere) causes the intensified sensitivity to the encountered spirit by which they were injured before. After each blow, the injury is deeper. This all causes the intensified accumulation of blows and tensions in the memory. The spirituality does not get stronger, it doesn't clarify, it doesn't integrate. Such person is spiritually weaker and weaker and broken. Every person with a stronger will causes cognitive confusion. It lasts for years and is deeper and deeper.

A general result of the injury is that the spirit instils himself more and more into emotions, into the emotional memory, causes the trouble in the will – disintegrates – and cannot be removed. Then he will invade the spiritual heart and cause the illness.

This stage – from the first changes – to the invasion of the spirit to the spiritual heart – I will analyse once more, on the basis of the diary written by the patient before the illness.

The evil spirit which will start to attack the future ill, first will ruin their emotionality, later he will touch the affection, then he will start to destroy the memory and intellect, after this he will paralyse the will, then he will finish destroying the affection, which he made unnaturally great, after that he will cause constant depression during which he will finish destroying the intellect and in the end he will invade the spiritual heart.

The evil spirit does this in such order, because this is how the person reacts to the activity of the spirit, whom they try to resist by the will.

When the reverse process starts, God will touch first the will, then the affection which He will fully satisfy, after this He will heal the emotions, then the memory and intellect, and later He will purify and release the will. After this, after the union of the will He will touch the affection again, but differently – He will injure them by his love and He will draw the person to Himself. And later God will transform by touches and by the forces of the spirit to achieve the full union. The order will be the same but reversed, because in such way a person reacts to the activity of the spirit – in this case – of God.

9.07.1976 Today I saw how lonely I am...I got lost. I was walking in the garden, the sky was cloudy...I have lost something and I can't get together. I am lonely, I haven't been so lonely for a long time. I remember many beautiful moments from this year when I had the goal – now I have lost it. I feel that something has gone away and it will never return – and I am poorer by this.

The original injury causes the accumulation of the spiritual contents but accumulated in the evil spirit. At some moment there are so many contents that they overload the emotional memory. As a result, emotions don't act freely, they hobble the will. **This is exactly the reversal of what happens with the simple union,** when the sensual contents coming from the lower part stop to influence the will. The will is liberated from their influence, and the emotions are released from the influence of the evil spirit – the emotional memory is purified from the spiritual contents.

Confusion and loss of sense results from the beginning of the hobbling of the will. Loneliness results from other reacting of emotions than of other people and from the beginning of moving in the direction of the spirit. The existing perception of the world disappears.

During the spiritual way this state ends definitively **during the simple union.**

Whether the evil spirit was present since the original injury and emotions and affection, as if submerged in it, stopped to react freely – or every next injury deepened the original injury and instilled the evil spirit deeper as it entered the spiritual heart? I will leave this question open.

5.12.1976 In November I did not sleep a lot – 5 hours every second night... this terrible sleeplessness ... I need to sleep. Yesterday I trained only to finish. I did not enjoy what I was doing – it didn't matter to me. The mental resilience has fallen down during this month by one third. I have first problems with the memory.

The appearance of insomnia is a special sign that there is too much of these spiritual contents accumulated in the emotional memory. The daily rhythms start to change. Around 10 pm. when the body naturally starts to prepare for the rest – intense activity starts, accompanied sometimes by anxiety and fear which prevent falling asleep. Such person falls asleep after midnight and wakes up in midday. There is great tiredness during the day which make any activity impossible. During the sleep the ill person gets tired and gets up tired even if they slept 10–11 hours.

Insomnia in schizophrenia is eliminated by **active purifications of the emotional memory.** After the first pair of active purifications – after the expression of anger at other people and at oneself – the ill starts to sleep much better. The new quality of sleep appears – sleep is deeper and shorter. The rhythms of day and night slowly come back to the old way. Sleep comes naturally in the evening – the ill person is more rested during the day. The periods of the activity appear a few days after each expression.

This state improves **after the expression of the second pair of anger at the devil – anger at God.**

The meditative expression of images associated with the affection restores all the other rhythms.

13.01.1977 The Christmas tree – I found myself a little with it, I sat near the tree in the evenings looking at the lights. I understood what the Christmas are about (their atmosphere) long time after they ended. I am looking forward to have a good May, June with the leaves on the trees, with sun bathing, with the library, with walks in the nut avenue – with all that was in this special year 1975. I would very much like to return to all this, to find again my own happiness and the joy of life.

1.05.1978 Mentally strange – I think I have become indifferent – I am empty though calmer. I am sitting in the garden – the trees have flowers – it is wonderful like in the painting of Van Gogh. All is awaking to life – but I can't wake up. The trees are 2 years older – me too. Some of them have cut branches – someone has also cut me – I am also 2 years older. The moon also is 2 years older and everything looks different in the environment of the trees. This fate is mean – moments, which should never pass, pass.

15.05.1978 I have died, I have become indifferent. I felt like as if my soul had been turned upside down and shown around.

The slow entrance of the emotional memory in the space occupied by the spirit is a reason why reality is not perceived as before. The sensual world – full of life, coloured, joyful has finished and its existence will not return.

The beginning of active purifications will return colours, but this sensual perception will change to the spiritual – deep and full of reflection. The vital colours of nature, spontaneous reactions of other people will not touch as before – they will stay in the world which was lost too quickly.

Active purifications will liberate the emotional memory from the influence of the spirit – they will give it under the authority of God – but they will never return to sensual perception.

22.07.1978 Mentally I am destroyed again. Again I did not know what to do with myself. It's bad. How is it possible to enter into such blind alley. The worse is that nothing changes.

31.08.1978 I can't sleep. I fall asleep at 4 o'clock in the morning. Simply I can't sleep.

15.09.1978 I reached another bottom. I learnt the whole month and I didn't take the examination. The worst is that I am alone and I have no results (in sport, studies, personal life) – I fail in everything. I feel stupid and I want to cry – this is nothing new. Somebody made a huge mistake giving me life – only for being a laughing stock to others.

There comes a moment when the future ill person starts to see their real failure in the natural life. They also do not see the exit from this situation.

An antidote to this situation in their opinion should be the continuation of the natural way. They think that the success on this way will change their life. They are very diligent in their actions to achieve success.

They are not aware that they deal with the evil spirit – and if they do not start to fight against them consistently, they will not change anything in their life. This is the time of breakthrough, the time of breaking the logic – "I didn't succeed in the world, but there is no other way than to come back to the world and to start the next attempt"...

The opposite of this state are **the first contemplative prayers.** A totally new way, which the future ill hasn't seen yet, opens up. And automatically, the ruthless logic, which does not allow leaving the blind alley, the logic of the old way and of the old man disappear.

13.10.1978 I have been nervous for one week – I don't know why. My life has no aim – I just walk and get nervous. In the morning I wake up very early – nervous. I noticed that all the time I am "under the pressure", I am always in the hurry and I can't stop – although I don't see the reason for such hurry.

Such a way of life with inability to stop is **a symptom of the spiritual insatiability.** This symptom is in the group of symptoms which disappear very late – **in the beginning of the unitive way.** Satiation occurs after the active purifications. The ill person gets slower, reflects. They notice that 60 – 80% of their activity was not necessary and senseless. They get calm – the necessity of fight, conquering stops in them.

2.11.1978 Tomorrow I will not go to French and Russian because I was not able to learn them – although I had a free day yesterday and today.

6,12.1978 Something is wrong with my memory. I have something like memory loss and I am not able to say anything correctly in Polish.

23.12.1978 The mental resilience is very low. I easily get nervous.

24.12.1978 I was very sad today. I felt that my parents are tired and slowly all burden of life is transferred to me – but I will not bear it, because I have no vital forces – dead. Any sparks of hope, joy, expectation have burnt put in me. I feel that I will infect people with discontent. Everyone in my family wants that everything would all right, but they (and me too) are covered by the stoned shells – and they can't be different. I am not myself too.

24.02.1979 Many things vanished from my memory.

The ill person sees that something is going on with them. They would like to be different but they can't. They are drawn into the space dominated by the evil spirit which attacks them more and more from the side of emotions and emotional memory which is possessed by it in a major part. The future ill person cannot diagnose their state and they are not able to change this state.

The undertaking of the spiritual way can start to reverse this state.

19.04.1979 Something is wrong with my memory. At school doctor pointed to me and said – this miraculously distracted gentlemen will answer this question. And I said – with pleasure – but I couldn't find anything in my memory.

12.06.1979 I have trained very hard for 4 years and have no results. I have no influence on anything – because all will go on as it was destined. Everybody will play their own part and the end. A man has no influence on anything.

The statement of the fact that a person has no influence on anything is a characteristic of the beginning of stage which is **the hobbling of the will.**

In the spirituality the undertaking of the spiritual way will lead over time to the night of senses. The authors of the spiritual texts compares this period to the evening. Then the reason with its natural analyses starts to disturb the spiritual way. This is compared to the midnight. After this the night of spirit happens which ends by the dawn – it means by the new level of unification with God. The night of senses and the nights of spirit can be few – despite this scheme is characteristic. Such stages follow one after another and each of them results in a deeper union.

For schizophrenia sufferer it is similar. The majority of described states one can compare to **the night of senses.**

Now the reason defects. The following are observed: loss of memory, lack of concentration, difficulties in associating and learning new content (because it is written in other spiritual perspective). The future ill person quickly gets tired. They also lose a global perspective and are focused on details.

This state disappears **in the beginning of the unitive way – after passing through the nights of spirit,** when the cognition clarifies (it concerns only the spiritual cognition).

The next stage will be depression which is the equivalent of the night of spirit. After that, the evil spirit will invade the spiritual heart.

The conclusion from these descriptions is that when these first states appear – one should rapidly start the spiritual way. If it does not happen, the reason will defect. If after these first symptoms the future ill does not start the spiritual way, the evil spirit will pull them into depression. If the radical spiritual reversal does not take place – the evil spirit will invade the spiritual heart. This will cause the terrible suffering comparable to the infernal suffering which many people won't stand.

And because the evil spirit over time breaks the structure – the physical construction on which the physical and spiritual life is based – it is good to start the spiritual way – to protect oneself from this state. In other case one should start the spiritual way from the beginning – but the breaking of the physical structure causes permanent damage and no therapy will be able to reverse this state.

27.06.1979 In my fucking life nothing has changed. Nervously I sat down. This year has been tough. I see the future in dark colours. I am tired with life. I am fed up with constant problems. I would like very much to speak to my father, but he was so hounded against me that we will not understand each other, it's a pity. I will regret this, but I can't do anything about it.

7.07.1979 Today I woke up very late – about 11.30am. I listened to the scenes from the "Faust" by Gounod, and I went to the shop. I met A. – very pretty. My heart was shaken, I felt faint for a moment. I have the internal injury which is not healed – somebody hurt me deeply some years ago.

4.08.1979 I start to see the future in dark colours – the problems are stuck with me. I am happy when I go to bed, but my dreams are very heavy.

2.09.1979 My father said that he is fed up with my boorishness and he wanted to beat me. He told that he would call the ambulance to take me. That I should start to work, because he doesn't want to support me any longer. I am alone – I cried after this for one hour – I was sorry – so sorry that nobody can't imagine.

12.09.1979 I felt really bad mentally – very bad. I learnt – actually I talked to myself, gave interviews. I have a piece of wood instead of brain. My memory fails, my hands are shaking. I have no luck for this. I haven't been so unlucky for a long time. I read that the rats closed in the maze and shocked by the electricity are very nervous. It is the same for me.

23.09.1979 Tomorrow I have the examination again. I did not learn because I was as if indifferent mentally. My wooden brain couldn't learn more.

20.10.1979 Sometimes I think that I would like to die – everything goes terrible in my life – my brain is getting wooden. Again they told me that I am a boor. My soul is ill. I feel very bad for no reason.

I always feel bad in the autumn time, but now these periods are longer – they surround me like hyenas.

2.12.1979 I have no aim. I am suspended in the vacuum. I don't know in which direction to take the step. I will see which direction the life will go.

These states of the vacuum are equivalent to the states which take place with **the union of the will.** The will goes through them to liberate from the influence of the lower part and from the natural will. Here the natural will is totally hobbled – without the possibility to move to the next state. Now the evil spirit which hobbled the will changes the tactics of his attacks. The "black series" appear – series of spiritually bad events and the total frontal attacks which causes severe damages and leads to quick exhaustion. It is now, after the hobbling of the will, that the illness accelerates rapidly.

14.03.1980 I have been feeling very bad for a couple of days. Last that I felt so bad was 2 months ago. On Saturday during the training I quarrelled with my friend, later police pursued me by the police car, on Wednesday I quarrelled with the trainer from the Academy of the Physical Culture, on Friday (it means today), I wanted to beat the workers near the club. This, that I start to beat somebody, these are the movements of the drowning person. This growing mental tiredness will lead me to the choice, and I am afraid of this, because I have lost in my life and I can choose only this second option. And I am afraid of this moment.

10.05.1980 I feel bad again. It is 0.20. More and more often I think about death, and more and more often I have tears in my eyes. I can't stand it any longer. Such periods are getting longer, more violent. They appear again and again. I am finished. Every moment of my life is a torment. Nobody knows how terrible one.

24.05.1980 Today I have reached a bottom. After a very hard training I injured my leg in the first jump of the season.

10.06.1980 The worse thing is that I suffer. The time passes slowly now – and I suffer. I don't know how to cope with the situation – and this is the worst. Even in a sleep I have no rest. Every moment of consciousness now is a terrible suffer. And the worst is that I don't know what to do.

1.09.1980 I met her again. My life was thrown out from the orbit. I can't find the solution. I have tears in my eyes. This 3½ months was one bad dream. The death chases after me. I don't know what to do. I am tired, very tired. After half an hour I get calm. I haven't been so calm for a long time. Two hours later I feel strange. My motions are slow. I don't care about anything. I feel like dead but, in my soul I feel very light. This day was peculiar. I died, but I want this state to last longer.

12.09.1980 This stress does not end. At night I almost didn't sleep. My physical powers went out. I am week, terribly week. I walk down the streets and I see that the world is not as it was.

This sequence of negative events was finished by the experience (looking from the spiritual side) **on the level of the violent ecstasy**. By the attack of the evil spirit the ill person has been taken out of the preceding state – to the deeper spaces of depression. The fact that the world is not as it was before, indifference, strange as if supernatural mood, total loss of forces, slow motions, loss of motivation, consciousness of the spiritual death which is a sort of liberation – these are all the equivalents of **the level of the ecstatic union.** And only this level can be a therapy for this state. The ill person is extracted from the schemes of the world, partially liberated from them, but pushed to a contact with the evil spirit which will deepen these states. The polarisation starts – the bad days alternate with better days and so forth. In this case for the first time **the physical-spiritual structure is torn.** The body loses its properties, for example the power in muscles is broken. **From the side of a body this is the worst – irreparable result of schizophrenia.** From the spiritual side – also there will be no return to the natural and real state. The ill person is pushed into unknown spiritual spaces.

29.09.1980 This periods of good and bad as if intertwine. Good 1-2 days intertwine with 2 – 3 bad days – and so on.

14.01.1981 I am mentally tired. I am tired and that's all. I am very nervous during the classes. At home a little thing shakes me up. I am like a tortoise without the shell. I feel every smallest hit. I can see the animal selection, cheating. Sometimes I don't want to go out to the street. My memory fails more and more. In I can't speak well in my native language – I cut the sentences, I suspend them, I use strange syntax. I can't articulate what I think. During the classes I don't open my mouth sa as not to ridicule myself. Alas, I don't feel the need to tell anything – rather the need to sit in silence, thinking.

The will hobbled nearly to the end causes that the ill person has no defence – every knock touches the depth of their soul – and the ill person is aware of this. The desire to stay in the silence and thoughtfully allow to consider that these states are adequate to **the states from the second stage of the ecstatic union.**

21.01.1981 I thought that I rebounded. But there is another force which has been keeping me from the childhood and because of it everything goes in one direction with a terrible regularity– as if in the background – but when the curtain in unveiled I can see that it consistently moves forward – the death.

21.02.1981 I scoff a lot other people. I am cynical, I feel that this plasma cast in the dish of resignation will congeal finally and if I don't shake it, I will remain like that till the end of my life.

24.02.1980 Now I had a very strange period of terrible illusions. I dreamed during day and night. I felt very well for a couple of days – of course living in the unreal world.

The depression still lasts – the changes for better are illusory. The evil spirit occupies and fills the emotional memory at that time. **The imagination produces false, untrue images, so as not to be dominated by the spirit.** Only the fragments of the will, which is more and more hobbled, defend themselves. The mood clarifies in this way that the periods of bad mood are longer and longer (2-3 days) – whereas good periods are shorter and shorter – violently broken by the attacks of the evil spirit.

Now a period of preparation of the evil spirit to the invasion to the spiritual heart will take place. The characteristic traits of this period are: permanent tiredness, lack of the physical and mental powers, attacks of the evil spirit through the closest people, the change of the relation to them (or breaking), indifference, passive observation of external events – without any reaction, being conscious that there is no exit – and later with thoughts about inevitable death. **These states are equivalents to the nights of spirit.**

14.03.1981 Resignation, resignation. I am very tired – tired with life.

1.04.1981 Sometimes it happens and it is very sad, when something that gives sense to somebody's life does not work out – the man is finished.

13.04.1981 I haven't passed the examination for the second time. Mentally, I am devastated. Difficulties in connecting things, no memory. In the morning I get very nervous for no reason.

21.04.1981 I have absolutely no protective barriers. I am totally destroyed, totally – to the end.

23.04.1981 All day I was thinking about death – that I can't avoid it. I passed the examination, I didn't get nervous at all – I was only thinking about death. When I was answering, my heart started to beat much quicker. I thought that my head will fall down on the table – I supported myself with hands. I received a good note – but it doesn't change anything. I am useless. I would like to fall asleep and to live in the world of dream. That's all I have left.

1.05.1981 All night I quarrelled with my mother.

18.05.1981 Two nights I haven't slept. The springtime has passed. The magnolia trees in the Wilanów Palace have finished to bloom. Something has finished.

6.06.1981 For the examination of Finances I went only to the doors of the examination room – I was feeling bad during last days. I was really nervous. My heart is very bad. For the first time in my life I haven't tried to take the examination. I was feeling bad. I will never achieve anything in my life.

3.07.1981 My mother started to quarrel with me. I wanted to go out to never get back home.

9.07.1981 The invasion of the spirit to the spiritual heart at 2.10 pm.

The invasion of the spirit (in this case), was a sudden inflow of the consciousness – that all had been finally lost. There is no a simple exit from this situation.

Previous states passed after some time, but here the tragic consciousness has entered – and will not leave. This reminds falling one level down and this fall is accompanied by a very painful awareness that there is no exit from this state.

There is an incredible struggle in the man of what is left of life against what is death.

The subsequent now bottoms of depression are very deep and painful. The ill person does not feel it only when his mind defects. The world shown by the spirit and the pain caused by him are impossible to stand. This pain passes only when the mentality can't stand this consciousness – and it defects. There are only two states. The painful consciousness or the absence of perception – either one way or the other.

This is a horrible struggle of the ill person who does not know who is the reason for this situation, and who causes such terrible pain. There won't be a quick improvement because the ill person is in the sphere of the natural perspective and these unrealised natural desires don't permit him (apart from the invasion of the spirit) to change his state.

These "prescriptions" of the natural man and this perspective should finally disappear. Only at that time God comes and starts to create His new logic constructions in a man on the basis of His grace. And because the evil spirit is not a match to them with his false ideas and lies, is at a certain moment thrown out by God from the heart of the ill person.

CHAPTER 7

THE EXPLOSION OF THE ILLNESS

A man is a creature created for the union with God. He has the immortal soul which God created in him in the moment of conception. He has upper powers of soul – the will and the intellect, by which he can unify with God. He has the spiritual heart which allows feeling the presence of God. The heart is also the base for the will. Through the heart the experiences from the lower part (through emotions and feelings) pass, to later go through the filter of the lower part of the intellect.

When devil guilefully invades the spiritual heart, he occupies in a man the place designed for God – the place to perceive God's presence, the place where a man can hear God's inspirations or His voice. The devil enters with his presence – unfriendly towards a man, strange – he causes pain, he torments him. He tears a man away from God and from other people, he closes the ill person in the autistic circle of his own spiritual problems. He paralyses with his own false comprehension, from which the man can't exit. The man feels this tearing away subjectively, very often he can notice a moment when the invasion has happened. The devil does this after the long pressure on the emotional memory, after he has possessed a great part of the will – when he wants to ruin the man spiritually in this life and to bring the man to destruction (as he thinks) in the future life.

The ill person doesn't understand the depth of this invasion. This is a totally new experience to him. The ill person has no comprehension of God, no comprehension of the devil and his activity, no comprehension of himself, which would enable him to understand correctly this experience, which can be interpreted only with God's grace, because it relates to the spirituality. The ill person has also the difficulty describing this experience. The human language is too poor to fully express it. Also the ill person loses contact with the reality and only when he has it again, he can partially reflect over his own situation.

The person after the first injury was against his own will joined with the external world, with the area possessed by the devil. Now together with the invasion of the spirit, all this external world invades the consciousness of the ill person. The ill person perceives other people as if somebody persecutes him, watches him, prisons him, influences him, steals his thoughts – although he has no physical contact with him. This external world which affected him so much before – has now **entered inside together with the evil spirit.** Entered and started to torment him – making it impossible to function correctly. Tormented by strange thoughts, which come against the will, which persecute him days and nights and it is not possible to get rid of them, persecuted by voices or thoughts, which present to the ill person strange contents, by crippling fear against other people, perceived spiritually.

The evil spirit invades through such events as being frightened, beaten by somebody, death or suicide of members of the family, love disappointment, extremely difficult life events (emigration, prison), humiliation with no possibility of exit (military service, university).

In all such events the spirit behaves in a cruel and ruthless way. The future ill breaks down under **the acts of the spiritual brutality.**

Very often parallelly **the physical and mental forces go away.** A person without forces, with slow movements looks characteristically.

The activity of the spirit can be recognized by the cognitive falseness, the theological errors, by the lacks of the unity in comprehension, by the great supernatural comprehension, by harassment, by false inspirations, by false pressures and by the force which accompanies them, by the helplessness when the ill person can't undertake any intellectual or physical activity, by obsessions (disturbing something that was before the war), by internal dialogue – the ill person gives the answers to the internal inspirations provoked by the spirit, by merging with the environment (the ill is persecuted, invigilated, observed by somebody or somebody influences his thoughts – all these cases have one common background – **the ill is spiritually merged with the spirit and with the environment.**

To describe what is going on in the moment of the explosion of the illness and during the illness, **I will compare the results of the birth of God in the spiritual heart to the results of the entrance of devil with his presence to the spiritual heart.** Thus, I will compare what is going on in the spiritual heart of the mystic and of the schizophrenia sufferer.

The birth of God	The invasion of the devil
God is born in the spiritual heart with subtlety, mildness, delicacy.	This is a brutal invasion against the person's will.
God respects what He has found in the human heart – He purifies and refines by His grace.	The devil destroys everything – he ruins the natural human gifts.
God by his presence doesn't limit the will of a person	The devil torments in a terrible way, he wants to dominate a person.
God rises a person to Himself, He strengthens internal powers of a man. A man becomes internally integrated.	The devil degrades, he blocks the internal integration and unification of a person, he causes even greater disintegration.
A man takes individual traits, God gives him the identity	A man gets lost in cognition, hesitates and is not sure about his judgement.
A man experiences God's presence and acting in the world with logic and power.	The devil paralyses with the evil, from which one doesn't see any exit.
The experience of power and omnipotence of God. Increasing consciousness of your own weakness, fragility and dependence, but also of the love of God.	The feeling of the huge imagined power with parallel escalation of the anxiety.

Greater and greater supernatural cognition.	The cognitive emptiness or the impossibility to construct any consistent theory. False cognitive illuminations understandable only in the moment of appearance, and only to the mind in which they have appeared. The devil deceives in cognition – he tries to introduce false contents.
God shows the meaning of existence, shows the role of past events in the formation of a man.	Progressing fear of God and others. Introduction of the hate of God, yourself and others.
Experience of the God's love care. Opening to other people.	The devil hits a man by the false image of the man. He does this to destroy the man.
God gives the grace of cognition of Himself and oneself, as far as a man is ready to accept this cognition. God leads by the new ways of cognition.	The devil does not lead out from the autistic stereotype. Experience that does not teach anything.
God gives a place in the Church,	Inability to find a place in this life and in the future.
Experience of greater and greater emotional balance.	Changing and swinging mood. Powerless scuffling and tossing from one extreme to another extreme.
Experience of loving presence of God.	Lost control over sexuality.
The deep joy because of the supernatural presence of God.	Gaiety without any reason or extreme spiritual force.
Subtlety and delicacy in relationship with other person.	Insistence
Supernatural peace.	Tormenting trouble from which one can't be liberated.

In the mildest form of this invasion, the ill person starts to feel strange. The word "strange" is repeated in many opinions. Something that the person has not felt until now. The way in which he perceived the reality has been undermined. Suddenly a person loses the previous manner of perception used for the entire life. They see that this is the same reality, but perceived otherwise, as if they were found in another reference system. They lose themselves in this system. They also lose the aim of this life, to which they strove with a great effort. They are surprised that this was their aim. They are totally disoriented in this new situation. There will be no return to the perception of the reality of the world. The new perception entered which the ill person hasn't known until now and they are totally lost in this perception. The "old" world stopped to exist.

Polish poet Jan Lechoń writes – *I feel that I woke up from the dream of almost all my life...*

The accumulation of pictures and the invasion of the evil spirit is one problem – and the invasion and in dispositions to which spiritual gifts the evil spirit entered – is another problem.

Thus, the next question after the invasion is – **the dispositions of which gifts the spirit has found himself in?**

There are many types of spirituality – many characteristic spiritual ways. There are also many spiritual gifts and charisms in spirituality. Somebody can have a gift to hear the supernatural voices, another person will be taught by God through visions. Everybody has their own spiritual way with the characteristic trait of spirituality – everybody should recognise and undertake in the mystery of the cross their vocation prepared by God.

There are no better or worse gifts in spirituality, there is no bidding of gifts, because the natural order is inverted. Very often God bestows a lot to people who are weak in the natural order to make them stronger. With these gifts they should serve to build the Church – not to show off with them. A person should be conscious that this a gift.

Thus, in the spirituality there is a disposition to different gifts. One can compare this to an undeveloped photo, on which you can't recognise a picture until it is developed. Only the spiritual life undertaken will slowly reveal this picture.

In the schizophrenia the evil spirit enters to these dispositions – and this is a paradox, that it is him who shows the existence of them – by entering to the spiritual heart he exposes them. As in the spirituality there is a characteristic spiritual trait – just because of these dispositions – the same in the illness – there **is a characteristic trait of it.** As one spirituality exists – one illness exists – even with the numerous experiences.

And if somebody has the disposition to hear the voice of God or the disposition to ecstasies or visions – during the illness the evil spirit will speak to him by the voices or he will cause him the psychoses with the great supernatural false cognition or he will present him false visions. If the person will be ill many times – such characteristic symptoms will repeat. Other people who have the disposition to admirations or ecstasies, will rather not hear the voices. But during the illness they all will have the exultations of the spirit with the ecstatic false supernatural cognition – equivalents of the states from the stage of the ecstatic union. The false pressures will cause strange acts which will be difficult to explain when the psychosis stops.

And these states not the other ones will repeat – if somebody will be ill many times.

In the case with voices the difficulties are that the devil also proclaims the theological contents, he gives advice – this all is a sort of the false private revelation. And because the ill person is not proficient in the theology of the internal life, and also they have a contact with a spirit with a great false cognition, which tells them about the problems which are beyond the capabilities of the ill – usually the ill is quickly deceived by the spirit. For example, a 19-year-old man heard the voice, which told him – 'You will be a priest'. He went to the seminary and he became ill in the end of the first year of studies. He did not verify his vocation on other grounds, but did only what this voice ordered him to do. To another ill person the voice has told that there were 7 such women as Mother of God in the history of world, that Buddha also had such mother and another great reformers of the spiritual life had such mother too. But from the dogma of the Immaculate Conception we know that there was only one such mother in the history of world.

Thus, to notice the theological contents in the voices and their verification are important. The devil besides the theological false contents introduces banal contents. The contents which seem to be advanced theology have a banal, literally garbage contents. Unfortunately, the ill person very often believes in them. But the manner of transmission of the voices is really extraordinary. I know the ill person who wanted to run away from home to the solitary place – to hear and to discuss with the spirit many hours daily. It is very often difficult to break this extraordinary contact and with these extra contents proclaimed by the spirit. Of course in many cases the contents proclaimed by the spirit start to be very troubling for the ill person.

The next factor which one should take over consideration is **whether the emotional centre has broken or not.** After the invasion of the spirit to the spiritual heart the devil attacks the man in a particular way. It is received by the emotional centre of man. Till this centre functions as before, the manner of attacks does not change. Very often in the illness there is a moment when this stupefied blocked emotional centre breaks down. It defects, it doesn't withstand the pressures of the spirit and the pressure of accumulated contents. A person is liberated in this moment not from the spirit, but from the manner in which the spirit harassed them. They are liberated, because the emotional machinery by which man perceived the activity of the spirit defects, but not because the spirit has gone. **The spirit can't repeat the manner by which he persecuted the ill person.**

Different types of illuminations accompany this breakdown. The sudden change of the nature of the activity of the spirit joined with his presence causes that the ill person suddenly has a very clear (but in a great part false) cognition of different subjects, personal, historical, social ones. Suddenly the ill person understands all, all becomes clear to them, they penetrate all the mysteries with their mind. The psychiatrists maintain that the more of these contents go outside – and the greater the breakdown is, the better. And so it is. It takes place usually later when the emotional memory is overloaded.

The breakdown of the emotional centre on the one hand liberates partially from the autism, but on the other hand it can cause an inability to feel empathy. The ill person is closer to other people – whom they couldn't understand well because of the emotional differences – but they will live among them "painlessly" – their great joys or their great tragedies will not make on them such a great impression as before.

In the Holy Gospel according to Luke (chapter 8 verse 2) one can read about Mary Magdalene *from whom seven demons had come out*. (NIV) One can ask a question – how did the evangelist know that there were seven devils?

He knew that probably because when Jesus liberated from the spirit, he materialised him for a moment – showed him. He did this to show from what kind of spirit the person had been liberated. Or Jesus showed the spirit only to the liberated person in the form of the internal vision – and this person transmitted it to the evangelic description.

We know that the hierarchy of the evil spirits forms some kind of a pyramid. These united together spirits invade the spiritual heart. But the cases related to this supernatural cognition can be showed only by God by His grace. One cannot learn them by the experimental knowledge. The knowledge about which was the structure of the spirit which entered to the spiritual heart in not necessary to the healing. If God shows it – it will be additional information useful during the spiritual way and during the active purifications.

There are many types of schizophrenia. In all types there are:
1. The first injury which causes the overloading of the spiritual contents in the emotional memory and later the slow isolation and cognitive deficits.
2. The invasion of the evil spirit to the spiritual heart upon the explosion of the illness.
3. Existence of the complicated nets of tensions in brain and transmitted to a body.

What causes the difference in the image of the illness?
1. When the first injury has taken place – if earlier – then the external world to a greater extent enters, hurts and disintegrates.

2. What type of the personality is touched by the first injury, i.e. what is the proportion between anger at people, anger at one-self, the devil and God.
3. What type of the spirituality found the devil which made the invasion. It conditions whether the ill will have voices, visions, psychoses with the ecstatic false cognition etc.
4. If the emotional centre was broken down or not.
5. Which structure of the evil spirit has entered the spiritual heart – how many spirits joined entered the spiritual heart?
6. How much the material structure on which the spiritual and physical life is based has been damaged?

The example of the simple type of spirituality with a great part of the sphere of feeling without breaking the emotional after the invasion of the spirit can look as in the following example – the ill persons recalls:

I went to the examination after the 4th year of studies, I was standing in the narrow corridor for over 8 hours, because we were waiting for the professor. To the first and only one question I got the wrong answer, because I couldn't concentrate because of long waiting. My entrance to the room, the question, my answer and the inscription of the bad note to student book took about 1 minute. I went out of the room and got very nervous.

When I was walking down the street, I started to feel mentally bad. The thoughts full of pain started to flow to my consciousness. They lasted 4-5 minutes, and later there was 2-3 minutes break – and then again pain and break. It was for me quite a new experience which I haven't had before.

This acute state has passed after 2-3 hours, but in the next days I noticed big changes in my frame of mind.

When walking down the street I observed passing cars – everyone had the goal which they pursued.

I was walking totally confused – aimlessly. A few days ago I didn't even think that there was any goal. Now I felt mentally exhausted, lost, solitaire and without any chance in this life. I had to force myself to sport training which before was a great pleasure for me. After a greater effort I had low mood for several hours. I was learning and I was training by the impetus, by force trying to make a sense of my life. I hated such behaviour, but I couldn't stop it so as not to fall into greater emptiness. I felt that I will receive the next blows, but I didn't know from which side.

There were the examinations for the secondary-school certificates, again the trees were blooming beautifully – but this all didn't make any impression on me. On the street I met my friend. I was feeling that our life paths go separate ways and that something in our lives has finished and will never return. I couldn't reconcile with this and find myself in this situation. All the meetings and partings were similar – we were parting ways and we shall never meet again as before. My friends leave as if to another space and forever, even if I shall see them again.

I took the written examination of the Russian language. I felt that all my physical and mental forces wore out. I was late to the oral part of examination, because I couldn't prepare myself to leave home. I was distracted, I couldn't shave quickly, I couldn't dress up quickly, quickly (as normal) eat breakfast. The board was waiting for me, because they had examined all my fellow students.

During the nights I woke up and I couldn't sleep for 2 -3 hours. In the next days I got very nervous for no reason.

I went to the stadium to train, but I had to be careful, because my heart started to work in a strangely. The next night I slept only 5 hours. I woke up with heart like a stone – for a half of a day I got very nervous. I didn't care. I knew that I would not achieve anything in my life.

Next day I went to the triple jump competition. During the warm-up I was very tired. I was unwilling to jump. During the competition I had no power to run to take-off board. Despite that, I jumped 3 times breaking the terrible tiredness. After the competition I started to feel mentally bad. There was a consciousness that in the sport I will not achieve anything – despite so many years of training. There was a sharp mental pain, which has not passed. I was feeling that I entangled myself in the net without any exit. I was thinking about death. All nonsense of my life went on the top. In the night I slept only 3 hours.

Next morning, I was walking down the street where I was always walking and I was crying. At home I was walking for a few hours in the room and I didn't know what to do with myself. In the evening unexpectedly I started to feel better. I started to think about the organisation of my life. I was afraid to go to sleep. In the morning I woke up in a terrible mood again. I trembled and I had pain in my heart – I was full of anxiety. The plans from the evening have disappeared. I went to the park, but a burning mental pain had not disappeared and the tears continued to flow for no reason. In the evening it was better again. I started to think about work, family, children, plans and the joy of life. About midnight (because I couldn't sleep), the mental pain came again and I didn't believe that I could ever leave this tragic situation.

At night I slept badly and I woke up 2-3 times. This cycle repeated day after day. There were moments when I was thinking that I would get up and I start a new life. In these moments I was full of optimism. Few hours later I was terrified by the dark future. I trembled as if I were cold even though it was the middle of summer. Such states changed but they didn't pass. I saw that with my own forces I will not deal with them.

I went to the psychologist and to the psychiatrist. During the psychologist appointment I couldn't concentrate to do relatively simple tests. I did in over 1 hour something that before I was able to do during 10-15 minutes. The psychiatrist asked me – where is my 'self'? I answered that if all is going well during the studies, in personal life, in sport – I am fine, but otherwise I feel bad. And my self hasn't existed for a long time.

At the afternoon something happened to my mentality. I didn't care about anything. During the training I was stupefied and I didn't care about anything totally – I was not myself. The next day I started to take the medicines, but they didn't help me. In the bus the tears flowed by themselves. Every day the extraordinary clear awareness came to my mind that I have lost everything. These clear thoughts caused terrible mental pain. I had known that I will be forced to take my own life. These thoughts lasted for some hours – later my head defected – stopped to receive them. I was feeling as if my brain was full of cotton wool – and I was not able to think about anything. This changed in the same cycle – all around. If the depression appeared in the morning – in the afternoon there was stupor. If I didn't feel anything in the morning – the evening was full of the clairvoyant thoughts full of pain. These depressive thoughts become deeper and deeper. I concluded that these were critical days in my life and all goes down and down and doesn't want to stop. I was falling down deeper and deeper and I didn't know what to do. After a month the psychiatrist referred me to the hospital.

The thoughts entered to my consciousness more powerfully than ever before. They caused pain, they were tearing my head day and night, they were burning like a hot iron. The main thought was – you are lost in this life – you have no chance in this life. The pain was so terrible and it did not end that I wanted to shatter my head up against the wall. During the night I slept 2-3 hours. I had such nightmares that after I woke up for a moment I felt relief, but soon these disquieting thoughts came to me again. I had the impression that this was the end of my world – a great catastrophe of it. That the machinery by which I perceived the world crushed and I would never perceive it as it was before. For me this previous world stopped to exist.

I felt as if I was on the bottom of the dry well, from which I couldn't escape – and somebody was kicking me at my head – and I am totally helpless, and I can't do anything against them.

The example with broken centre of emotions with disposition to visions with great supernatural cognition can look like this – the ill person recalls:

I was working in the Botanical Garden as a seasonal worker. I was digging by shovel the old rose garden. It was August and hot weather 35 – 37 degrees. I was working in the open air. After 3 days of digging my physical and mental forces wore out. I started to feel very bad. I took a day off. During the night I slept very deep. In the morning I woke up rapidly. I looked out of the window. The whole city was in the fumes of the violet clear air. In a moment I thought that everybody who would breath this air and who is not in a state of grace would not survive till tomorrow morning. It would be a great cataclysm and nearly all people would die.

I went quickly to my workplace and I warned everybody that I met that they should leave the town before the night (but only till tomorrow). All people were very surprised. I saw they tried to wriggle out of this – but they also didn't want to be unkind to me. I went quickly to my old parish church to the chancellery to warn a priest – that he should warn the others. But the young priest answered, that he was here to cover for someone and he must speak with the young couple who came to order their wedding. I didn't wait until he finished. I went to the parish church but I didn't meet any priests. One man started to shout at me terribly and he wanted to drive me out. I was really frightened of him.

I went to the psychiatric hospital in which I was treated, to warn my doctor against the catastrophe, but she was not at work that day. Even though I stopped the treatment 1 year ago, I liked her very much. What should I do – I thought – And I was looking for the last time at her office – I am so sorry that she would die. Feeling helpless, I returned home.

In the afternoon my father took me to the garden plot 15 kilometres out of the city. I didn't want to go back home. I went to the neighbour who worked near our fence and told him not to return home for this night. My father also wanted to go back as always, but I was against this. I wanted to stop him by force. We started to beat each other for the first time – but each of us didn't want to knock stronger. But after 2 hours of such fight the skin on my hands was cracked and bloody – because of punching my own father. At last my father said that we would stay.

At night I couldn't sleep. Very often I switched on the radio to hear if they were broadcasting or not – if they were killed already or not yet. My father said – let me sleep a little – I must go to work in the morning. About 4 o'clock they said on the radio that in Argentine a truck with eggs crushed. After a moment it will be the same with you – I said to the radio.

But in the morning the beautiful August's sun rose and nothing happened – which surprised me a lot. My father tired and mentally crushed, brought me to the hospital. In the admissions a young likeable doctor asked me very surprised – What is wrong with you? I answered – I translated the Mythology into the Bible and I feel bad. For the last 2 months I had been thinking about the theory of religion and this answer seemed adequate. I had such "gas" in my head that I thought that I could easily do this.

I was brought to the ward, where I spoke to the doctor who treated me before. The nurse made me an injection, after which I fell asleep. I woke up in the late evening in terrible anxiety. I removed the hospital window with the chain, jumped out and I escaped. I was running barefoot in pyjamas and I jumped the hospital fence. When I was running the 3-lane road at the red light – and I raised my hand – all cars stopped immediately. How great power is in me – I thought. I was walking home – but I remembered that about 1 kilometre from here in the housing estate my doctor lives. I will go to him – I thought – so that he would not worry about my health – because in the morning he looked depressed. His block of flats had 6 staircases and I didn't know the address. From one of them a women was going out. It's here I thought. On the third floor I started to knock at the doors, but somebody attacked me rudely and I was surprised that I didn't find the doctor. It was about midnight when I went to my home. The gate was closed and I thought – I would not awake my father – when he would go to the work I would enter. I sat on the kerb and I was waiting.

After 30 minutes 2 nurses came. They held me and brought me to the hospital. There they attached me to the bed with belts. I was very afraid, and because of the anxiety, and because of the mental pain I was howling like a wolf. In the morning I detached myself with the teeth from the belts, reaching under the frame of the bad and I calmed down.

I don't remember too much of this day. They took me to the music therapy, but soon I came back because – as they said – I disturbed others during the classes. Really from the first moment I couldn't stop commenting and I dominated this music therapy. Later I slept all afternoon.

In the morning I woke up early, well-rested and I felt in me a great mysterious spiritual power which embraced me and the whole world. Somebody turned on the radio. I noticed that the same *power which was in me, was broadcast on the radio. Also, very surprised I discovered that the source of this power is just in me. That it is also me who directs this all – being also the part of it. I had a great mysterious power, but this that I am the source of it, is only me who knows it. I felt free, liberated, strong, even powerful and finally fulfilled. I dominated over everything.*

On the ward one of the patients thrown an apple at me and said – help yourself. I got scared and with a great power I thrown him out this apple and said – Oh devil – you wanted to cheat me.

Through the window I saw the hospital ambulance with 4 men. I was very afraid of them – because I thought that they arrived just to take me away. That they would take me and nobody would find me.

My doctor came and invited me to the room where a group of students were. For 10 minutes I was speaking to them in a form of a lecture, I don't remember what about. They were sitting without any move and were looking at me as fixed to their chairs. The doctor thanked me and I went out. I was very surprised that I had the possibility to speak to them only for such a short time. I felt a great "gas" in my head and I was able to speak for many hours. I was brilliant, eloquent, humorous, and thoughtful. It was very easy for me to articulate any thoughts.

Finally, after many years, I felt healthy, but the tasks in this world overwhelmed me. Gorbachev visited Paris, London – he talked but he also threatened a little, I saw that the situation could explode – but how I will protect against this all – and I must do this. In the beginning I decided to write a letter to the pope – to cheer him up.

What is going on later with the spirit? Generally, there are two possibilities – he entered and stays – the ill person goes from the psychosis to the psychosis. Or the spirit entered, disturbed the consciousness and went out – but the traces after many attacks remained and by them the spirit can influence the ill person – the spirit can even return. And surely he will use these traces to fight against the ill person when s/he starts the spiritual way.

CHAPTER 8

SCHIZOPHRENIA AND DISPOSITION FOR CONTEMPLATION

In the beginning I would present a thesis **that a person with the disposition for contemplation will suffer from schizophrenia.** Previously, I compared the consequences of the nativity of God in the spiritual heart with the invasion of the evil spirit to the heart, and now I will compare the special graces which accompany the contemplative life to the phenomena found in schizophrenia. I would present that **the illness has a key clearly visible from the perspective of the spirituality.** But the partial unpredictability and partial absence of logic derive from the fact that free persons are involved in this illness – a person of God, a person of devil, a person of man.

In a man the spiritual, the supernatural level exists. By the biochemistry one can't explain the existence of it. By the will (upper part of soul, which opens at the spiritual right and good and unites with it), a man who is free can choose in the final way God, or s/he can choose the devil. **There is no other choice and any feeling of freedom is illusory.**

I will notice later and I will suggest that if the spiritual factor plays an important part in schizophrenia, a therapy of this condition should be the spirituality.

But I will start from the two definitions of contemplation. First by the Hugh of Saint Victor, second by the Richard of Saint Victor.

Contemplation is a penetrating and free gaze of soul extended everywhere in perceiving things.

Contemplation is the free, more penetrating gaze of mind, suspended with wonder concerning manifestations of wisdom. *

In the first definition Hugh pays attention to this gazing of soul. If the soul is gazing on something or on somebody, it means that this somebody or something exists and attracts the gaze of the soul.

In the second definition Richard adds what is going on in the mind during the act of contemplation. Thus, in this act cognition is put in the mind. God during the act of contemplation puts cognition directly to the mind of a man. The cognition which is in Him. But not by the activity of the intellect, not by analysis, but by the direct putting of spiritual contents in the mind.

It will be characteristic for the people with the disposition for contemplation – possession of knowledge which these persons have not read in the books, have not heard from anybody – the contemplation which was directly placed by God even though this person was not aware of it.

Following to these two definitions, I will present the definition of the contemplative prayer as a prayer when **God touches directly the soul attracting additionally the will by the act of His love – and the soul which is gazing with admiration at Him, revives given by the spiritual way the new admiring cognition accepted by the mind.**

These states of touching of the soul last for certain time and they are repeated and exchanged with the states of abandonment. This has further spiritual consequences, the spirituality attracted will is purified from the influence of the lower part and is directed to God and the flowing cognition concerning the spiritual things is more and more perfect.

What the development of the contemplative prayer depends on?

---

* Excepts from Richars of St. Victor: The Twelve Patriarchs, The Mystical Ark, Book Three of the Trinity. Translation and Introduction By Grover Zin, © 1969 by Paulist Press New York/Mahwah,NJ Used by permission of Paulist Press.

It depends on two factors – the disposition for contemplation and God's grace. Not everybody possesses the disposition for contemplation. Not everybody is led by God through contemplation. In the Church there are vocations to contemplative life and to active life. People are not endowed equally with gifts of grace and nature. One can observe a great difference between people and also a huge number of possibilities in which everybody should find their place and answer to God on the level of their natural and spiritual capabilities.

About the disposition for contemplation in a young person one can't express the opinion with the absolute certainty that they exist. But one can estimate the existence of such trait with a great probability. It is important to parents, teachers, educators – to lead otherwise a young person who possesses the disposition for contemplation.

How one can recognise that such person possesses the disposition for contemplation?

The first trait is **the ideal image of the world** which exists in the mind of a young person. Shelley, who had the schizoid trait, in the preface of his drama *Prometheus unbound* writes – *My purpose has hitherto been simply to familiarise the highly refined imagination of the more select classes of poetical readers with beautiful idealisms of moral excellence; aware that until the mind can love, and admire, and trust, and hope, and endure, reasoned principles of moral conduct are seeds cast upon the highway of life which the unconscious passenger tramples into dust, although they would bear the harvest of his happiness. (..) The having spoken of myself with unaffected freedom will need little apology with the candid; and let the uncandid consider that they injure me less than their own hearts and minds by misrepresentation,*

For the person with such disposition all situations, events, plans, all people and **their acts are compared to the not conscious ideal model which exists in the consciousness of the person** with the disposition for contemplation. This model is read, reflected by soul directly from God – it is difficult to explain its existence otherwise. Disposition for contemplation is the ability to reflect in yourself this existing ideal model. Such person tries to aspire to this model, by this model such person judges other people. This person has also high expectations in relation to oneself and in relation to other people (ethical, aesthetic). These expectations are so high that it is no possible to fulfil them. Such person can't rationally explain why s/he behaves in such way. Because of this ideal model very often s/he feels better than other people. But whether s/he will be a mystic or a clever artistically blasphemer will depend on the choice of their will.

The second trait is **the intuitive feeling of existence of the objective truth.** Van Gogh writes to his brother – *"I don't believe that my opinions are any better than other people's opinions. Yet I'm starting to believe more and more that there's something compared to which all opinions, thus including mine, are as nothing.*

Certain truths and facts, on which our opinions have little or no effect, and which I hope I don't confuse with mine or others' opinions, which would be a mistaken point of view.

Just as weathercocks have no effect on the direction of the wind, so opinions have no effect on certain standard truths.

The weathercocks don't make the wind east or north, any more than any opinions whatsoever make the truth true."

"There are things that are as old as mankind itself, and that won't cease for the present."[**]

The third trait is **the sensibility and openness to beauty.** The scientific researches has shown that this openness is not destroyed even by many returns of the illness. Even with the illness the capability of reception of high aesthetic values doesn't disappear and the need for beauty and aesthetic taste (as it was) still exists and is not distorted.

The fourth trait is **openness to the mystery, to its existence**. Such person is fascinated by the mystery. It is a deep intuitive conviction about the existence of other planes where life exists beyond the natural plane which is real and visible. It can be a capability of the reception of a mysterious beauty. It is a gift impossible to learn.

** *From letter 419 – To Theo van Gogh. Nuenen, on or about Friday, 4 January 1884*

The fifth trait is **the perception and feeling of the changing image of God during the Liturgical Year.**

During the Liturgical Year we reflect about the mystery of Christ's life. This spiritual picture of mysteries is perceived also in contemplation. The act of contemplative prayer will be perceived differently in the Advent, differently in the Christmas Season, differently in the Lent, differently in the Season of Easter, differently before and after the Pentecost, differently during the Marian and others solemnities. The person with the disposition for contemplation will perceive this image of God differently during this periods.

The first Sunday of Advent, Christmas, Ash Wednesday, Easter, Pentecost – from the spiritual side – are quite different days from the days preceding them. If one can make a photo of the person after Christmas, after Easter, after Pentecost – from the spiritual side these will be different photos of the same person. In each photo different mystery of the Liturgical Year will be reflected in the same person. This difference results from the different image of the picture of God contemplated in the Liturgical Year.

These mysteries of life of Christ are present also in the life of a person with the vocation to contemplation, even if such person is not aware of this. The ill person recalls – *I was training in a stadium with green grass and the red track, but after some days I noticed that the same grass and the same track, the same seating and the same sky which before were pale – suddenly got the intensive colours full of saturation and practically it was another stadium. Many years after I understood that it was the image before and after Pentecost.*

Thus, this spiritual background changes during the Liturgical Year – and this is a reason for sudden changes of the frame of mind – and one should know it. The same relates to people after the original injury where the changes are dramatically great. The reason for it is not only lack of the sun, but also not purified emotional memory. The evil spirit which has injured the emotions and feelings (and the marks of these injuries are still in the memory), is also not indifferent on this spiritual background of the Liturgical Year. This is also a reason for these dramatical changes.

Relatively the best period is the Ordinary Time. Many ill people feel well before 15 January to the beginning of Lent, and from July to 15 October – during the other time – worse. After the purification of emotions and feelings – the person will react normally – it means the ill person understands this dynamics of contemplation, colouring of the contemplation during the Liturgical Year and the changing of the dynamics of the calendar seasons which was before difficult to bear for them.

The next symptoms of the disposition for contemplation are also **the consciousness of God's presence and the very strong consciousness of the sin.**

The consciousness of God's presence is a very strong conviction that God knows each situation, that He sees it and observes. This is not a presence of God in the spiritual heart, but a very strong conviction that God knows all circumstances of the act of person, that they are such not others. One can't change here anything, one can't falsify, and one can't lie.

A **very strong consciousness of the sin** can't be stifled, even by the creation of a mini society which would accept the sin or which would glorified a sin. This consciousness of the cognition of this is so deep from childhood – one doesn't need any special lectures to form it. All the therapies which will not take this under the consideration, or therapies which are based on other values, are not able to achieve anything positive in the person with the disposition for contemplation.

The disposition for contemplation is a sort of a hidden talent. Many people haven't developed it, because of negligence of prayer. Despite this, these people possess psychological depth – they can understand the situation of somebody, they are unconsciously hold by the internal inspirations. They have also the aspiration to noble things, greatness, beauty, to unconventional behaviours. They are unique individualists. They have also **the extraordinary subtlety and delicacy in the will.** Their actions, behaviour, life prove the existence of the model deriving from the ideal world.

A symptom of the disposition for contemplation is also **the desire of the greater solitude, but also the condemnation to the**

greater solitude. Such people do not have many trivial relations which have the people with the disposition for active life.

Thus, the need for having not many relations, but relations very deep and unconscious creation of the space for God – this will be a characteristic trait of such people. During the illness, especially in the schizophrenic depression it means total emptiness which will be in the mind of and around the ill person. It is partly derived from the disposition for contemplation and from the openness only to God, but partly from the condemnation of the will.

The solitude is a very tough experience, which the ill person should undertake and wait when God will fill it.

The disposition for contemplation usually accompanied by weaker active life. These two kinds of activities are usually in opposition. Thus, the ill people will never be masters in the active life. Usually they will not have in this life such practical traits as resourcefulness, smartness. One can't expect these traits from such people at the highest level. Such people are lost in active life and after the illness they will also be lost. Active life is not their vocation. Their talent is openness to the truth, beauty, mystery, supernatural problems – and this is where they should fulfil themselves.

To such people one should explain that such vocation exist. And if they have a disposition for contemplation it would be good to discover it. Parents, teachers, educators, priests would be able to notice, discover and form in them this sort of vocation. In opposite way the society will be full of deeply not fulfilled people. One can observe today that in a queue for a free soup in front of the Capuchin's cloister one quarter of these people are the people with the disposition for contemplation. If one can add to this the original injury which causes the disintegration like in schizophrenia – for such people it is practically impossible to find the proper vocation, the proper place, the deep proper fulfilment.

From the spiritual side the original injury causes the inscription of the evil spirit to the sphere of emotions and feelings or after the subsequent knocks – a greater number of his traces in the emotional memory. In the case of the disposition for contemplation this inscription of the spirit (in which there are theses opposite to those existing in the ideal image) causes the division and later the hobbling of the will. Goethe writes:

Two souls, alas, are dwelling in my breast,
And one is striving to forsake its brother,
Unto the world in grossly loving rest,
With clinging tendrils, one adheres;
The other rises forcibly in quest
Of rarefied ancestral spheres.

Then, it results in the conflicts of the consciousness which had no time to form itself correctly and additionally very early it was taken under the tension between the ideal and real world. People who have no disposition for contemplation do not experience this tension. And this is one of the reasons of their mental health.

Disposition for contemplation is accompanied with such states mentioned in the psychiatric literature like: the ideal image of the world, dealing with philosophical problems – only later with real interests and problems, dealing with absolute truth, aspiration to unattainable things, perfectionism, superiority, avoidance of social conflicts, solitude and being misunderstood, retreat from the community, the feeling of emptiness (internal and external), the ideal love and opinion that sex is something low and dirty.

Generally, a man has 2 principal manners of the cognition – **the cognition through analysis and through contemplation.** These 2 manners are opposite to each other. Both of them are possible, because a man has the reasonable soul created by God in the moment of conception.

Cognition through analysis relies on the operation of the pure reason. Usually one can situate it on the level of natural gifts. Because of this, it is easy to create the hierarchy and compare oneself to other people.

Cognition through contemplation is a spiritual cognition poured to the mind. The reason behaves passively during it, passively accepts the contents poured to it on a spiritual way. **In the contemplation the spiritual heart and the reason (passively) take part. In the analysis only the reason takes part actively.** Because the spiritual cognition is the reflection of life, in the contemplative life the most important are the choices by the will. They affect the increase (or decrease) in cognition. This criterion doesn't exist in the natural cognition through analysis.

During the contemplation, the spiritual heart is touched (for example by God), and these touches influence the poured cognition passively registered by the reason. But the spiritual heart which is also a centre of the sensitivity can be moved also by other aesthetic experiences, for example the beauty of landscape (of the falling waterfall), the beauty of the architecture and so on. These acts of cognition mentioned above belong also to the cognition through contemplation.

So, more or less we know what the contemplation is, but it is very difficult to write a good definition of it.

The people with the disposition for contemplation encounter some problems in the social life. I remember the sentence told by the friend of my father, who recalled the lesson of chemistry in the high school. He said – *The most stupid person in the class was not able to answer this question – the future Jesuit...* Yes – this man was the weakest in the cognition through analysis, but he was the best in the cognition through contemplation – and he joined the Convent. Unfortunately, the secondary schools and universities do not teach and examine in the view of the cognition through contemplation, they rather teach and examine in view of the cognition through analysis. Therefore, people with the disposition for contemplation, very often are considered less capable (even stupid) at school, and it is demonstrated to them on every opportunity – by the assessment system, teachers, professors and friends. Whereas people with the disposition for contemplation (very often pushed back on the margin) think that their friends are very simple (even primitive) spiritually and culturally, but because of the subtlety and delicacy in the will, they usually do not demonstrate this to them.

If somebody has the disposition for contemplation and s/he wants to develop it in the spiritual life, s/he must know that

to develop it, the God's grace is necessary. It is told in the parable about the foolish and sensible bridesmaids (Matthew 25:1-13). If somebody has the lamp (the disposition for contemplation), s/he should have the oil for it (the God's grace). This is an obvious conclusion.

Can anybody have the disposition for contemplation and a great ability of analytical thinking? Yes, one can find such people, but generally, all possible gifts of nature and grace are not given to one person. There is a contemplative life, contemplatively-active life and active life based on analytical thinking. Every person should discover their own ability (and one should help a young person to do this), and develop it as a leading one.

The advanced internal life based on contemplative prayers is accompanied by the graces and special states such as **supernatural words, visions, ecstasies, being in God's presence, and earlier nights of spirit, internal emptiness, presses.**

Saint Teresa of Avila in the book *The Interior Castle* presents a very clear description of such states. But one can find similar states in schizophrenia. The devil introduces them using the disposition for contemplation. It is a paradox that he discovers in the ill person these possibilities. One can easily find in the illness these parallel states to special graces and special states.

These states give false spiritual cognition – contradictory to the theses which are in God – and one can easily find in them these contradictions.

The **supernatural words – in the illness will be the voices.**

These are extraordinary feelings. A man can possess the instrument by which the spirit and God can transmit the contents which man can hear in their spiritual heart and in the head. This phenomenon is well known in the mysticism. The sort of voices and behaving on them is described by Saint John of the Cross in the book *The Ascent of Mount Carmel* (part 2 chapters 28-31). After the invasion to the spiritual heart the devil uses these instruments (in the person who possesses them) to transmit his contents.

There is no greater theological problem (except the complaint of the phenomenon), if the voices are speaking without any sense.

The problem exists when the voices are speaking – as the ill person is thinking – with sense. This phenomenon is in itself extraordinary – that the ill person thinks that s/he speaks to God. S/he asks supposed God about different things and receives answers. In such dialogue s/he finds a pleasure – s/he can't stop it. S/he lives according to the teaching of the voices and he introduces to his/her life this false cognition.

The point is that the ill person usually doesn't hear the voice of God and s/he can't differentiate it from the voice which is speaking to him/her. S/he is not able also in this state of mind and cognition to appreciate the knowledge which the voices presenting to him/her. From the external observation one can see that the devil leads such person to possession. Very often, after some months of such teaching, the ill person is not able to the single-handed life – such is the value of this teaching. The voice of God would enlighten him/her and would integrate him internally and the false contents which have inspired the ill person till now should fall off from cognition.

Not every person is led by God in the spiritual way by listening of His voice. It depends not only on the grace of God, but also on this person's disposition. One can obtain a high level of the spiritual cognition without listening to the voice of God. As I have written, in the case of schizophrenia this disposition is important – because if somebody doesn't have it – they will not hear the voices of the evil spirit too – even when the spirit invaded their spiritual heart. The situation of such person in the illness is much easier.

In spirituality around 10 -15% of people have such disposition to hear the voice of God. The same percentage of ill people will hear the voices.

Visions appear in the spiritual life and in schizophrenia. Visions are pictures or sequences of pictures which are inscription in the visible reality (and one can see them there), or the pictures perceived by the internal sign in the spiritual heart or shown during sleep. These pictures convey the message – God teaches by them

– showing something. This message is easy to understand – evident to the receiver. It is materialized in the form of a vision about the spiritual reality. The dream – vision one can remember after many years – the picture doesn't disappear after awaking – as it is in a normal dream. Hallucination will not be an instruction – will be only a false presentation without any deeper sense.

Saint John of the Cross divides visions into those appearing through senses and without them. The most popular vision is of course the Apocalypse of Saint John. In the illness visions are full of spiritually false elements. The ill person recalls:

I had my head burdened by the prayers. I was very tired. I was walking down the street. Suddenly I felt explosion in my head. On the front of the church suddenly I saw two monstrances – one with the white luminous centre, the second one with the black centre. After this they joined together and became a luminous mark. It was divided by half – when I was closing and opening my eyes. I perceived that it was not a good sign.

I ran quickly to the sacristy and I saw a photo of pope Paul VI and a photo of cardinal Wyszyński with the mark – a letter P cross out on their foreheads. The priest had also this mysterious mark on his forehead.

I went quickly home to see myself in the mirror and I saw that I didn't have this mark. Later I saw that I had – but the letter P is on the one side of the forehead – the cross out on other side. I noticed that my mark is false. For the people whom I saw on the street this mark was correct or some people didn't have it.

I was convinced that the humanity is divided into two parts. The person who has the correct mark will be redeemed, the one who does not have it (or has the false mark) will be condemned.

I presumed that I am condemned. I was afraid that I would go to hell. I started to feel the torments. They were terrible similar to the fire in my soul.

The priest to whom I went with my mother said that I am ill and I should go to the hospital. When I drove in a taxi to the hospital I saw around the lights which before I have seen on the front of the church – they were lighting and switching off. This all was accompanied by the conviction that I am the Antichrist. That there

– where the Antichrist passes (it means me) – here will switch off the light of the faith. I thought that the taxi is driving me to hell. I was extremely afraid and I suffered terribly, because I didn't know how to defend myself against this all.

In the spirituality around 1-3% of people have the disposition to see the visions. The similar percentage of ill people will be exposed to the spirit which will utilise these possibilities to transmit his false cognition.

The night of spirit is another type of phenomenon. Through the night God leads a person to the union with Him. The night has its equivalent in the schizophrenic depression.

It should be mentioned here that **the total abandonment by God is common for the depression and the night of spirit.** The difference is only that in the night of spirit the abandonment is only subjectively felt, whereas in the depression the real invasion of the spirit to the spiritual heart takes place.

If the person has the disposition for contemplation – such type of the spiritual cognition as contemplation **requires ways through nights.** Every new spiritual stage will be achieved through the night. God pulls the will of a person to Himself, but the spirit present in the emotions and in the sentiment, in the reason, even in the will – if he wants to change – to pass to the higher level – to adapt to the spirit pulled by God will – must experience a sort of a shock. This adaptation is unfortunately painful. Every change of the spiritual level is compensate through the night, or by depression if the changes go in the opposite direction. The more emotions and feelings, the more contents are accumulated in the emotional memory and the nights are more numerous or more painful. In the spirituality on certain levels there is no other pass from one level to another than the passage through nights.

Therefore, people who suffer from permanent depression should examine themselves:

– If they have the disposition for contemplation?

– if not too much contents are accumulated in their emotional memory?

– If emotions and feelings are starting to hobble their will?

Here also every stage of the way opposite to the spiritual way will result in depression. If such person started the spiritual life, s/he would experience nights in the same moments of passing to the higher spiritual level. Such depression is not an illness, but only a reason of extreme unconsciousness of own spiritual dispositions and the lack of adequate spiritual way for these dispositions.

The experience of **internal emptiness** is well-known in the spirituality. During the spiritual way one can place it before the union of the will, when the mystic breaks all the schemes based on nature – when the order based on nature is replaced by the supernatural. Emptiness is a sign that such change is making happen, and that a new spiritual quality is being created. **The abandonment of nature and life based on its logic is accompanied by going through the emptiness.**

The emptiness is a bothersome subjectively perceived experience which can last during the nights even for a few months.

In schizophrenia the emptiness dominates the ill person and their surrounding. In the ill person, because the evil spirit introduced them to the sphere out of nature – additionally he hobbled the will – and because of this hobbling the ill person can't leave this space. This sort of emptiness is not accompanied with the night – it will not be a stage before the next step of the union. It is a durable state of isolation very often accompanied by the schizophrenic depression.

In the spirituality one can also observe **pressures.** A pressure means that God forces a person to do something with the use of internal power, for example to testify about something, to read a sentence from the Bible etc. God wants to convey certain contents by internal pressure, draw this person's attention to something.

The equivalent of pressures exists also in the illness. The ill person recalls: *I lived on the 5th floor in the block of flats. The voice started to repeat to me persistently – go out to the balcony and jump down. Simultaneously, the unknown strong internal power started to push me in to the direction of the balcony. I held myself by both hands against the frame of the doors – and I had to use all my power not to be pushed out against my will.*

Thus, on can compare these states existing in the spirituality to the states observed in schizophrenia.

In the spirituality it is God who triggers these states. In the illness these states are caused by a contact with the devil. The common trait is that they irrecoverably tear out from the natural life. But the transition is not simple. In schizophrenia because of the original injury, and because of the next consequences the wounded emotional and sentimental "instrument" will not perceive the devil like the mystic perceives God. However, one can observe similar elements of this perception. These states are well known and recognised.

Regarding **cognition** – in the psychosis and in contemplation one can observe a great perspicacity. It is a spiritual cognition as if over the possibilities of the intellect. In contemplation it is a clearly read from God, from His not contradictory cognition – in the psychosis it is the cognition read from the evil spirit – with all the contradictions which one can find in his mind. Additionally, it is read by the not purified human mind which results in additional absurdities. In the psychosis the ill person can see the extraordinary links between situations, events. This link can be known and observed only by him/her. Sometimes these links are so deep that they date back to prehistory or the mythology. The ill person is absolutely sure that they are true.

Analysing these links by pure intellect one can see visibly that this link doesn't exist, that the spiritual person served to the ill person a very suggestive false spiritual cognition which the ill believed in.

Thus, in contemplation and in psychosis, one can observe powerful out of intellectual cognition. In God – true cognition – in devil – false cognition. Cognition given by God exceeds natural capabilities of cognition, it rises and cleans the intellect – and therefore it has a great value.

The powerful cognition in devil does not separate the ill person from perceived spiritual reality. It draws into the reality as into whirl. It causes damages in cognition because of false contents and spiritual traces left in the intellect and emotional memory.

The cognition given by God in clear contemplations is accompanied by the feeling of God's love – this element is absent during the illuminations triggered by the devil in the psychosis.

The spiritual states deriving from God are generally accompanied by the internal silence. Silence is a background of these states. God comes with a relatively small internal movement.

In the schizophrenic psychosis the illumination occurs by the merger of the lower part (emotions and feelings) with the environment occupied by the evil spirit. There is no silence resulting from the separation from the external world. When the devil enters he does it with a great movement. The inspirations coming during illuminations force the ill person to give an immediate answer (because of the merger), and the ill person (who does not understand what is going on with him/her), usually answers immediately.

Which states are observed in the illness is an individual thing. Every person has a little different spirituality trait. Not everybody is led by God by supernatural words or visions.

But He leads in such a way as to take out from the natural life – and to introduce to the supernatural life. Devil also takes out from nature, but he pulls to his direction. He doesn't give cognition, no spiritual fulfilment – he is as if suspended – and does not allow the possibility to return to nature. Going in his direction is only a deeper entrance into illness and cognitive confusion.

Since there is no return to the natural state – spirituality should be the indication for therapy of schizophrenia. This is the only possibility for the ill person, where the spirit, which is God enters in place of other spirit – devil – throwing him out and taking his place. God enters in the dispositions for contemplation which devil discovered and economised – instead destroying and causing spiritual collapse – He rises, develops, ennobles a person.

And because in schizophrenia we deal with the devil – the spiritual way should be started by asking God for help – because nobody is able to liberate themselves from the power of the evil spirit.

CHAPTER 9

SCHIZOPHRENIA AND THE DEMONIC POSSESSION

In some country family a little girl started to behave strangely. As if seized by her own thoughts, she stopped to react to the instructions of her parents. She was brought to the nearest monastery and people tried to carry her to the church. To no effect. Four strong adult men were not able to carry to the church the girl who was 12 years old. There was a huge strange power in her and they were not able to handle it.

They put her on the ground and when the exorcist came, the girl started to insult him. She shouted – 'You are a thief, you are a thief'. The exorcist answered – 'Yes, I stole some eggs and I sold them, because I needed the money to buy a notebook'. He stole eggs when he was a young boy and it was the only robbery in his life. The devil remembers or rather he can see the sins which he inspired. Later, even after many years he makes accusations because of these sins. From time to time exorcists may experience this.

The girl was freed by the exorcist. The moment when the spirit went out was visible – he went out by the hand which for a moment got as thick as a thigh. After a moment she entered herself to the church.

I described here a classic example of possession. The devil entered, dominated the will, entered into the body. He was thrown out. This event was not long, therefore had no influence on the future life of the girl. Practically it was only a dramatic episode.

In schizophrenia the devil does not attack a man from the side of the will but from the side of emotions, feelings and emotional memory. These attacks (knocks) which start from the original injury can last very long – even throughout the years. This is not a singular entrance like during the possession. Schizophrenia is the result of the whole sequence of events (which one should notice), and one of them (when the spirit invades the spiritual heart) has a greater influence on the explosion of illness.

Depending on how deep the results attacks have, one can talk about the schizoid trait, about schizophrenia (where the devil invaded the spiritual heart), or about demonic possession where after the entrance the devil dominated the will and body.

The demonic possession is the third, the heaviest state which can accompany schizophrenia. But the possession is not the essence of the illness and it is relatively rare. The people suffering from schizophrenia and possessed are only about 0.5% of the population suffering from schizophrenia. The ill person consciously commits mortal sins and by this recklessly enters to the area of devil. The ill person additionally possessed, loses control over their behaviour. They are not able to liberate themselves from this state. Exorcist's help is necessary. But the liberation does not heal schizophrenia, because the whole sphere of emotional memory needs to be healed. **The exorcist will not remove the whole, complicated net of the emotional tensions additionally transmitted to the body.**

The schizophrenia sufferer has hobbled will (the feeling of being in a vicious circle from which it is difficult to get out). But this hobbled will has (even limited) the possibilities to move. One can call schizophrenia the possession of the centre of emotions or feelings – and nothing more.

The difficulties in schizophrenia are based on another problem – the structure of devil which possessed the centre of emotions. In the Gospel about the possessed (Mark 5:9) Jesus asks the devil *What is your name?* The devil answered – *My name is Legion ...for we are many.* (NIV) The question of the name is the question of the essence. The essence is that there are many connected penetrating themselves spirits. In this book I will examine the simplest example of such connection. It is created by 3 spirits.

On the top there is a spirit representing pride. It is always the highest in the hierarchy. It is very difficult to discover him. Its task is to keep the spiritual steer and reverse it from the will of God, out from the cognition which is in God. The second spirit is the killer. By encouraging aggression, it causes anxiety, spiritual pain. The third spirit represents the desire. This complex structure is of great importance, it causes the ill person to move in a circle, it is impossible for him/her to find the exit, s/he is mentally unstable, his/her mood changes from one extreme to the other and desires also change quickly.

The task of the spirit representing **the pride** is the dissuasion from the way to God which is the only solution for the ill. The spirit representing pride will block this way smartly. He will offer thousand doubts, he will try to prove, that such way has no sense. He will try to show the saints and provide the thoughts – look how great people they were – you will never reach their spiritual level. He can also provide thoughts that the spirituality is a waste of time and now nobody lives in such a way. He will smartly cover, block the place by which the ill person could exit. He will show here his extraordinary smartness – he can imprison the ill for many years. Because of his actions will, the ill person despite complaining about his/her fate, arduously discussing religion, will not take a step towards God.

The second spirit is **the killer.** It will try to introduce to the ill person aggressive thoughts against other people and against themselves. It also induces anxiety – it is in a large part responsible for anxiety states.

The third spirit represents **the desire.** It is weaker than the two others. Its task is to introduce impure thoughts to the consciousness – up to total losing of control over sexuality and the total possession of this sphere in the ill person. If sexuality is a therapy of aggressiveness and such person is not open to the cognition of God – it is very likely that such triple structure will start to enter to his/her spiritual heart and emotional memory.

Because in schizophrenia these spirits are conjoined – all these states which they cause will also overlap. This all will give a feeling of total hobbling. It shows how terrible illness schizophrenia is. That such structure will enter is a consequence of the original injury and disintegration. The spirit representing pride will enter, because the fundamental problem for the ill person is the struggle against the disintegration – rather than following God. Because of the original injury the ill person has lost the spiritual horizon. The devil inscribes into him/her the ill person searches for other goals in his/her life on his/her own.

God will throw away all spirits at once – it is not important for God how many there are. But it is important to the emotional memory – because such structure of spirits will deform the emotional memory in its own way. Later this should be taken under consideration during the therapy.

CHAPTER 10

THE MAIN THESES AND PROBLEMS OF THE HEALING ON THE SPIRITUAL WAY ON THE FIRST STAGE (ON THE PURGATIVE WAY)

Why schizophrenia is so difficult to heal and why does it degrade so much?

It is because a young person in the beginning of their life is knocked by the evil spirit from the very high spiritual level, which at the moment of the knock is not available to them. The devil knocks a defenceless, unprotected, helpless person who has had not time for spiritual progress in their life.

There is a great distance between the extremely malicious spirit which has huge cognition and the defenceless little or young person who is not able to defend or protect or respond to this terrible knock. To be able to do this one should go through all the years of spiritual development. This knock as well as the next ones are given with extraordinary premeditation – as if aiming at the existing wound.

Additionally, this knock is directed to the sphere of emotions and feelings. In the moment of the knock the devil is totally inaccessible, and the person knocked in the original injury is partially spiritually blind. Later the paralysed emotions and feelings start to perceive the world in a distorted, ill optics. They can't repair themselves, later they overload the emotional memory with the distorted perception of the reality. The overloaded emotional memory by the parallel block of nervous connections results in the sequence of negative consequences described before and in spirituality it will make impossible for example the union of the will with the will of God. Such union can't take place without purification and healing of the emotional memory.

The knocked person is not aware who made a knock and how great the depth of this knock is and in which direction s/he should go to get free of its results. S/he unconsciously follows the normal natural way and rhythm and as a result of greater and greater disintegration s/he fails. Unaware of the tragic nature of their situation, s/he enters the vicious circle with no exit.

To find the right way which should be additionally the way to God is extremely difficult.

Without the help of God the ill person will not get free from the results of knocks of devil. S/he will not get free from the spiritual factor at the emotion which the devil has written to their memory. This liberation can be done only by God with the active participation of the ill person. However, a great spiritual effort is required for this spiritual struggle – not by the moments of the spiritual comfort. The ill person should undertake this spiritual struggle and s/he should be conscious of this. All the spiritual way in schizophrenia is the everyday, huge, consequent effort (led by the help of grace). It is the struggle against the malicious, perfidious spirit, which blocks the way to God. With the spirit with a great supernatural cognition. Therefore, all spiritual tradition of the Roman-Catholic Church, developed during the centuries is useful here.

In the schizophrenia the relations to God, to other person, to oneself are cut. To restore them one should start to reconstruct the relation to God – as the basic relation. Other relations shall be restored on the basis of this fundamental relation.

The problem of the schizophrenia is a supernatural problem – the techniques and the means of the therapy which do not surpass the nature will not heal. In the moment of the explosion of the illness the devil extracted a man from the nature, sensuality, in which the man has stayed, moved and s/he acted. It was extracted forever and left the experience of the existence of the supernatural world. This experience has left a permanent trace and many people immersed only in the sensuality don't have this experience.

The ill person will never return to the life happening only on the level of the nature.

The natural cognition doesn't exhaust the cognition. To resolve the problem of the schizophrenia also the cognition of the supernatural is necessary, which is given by God as a grace, as a gift.

Also there is no cognition without the illumination and fortification by God. The events from the past are often very painful. The truth about oneself is very painful too. God shows it little by little, by some kind of illuminations. But He shows this to a man fortified before s/he is prepared to see it. Only a man fortified by God is able to accept the full truth about oneself. Only as the person progresses in the grace, God shows the successive fragments of the truth. God does not use this method of tearing the robe, which is used by the devil. The devil knocks with the fragments of the truth (and only for this he shows it), to the ill person who is not prepared to accept it. God acts otherwise – he protects and defends the man full of sins, or weak, showing him only such an image of Himself, which the man is able to undertake, to bear.

The spiritual way is necessary for the ill person to enter the supernatural life – that s/he will see oneself in the supernatural aspect. To see the way of their life – their faults, defeats, good points, successes – all in the light of God's love. In the aspect, in the perspective in which s/he has never seen oneself. In the light and in the fortification given by God, who exists, acts, takes care, protects – and has done this always in the personal history of life.

Moreover, all complicated problems connected with the person of devil one can observe only in the light of the Holy Ghost. Thus, a person of the devil who he acts and accuses God before a man, because of his hidden activity a man has objections to God. Hidden, because only in the light of the Holy Ghost this activity is visible – his activity reveals this. Not all the acts should be ascribed to the devil, but only exactly those acts which he inspired. One should see him exactly there where he has really acted.

In the light of the Holy Ghost **one can see exactly the elements of devil's logical constructions in different theories and the false**

points of them. Without the help of the Holy Ghost it is not possible to find them.

The manner of inscriptions in the emotional memory shows that the sooner one starts the spiritual way, the better. However, often in order to undertake it, one should experience total helplessness, the lack of the natural methods, one should recognise the personal defeat with the struggle against the illness. And paradoxically the cases of total defeat, of total helplessness are a good sign for the healing on the spiritual way. They facilitate a decision to submit the life to God as did the unjust steward who analysed his bad situation in the face of the powerful king and decided – *I know what I'll do...*(Luke 16:4). (NIV)

Such radical decision is always the beginning of the new spiritual opening, leaving the previous way of life. The radical choice of God, the radical transformation and reversal according to the words – *But seek first his kingdom and his righteousness, and all these things willbe given to you as well* (Matthew 6:33). (NIV)

Many people who have not gone through this radical reversal in their lives after the little successes in the beginning of the therapy have again fallen into the illness. They have lost the time without return, they haven't changed their relation to God and they haven't entered the spiritual way.

Schizophrenia extracts a person from their life, denies their plans, projects in the beginning of life. The ill person can't believe what happened to them. They move with the momentum. When they lose it and they will understand their situation, they are ready to change something. But until this time they remain in the absurdity, as they can't undertake life because of the illness (and they are very bitter because of this), but they will not undertake the spiritual way. They also do not expect that the way on which one can seemingly lose a lot is the way to liberation from the illness.

Everybody who undertakes the spiritual way will experience God's protection and God's leading. God will be their personal teacher and guide. He will teach them by the light of grace, by the internal inspirations, by the providential external events. The ill person from the beginning (because of the consequences of the original injury) will have problems to understand this teaching but later they will quickly learn to do it. They will experience God's kindness, mildness, subtlety, faithfulness, consequence in leading and the providential care.

God will not discourage because of their weakness, deficits, revolts, of sudden losing of confidence, crises. With great patience and gently he will lead and teach them. There are the traits which are totally opposed to the traits of many terrestrial teachers, whose relation to the pupil can be shown by the sentence from the Gospel – *they stripped him of his clothes, beat him and went away, leaving him half dead.* (Luke 10:30). (NIV) The experience of God – teacher who with extraordinary patience, mildness, and kindness leads from the depth of the illness is revelatory and new. Usually the ill person hasn't experienced anything like that before in their life.

Without the spiritual way there is no full picture of the illness. There is also no picture of God from the grace of whom all people live, who takes care of people, who protects them, leading and healing.

Also there is no possibility to recognize the devil – the source of the evil. One should reach to the devil to find the roots of evil which happened to the ill person. Without the spiritual way there is no perception of yourself in truth. There is no new relation to another man – relation full of evangelic love, which does not link a person with the evil which s/he has done.

The relation to God is the fundamental relation in the human life. The process of healing should start from the restoration of this relation. The basic way is not led by talks, workshops, physical exercises, the theatre or by cinema, even by work, although all this is important.

The reconstruction of the relation to God is the most important in the therapy and one should say it to the ill person. The ill person shouldn't be afraid to construct the individual relation to God – despite many mistakes, failures, and losses. The spirituality is trouble and toil where success is not and will be not the easy, perseverance and endurance are important.

The main theses of the spiritual way (and also of the therapy), on the first stage (it means on the purgative way), result from the two premises.

1. From the science concerning the devil – about the manner of his activity and about the way of fight against him.
2. From the great spiritual wounds of the ill person and from the spiritual disintegration.

From the science concerning devil and his activity against a person results that **the higher in a person he is situated – the weaker he is – the lower – the stronger he is.** Thus, the weaker he will be in the will and in the reason – by these upper powers a man unites with God. In these powers also as he is higher – he is weaker. Generally, the nearer to God – the weaker he is.

But in the lower parts of the soul in which the soul unites with the body, in emotionality, sentimentality, emotional memory – the devil will be much stronger.

Thus, one should remove him first from the upper powers not lower ones. First one should remove him from the will, from the cognition, later at the second stage – from the emotions, feelings, and the memory of emotions and feelings. **This order in the healing process should be strictly kept.** In the emotions and feelings the devil is so strong and so heavily situated that nobody from the beginning is not able to remove him – specially by the partly occupied will and cognition.

The devil is a spirit, over which only God dominates and only God by the power of his grace (with the active participation of a man) can remove him. And because this rule is not applied, there is absence of full consciousness, against whom the spiritual struggle goes on – practically all schools and directions of psychiatry fail.

Thus, the partial cleaning of the will and reason will fulfil the first stage of the struggle against the illness.

The second fundamental problem are the extraordinary injuries of the emotional memory of the ill person. And here one should utilise the rule mentioned before – that at the first stage of the therapy **– one shouldn't touch the emotional memory of the ill person.**

This sphere should be left to God that slowly through His grace will purify and heal the will. And only as much as it will happen, the ill person, will open themselves to their past and the external world.

And here one should have great patience towards the ill person. It is necessary to create the conditions in which they would open to the grace and accept it – to speak to them about the spiritual way, invite a priest, lead them to the church, help them to prepare for the confession or prepare them for the Sacrament of Unction, to pray for or with them, encourage them to read religious books.

One can hear the secrets of the ill person, but one shouldn't give them the subjects to think, because they are not yet prepared for this.

The role of the priest, psychologist should be of the subtle and consequent spiritual company, but not of breaking a very weak will of the ill person.

At this stage one should observe the progress made by God in the soul. One should not outpace this progress in expectations and not accelerate it by force.

What kind of problems one can meet in the beginning of the spiritual way leading to the healing?

1. The first fundamental problem is the **reluctance of the ill person to restore health and the life in the world.** The image of the world which the ill person had before the illness was not full. They perceived only its negative aspect. Such aspect really exists, but it is not the full image of the world. The ill person was tragically injured by this negative aspect in the past, fell to the bottom of the illness. The ill person will perceive the return to the world as the next struggle, for which they have no strength.

2. **Lack of knowledge that schizophrenia is related to the spiritual life and lack of awareness that God can guide a man through this illness.** In schizophrenia, if the ill person does not undertake the spiritual way, practically they have no chance of healing. By healing I understand the possessing of such perspective which is in God and undertaking the life according to such perspective. There are methods which can improve the efficiency of life, but they only trouble the spiritual life.

3. **The reluctance to undertake the spiritual way.** In the schizophrenia it results from the structure of the evil spirit which made the invasion to the spiritual heart and specially because

of the spirit which is in the top of this structure. It is him who is responsible for the isolation of the ill person and whose task is to dissuade from the spiritual way. This spirit blocks and covers this way smartly and in this way he closes the way to healing. The ill person will discuss for many hours, but they will not make any change in their life. They will not get free from the sphere controlled by this spirit. It is the additional internal barrier which the ill person must overcome.

4. **Disobedience of the ill person, submission to false cognition, false inspirations or false revelations.** There are the problems to reach to the consciousness of the ill people, because usually they disobey, they are obstinate – and they have no cognition about the illness. Additionally, the lack of full perception of the reality about themselves is weak. The ill person makes the same mistakes and is not able to draw the conclusion about themselves. For example, they hear the voices and trust them indiscriminately. In this way they waste time and are deceived by the spirit. They hear false inspirations and they can't recognise them. They are not able to go out of the sphere dominated by the spirit and out of the sphere of false cognition. They do not know that without leaving this sphere and without leaving the sphere of the world, they will not make any progress. Unfortunately, it can happen that the ill person will use all arguments possible, sometimes false and senseless to defend their attitude. Because the spiritual way should be rather exact – such disobedience can totally disqualify the ill person.

5. In the schizophrenia **mood swings** can take place during the day. The schizophrenia sufferer has the sensitivity of barometer. On one hand, they must strictly observe themselves so that the hesitations will not escalate and they must quickly prevent them – on the other hand, if they undertake the spiritual way, they must carry it out consequently. The ill person must know themselves very well, immediately diagnose themselves, quickly react to the changes. They should know the methods which are utilised in the spirituality, should know how to use them. They must smartly use them in the struggle against the spiritual problems and against their internal weakness. The ill person should also know

their actual spiritual possibilities and undertake the struggle only as much as they can bear – they shouldn't lead the spiritual struggle beyond their capabilities and forces.

6. **Because of the "perforation of the system"** it is very difficult to recover from schizophrenia in a city where 10% of the inhabitants participate in sacraments and lead life according to the faith, where there is practically atheism. Or, in the country where the ideology, or behaviours are far from the rules and the climate of the evangelic love.

As a result of the perforation of the system, the spirit which is really outside penetrates the spiritual heart and the limbic system of the ill person. During the progress in the grace and during the long periods, in the beginning of the therapy he seriously distorts the perception, makes the will weak, causes long periods of physical and spiritual faintness.

To prevent it, it is good to go away for some time from the place of living. To go away, to change the external spiritual conditions. After some time the ill person will not feel this change of external conditions, because the reason is in their emotional memory. But the change of these external conditions even for a short time, because of the perforation of the system, is recommended.

In this book I apply the stages of the spirituality as they are proposed by others books of spirituality. Thus, from the beginning of life in grace to the first contemplative prayers there is a purgative way. From the contemplative prayers to the ecstatic union there is an illuminative way. Later after ecstatic union there is a unitive way.

In the spiritual way of the ill person the stages will look little differently. The border point between the purgative way and illuminative way will be **a crisis**. This will permit to look more carefully and to change the theses of spirituality. Also, one can construct the border between the illuminative way and the unifying way in the **simple union**. This union belongs already to the perfect unions, and in a great part active purifications finish there. This will show also the greater part of the passive purifications (as the nights of spirit) which are important at this stage.

CHAPTER 11

THE PURGATIVE WAY (TO THE FIRST CONTEMPLATIVE PRAYERS)

The first problem which I would touch in the beginning of description of the spiritual way concerning the schizophrenia sufferer is the problem of undertaking it. To a healthy man, the spiritual way, the evangelical way is a proposition. One can choose it and undertake it or one can reject it. The Church doesn't force anybody to choose it – it tells only about the final consequences and consequences for cognition during the life which result from undertaking or rejecting it.

To the person suffering from schizophrenia there is no such choice. The liberation from the evil spirit will not take place without the way to God. The ill person will not liberate themselves from the influence of the spirit. Every ill person can undertake or reject this way in the Roman-Catholic Church (and happens very often). But they must be conscious already in the beginning of all consequences of such or another choice.

They must be conscious that in the struggle against the devil there is no free choice and there are no free methods. The devil is the enemy so consequent that to beat him one can't utilize methods at one's own discretion, as there is a big problem in the case of mistake.

The schizophrenia sufferer has no such possibilities, such liberty. They march to God, but in the struggle against the devil **which is a characteristic rite of their spirituality.** Therefore, there is no freedom and it makes the difference. The evil spirit will use pitilessly every discretion, every inconsistence. It is mainly him not the other person that is the main spiritual enemy of the ill person.

Thus, the way to the healing will not only be a way to God, but this way will involve the struggle against the devil. Therefore, it has to be specifically followed.

I will start from the repetition of classification of what a schizoid trait, a schizophrenia, or a schizophrenia and a demoniacal possession are.

There are people in schizophrenia possessed by the devil, who in a moment of clean consciousness want to change their state to undertake the spiritual way and can't do this. These cases where the ill people can't liberate themselves are not many. In such case, the help of the exorcist is necessary.

The role of the exorcist in the whole process of healing is not big. It is important in the cases of possession – to help in the first step of the liberation. But the liberation from the demoniacal possession is not healing of schizophrenia. It is the first and very important stage. A complicated process of the healing of emotional memory is necessary for the healing of the illness.

If the devil invaded the spiritual heart (and such are the main cases in schizophrenia), God will throw the devil away in certain time after the beginning of the spiritual way. One should remember that God is the best exorcist and He will liberate the spiritual heart of the ill person.

When one should start the spiritual way? – when the ill person is conscious and sufficiently strong.

One should not start the way to God during the psychosis. During this time the ill person can refer the evangelical texts to themselves and understand them literally. For example the text of the *parable to show them that they should always pray and not give up.* (Luke 18:1). (NIV) The ill person will perceive this text, that s/he will pray without stopping, but when the psychosis finishes, they s/he will stop to pray totally.

Also, very often the structure, on which the physical and spiritual life is based, can be broken in the moment of the first explosion of illness. This broken structure will not bear the full charge of the prayer and of ascetic life. In this case one should leave a margin of endurance so as not to permit to break this structure again and again.

In the schizophrenia until certain moment one should take medicines. They help in the relatively short time to calm down the symptoms of illness and return to the external normality. The medicines are the important invention which can help a person. But the whole system proposed by the psychiatry is effective only in the first phase. It will not resolve a very complicated spiritual and emotional problems of the ill person accumulated in this illness. It will not liberate from the spirit, it will not help in the troubled internal life and will not give a new cognition and this is all visible. One of the reasons why one should take the medicines is the quick stabilisation of the mental health which will enable to undertake the spiritual life. When this life will be in rather advanced phase the medicines can be taken away.

I will start from the differentiation of the problems of the relation to God and the feeling of God's presence.

Relation to God is the reflection of the picture of the Holy Trinity in the top of the soul. This relation is destroyed by the sin which is committed by the will. Because of this **the full relation is reconstructed by the confession.** There is no other way for the reconstruction of full relation. Without the confession a certain relation exist, but it is not a full relation. The confession reconstructs the picture of the Holy Trinity in the top of the soul, without the subjective feeling whether the relation exists or not.

The feeling of God's presence is the perception by the spiritual heart of the loving presence of God. It is an important question in schizophrenia, because the ill person's perception (unconsciously) will feel the presence of the devil who make the invasion there. The perception cannot be linked to the relation. There are people who never feel the God's presence, but they have correctly constructed the relation to Him. And also many people have the feeling of God's presence and mistakenly identifies God's presence with the correctly constructed relation to Him.

In the schizophrenia first one should reconstruct the relation – very often not existent – and later to have correct perception of God's presence.

To examine the relation to God **self-examination is helpful**, and the relation to God is reconstructed by **the confession.**

And one should start all spiritual way from the confession. There is no full relation to God without the confession. And here the ill person can make many mistakes. After the confession s/he can better feel God's presence, but this feeling has no influence on the relation which is reconstructed only during the confession. The ill person must know about this and does not speculate if there is a relation or not – and doesn't suggest what s/he actually feels.

Thus, **one should start the spiritual way from the confession.**

In the case of the schizophrenia sufferer one can meet here several problems.

1. The schizophrenia sufferer is a man more beaten than sinful. If it was possible to find the proportion between sinful and beaten – it would be like 1:10 or 1:100. During the confession one should not remind the ill person – look how sinful you are or one should not lead them by looking for sins or by the endless examination of sins (such schools exist). In the confessional it is more important to rise their spirit, to rise from the beating, to give hope, to show that Jesus resurrected half-dead Lazarus and the same He can do with the ill person. Later one should show that the ill person by the grace and by active purifications is possible to bring together this great disintegration which touched the ill person. It is important to give them hope which the ill person would not receive in any other place. One should not discourage the ill person by the spiritual severity, categorical behaviour and high expectations which one can meet in a confessional sometimes.

    One of the first advice to the ill person should be that s/he will not give back the knocks which s/he received from the friends, family, other people. This means that s/he opens to a great stream of God's charity over all their situation. A person who beats or gives back the knocks is totally closed to the activity of God's charity. This breaking of the scheme and opening to God's charity (giving the situation in God's hands) is one of the first important stages in the spiritual way of the ill person.

2. The schizophrenia sufferer from the beginning does not have the exact understanding what a sin is and what is not. **One commits a sin by will.** And this is a sin and this should be told

to the ill person. And very often during the confession the ill person tells about what takes place in their imagination – and only there. Such situation needs a great experience from the confessor, that he will not think that a great offender, a great sinner is confessing. And it can happen so if the confessor without any criticism will believe in all what the ill person tells him and what happened only in their imagination.

3. The schizophrenia sufferer doesn't see their sins, s/he has no feeling of the sin, s/he doesn't see the burden of the sin. S/he will tell for example, that s/he kicked the dog on the street, but s/he will not mention that s/he didn't help their ill father. In schizophrenia this ignorance of the value of the sin results from two reasons – from living in such a terrible reality where the conscience has not formed correctly yet, and because of the ill emotionality, which made impossible the correct perception of oneself. The ill person doesn't see themselves fully, s/he is not able to recognize their mistakes and sins and their depth. Not only because of the absence of the grace, but because of their emotionally troubled perception. The stable conscience forms for a long time and the temptation to work according to one's own rules, not according to the theses which are in God remains in them for a long time.

4. The ill person has the feeling of hatred to themselves. They expect a great punishment for their sins. And here a great role plays the feeling of the confessor – not to leave the ill person with such feeling and on the other hand, not to treat them too light.

5. The schizophrenia sufferer should confess to the confessors who are characterised by goodness and mildness. The confessional is a place of the extraordinary opening – not all the confessors are conscious of this. In the confessional, because of losing the delicacy, by censuring of the expression, by the impossibility of the free pronouncement, by the returning to the second side of the spirit of the expression – the ill person can be heavily beaten. There are many examples of this. The confessor shouldn't be a censor additionally surprised that the sin exists. By the attitude of the confessor the ill person should have the pos-

sibility to express their sins freely. The confessor should not return the spirit to the second side (often it happens so), not knock back the ill person with the spirit. His role was to liberate from the spirit – not to return it. The ill person should avoid the confessors who hurt in the confessional.

6. The problem of appearance of the thoughts is a very important problem in schizophrenia. These thoughts can be blasphemes, aggressive, impure. These thoughts appear in different situations, for example – on the priest, who is lifting the chalice, to an unknown man passing on the street, to an unknown women on the bus, etc. It is difficult to find any logic in it. These thoughts enter by themselves to the consciousness, they make trouble – and they live the consciousness by themselves – without any participation of the ill person. Partly this is the result of the perforation of the system. These thoughts cause the conflicts in the consciousness. And here one should explain to the ill person that such thoughts are not a sin – if the ill person does not find a pleasure in them. If they appear, the ill person should cut them off by the will. In practice, it is enough to say I don't want or I don't accept it, when the thought appears. This separation of the thought by the will causes that there is no sin. And this one should tell to the ill person. From the thought which has came by itself, and which was cut by the will – one should not confess. The sin is only in this case when the ill person accepts such thoughts – when they start to like them. In schizophrenia the important question in the beginning is to learn how to manage such thoughts and how to do it in practice. As the spiritual life will develop and the disintegration will be much smaller – these thoughts will disappear and only the echo of them will stay longer – but after some time (after the active purifications) – there will be no problem with them too.

7. In the case of a spiritually difficult situation – of a conflict, crisis, quarrel – or every similar situation – one not should not wait for confession. The devil with whom the ill is struggling reminds the competitor fighting on the mat. If he felt that his opponent has lost a balance for a moment, he tries to overthrow him. And here such incredible escalation of events takes place

around the ill person – which is possible only around the schizophrenia sufferer. Very often the environment of the ill person is so much directed by the evil spirit against the ill person and it doesn't understand their behaviours and doesn't make any reflection on this. It looks like a tempest around the ill who explodes suddenly, multiplying the attacks and problems – and later slowly calming down. And here one should have a great spiritual experience not to take part in the collective and unconscious attack against the ill person. This sudden attack from the side from which the ill person didn't expect it makes great damages in the weak mentality of the ill person. Every hour of such perfidious attack can cause the return to the hospital. The ill person (very often provoked), as the revenge starts to struggle with the evil spirit and against the person partly possessed by him. And here the method to cut the escalation is a quick confession. And in this case one not should not wait for it.

8. It happens very often that the most painful knocks are received from the closest persons – from the father, mother, brother, sister. Very often the ill person lives together with them or because of the circumstances they only contact with these people. The favourite and the most often utilised techniques of the devil is to lead to the clash. The evil tries to affect the will of two (or more) people in such a way that they will attack themselves in the most brutal way possible. If the ill person is one of such people – this attack can ruin the beginning of their internal unity. And here also the sudden confession is a way to cut such bilateral attack. In such case, one not should start to apologise the second side (the more so if this side has provoked this altercation). Very often this person doesn't want to apologise which causes additional conflicts of the conscience of the ill person. And here one should not try to apologise by force. In this case one should go to the confession. To the question of the confessor – 'Did you apologise?' – the ill person should answer – 'I will do this'. The practice shows that the evil spirit cut during the confession automatically retreats also from the other side. The problem of apologising, reconciliation and the normal change of opinions is much easier.

9. Until the crystallisation of the conscience, the confessions should be done often, 12-18 times during a year. As much as the ill person feels the need for confession – they should do it. The confessor shouldn't discourage or dissuade them from frequent confessions. After the purification of emotions the confessions will be less frequent. Such process shouldn't be accelerated by force.

10. The ill person should learn the self-examination. By the method of Saint Ignatius of Loyola every day in the evening or by another method, but frequently. It is a question to form the right conscience as if from outside – which s/he has not from the beginning because of the weak formation of spirituality.

11. So as not to be exposed to the misunderstanding or the unexpected knock in the confessional, it would be good to the ill person to have their own confessor. If the ill person finds someone before whom s/he can fully express and s/he feels that such person understands them – s/he can ask for such spiritual direction. The opening in every confession poses a risk of unexpected reaction, and one should avoid this in the beginning of the spiritual way.

12. Sometimes it happens that one can receive a very brutal knock as a result of a certain situation. This knock destroys all the spirituality and causes the resentment in all possible relations. Even if that knock (or situation) was not provoked by the ill person and s/he does not have the mortal sin – s/he should go to the confession, to reconstruct the relation to God and from this reconstruction to start to construct the spiritual balance. And it may happen that in the confessional the confessor will knock them as strong as the knock before – by accusation, scolding, rude answer. In the confessional which is the place of the special asylum, the confessor can give the extra knock to the knock received before. It is a very interesting phenomenon where the devil with his hate even during the confession can reach the ill person. One should simply know that such phenomenon exists. By the personal sin of the confessor, by the losses in the spirituality or through the simply sight the devil can act even there. After such confession the ill person should

return to the normal state, because of the reconstruction of the relation to God. Unfortunately, the trauma after such confession and the feeling of lack of defence can stay in the ill person for a very long time.

13. During the confession after the expression of the sins one can talk about the current spiritual problems, plans, (pilgrimages, travels, examinations etc.) and about other personal problems – to confess them all to God also during the confession. It is unbelievable how God, who entered in the human life will answer to such confiding of problems and in which extraordinary manner He will answer and the life this answer will bring. Such person who once experienced this will have no doubt with Whom s/he meets in the confessional and what is the dignity of this meeting.

One should remember that the confessor (despite some objections) is the instrument of God. God has chosen him, appointed him to this function, cooperates with him, inspires him in the confessional, corrects his faults, if any. It is a mystery which one can experience when somebody will enter in the spirituality and will accept the leading of God.

Also the basis to construct the relation to God is the **everyday Eucharist.** Why everyday? Because the day is a basic period in the life, in the life of the ill person too. Because in the schizophrenia there is no continuity. Every day is a separate unit – every day is different from another. The mood of one day is fleeting and is difficult to repeat during next day. The plans and decisions of one day very often are not real the next day. The hesitations are so great that from the beginning a day should be a unit of accounting with one's own life. And a day should be sanctified by the Eucharist. Also at the end of the day the ill person should make the self--examination of conscience. The everyday Eucharist from the beginning would be the ideal to which one should aspire. But to the ill person, it will be such great spiritual charge that it will be fine if s/he will take part in the Eucharist two-three times a week. The ill person must overcome many barriers – to find the time, to force the internal weakness, to break the pressures of the environment to start to live by another spiritual rhythms than one's own family, environment, nation. In the Roman-Catholic Church one can take the holy communion twice a day, but the second time one should take part in the holy mass. One should not discourage the ill person from the idea of the everyday Eucharist. This illness demands the life of prayer and asceticism nearly like in a monastery.

The form which can everyday help to construct the relation to God is **the prayer.** The prayer as the form of being in the presence of God and the form of the conversation with him. And here the ill person will notice that all their problems s/he expresses by gestures or by words in all possible directions nearly to all met people, but no to God – the only who can remedy them. The way to God was in this illness closed by the evil spirit. The picture of God troubled by the spirit, the spirit has isolated the ill person, had cut out their relation to God – and during all the next years this is all visible.

One can start the prayer by the expressions, confiding, describing and presenting to God their own problems. The ill person should repeat this expression for as much time during a day, as much s/he feels such necessity. The ill person should introduce such forms of prayer which s/he knows, which s/he remembers from the childhood from the catechesis. The life of prayer has one general rule that one should go through all forms of the prayer – from the simplest ones to the more advanced. One should do it really, by themselves, making all possible mistakes. One should go through them like through the childhood diseases to quickly find the reasonable conclusions. One should start by the prayers to Mother of God or by the prayers through the saints for example to Saint Anthony of Padua or Saint Teresa of the Child Jesus.

The prayer should be the main factor in the life of the ill person. The life should pass between the prayer. This transformation should be visible. Going out from the active life to the prayer which is real and visible.

It is not possible to start the spiritual life without the visible and real living the world. Especially in this illness it is necessary to isolate oneself from the knocks given by the world. The time of the ill person should be really offered to God by the prayer, by the lecture, by the pilgrimages – should be really offered to God, because in the schizophrenia the daily rhythms are totally disordered. One of the form which can return them is just the prayer. From the beginning it is good to pray in the fixed hours, for example at 8 am, 12pm, 3 pm, 8 pm and to respect these times.

What problems related to the prayer are encountered by the ill person.

1. The ill person's **structure on which the physical and spiritual life is based is broken.** One should pray in such a way as not to break this structure again. Thus, s/he should arrange and realize the rhythm of the prayer, but when it will start to burden the structure – to change it, or stop it for a certain time. Later the burden of the prayer can be greater, but generally one should be wise, which is very difficult in the beginning of the spiritual way.

2. In the schizophrenia **the reality doesn't reach to the ill person, because of the troubles in the emotional perception.** Also the meeting with God (and this is a prayer) during the long time will not have a factor characteristic to the meeting of two people who react to each other. In the prayer of the ill person, there will be from beginning only the quantitative factor of the prayer. There will be not a meeting with its all complicated subtlety.

3. Next to the extraordinary **distractions** which appear during the prayer, the presence of the evil spirit appears which enters with his own inspirations, false consolations and presence. The distractions during the prayer concern the current matters, personal matters, people met during the day, personal problems. These problems appear during the prayer one after another. It is amazing that they are so alive, as if they lived their own life, in the consciousness even after many days. It happens that after the prayer of one hour only for the last 10-15 minutes the ill person is concentrated on the not troubled image of God.

4. **The schizophrenia sufferer is scrupulous.** If s/he misses one of the hours of prayers – s/he will try to make it up. If s/he misses the Hail Mary in the rosary, s/he will pray it even if all the church prays the Glory Be To The Father. S/he will tell the parish priest

that he didn't say the prayer connected with the indulgence. Even during the solemnity s/he will fast as if without their practices the church will get destroyed. The scruples are the oppressive spiritual problem. By introducing the irrational anxieties they take out the spiritual peace. The ill person will be healed from the scruples after the purifications of emotions.

Despite these problems, one should undertake the life of the prayer being fully conscious of them.

What advice concerning the prayer can one give to the ill person?

It is good to pray by the Liturgy of Hours. From the breviary for priests and monks. By such rhythms as the Church prays. It will be good that the ill person entering the church could also enter the rhythm and manner of its prayer.

One should increase progressively the burden of the prayer. One should be regular in the prayer if it was not possible to pray – one shouldn't make up this hour later. In the bad mood one should pray less.

The intentions of the prayer should be simple and general – for salvation, health, family, church, the country. One shouldn't pray for the complicated or global or political problems, even if they affect the ill person. The intentions should be comparable to the weak powers and forces of the ill person. In the case of undertaking intentions which are above the possibilities – the evil spirit can incite the ill person to aggression. It is important not to destabilize the weak spiritual powers by wrong intentions.

It would be good to take part in the group of prayer for example of the Catholic Charismatic Renewal. The presence in such group does not protect from the knocks which one can receive also there. One should in the reasonable way consider if in the life of the ill person there is a time to for greater opening or not. One can construct the spirituality also without the presence of the group, but the experiences of the prayer and of the presence of the group, even partially negative, are also useful.

One should learn prayers by themselves, one should like the prayer, one should find the time to pray, one should start to pray in such a way as one can do it and to continue such prayer. The Holy Ghost will lead the prayer and teach the prayer. One should permit that the prayer will change. The change in the nature of the prayer shows that the prayer is developing. The ill person should not to stick obstinately to the plans, schemes of the prayer. The prayer at this stage corresponds to the sensitive level of the man – there are the simplest forms of it. Later one should complete or change them – so as not to stop the spiritual progress.

Also **the asceticism** shows how complicated and full of contradictions is schizophrenia.

There is a necessity of asceticism, because the rhythms are very disordered in this illness. It is necessary to introduce even the simplest order – regular practices – to do it as if by force, from outside, to mechanically restore these rhythms.

On the other hand, there is the breaking of the structure on which the physical and spiritual life is based. The structure which will never endure the burdens like a healthy person. By the ascetic exercises such structure can be broken again, but on the other hand the spirit will hide himself behind the unmortified functions. There is a necessity to treat the body and the emotional memory severely so as not to permit to receive the new, false spiritual contents. But this not liberated (because it will take place later), but overloading structure should not cause the appearance of the element of psychosis.

The hatred towards oneself, the characteristic trait of schizophrenia is transferred also to the asceticism. And also enjoying great expiation, non– acceptance of one's own spirituality without such tough elements is characteristic. In the asceticism it is important not to cross such point, not to make such subtle mistake, when asceticism, because of the great hardness, should destroy the spirituality.

The schizophrenia sufferer is the person with the "killed necessities". S/he hasn't developed them, because of the original injury, and because of the early illness. In the asceticism one should differ undeveloped necessities from renunciations. One should remember also that at this stage of development it is difficult to use another asceticism than this relating to the body.

Even the greatest asceticism will not remove the contents from the emotional memory of the ill person and one should remember also about this restriction.

Despite this fact, I want to mention the corporal ascetic exercise which is **the discipline**. The discipline is the group of whips or one whip 70-80 cm longs one should utilize to hit oneself, at the shoulders or the buttocks. In one round it should be 4-6 knocks and rounds from 6 to 12. Between the rounds it should be 5 minutes of break. The exercise can be finished by the visible breaking of the activity of the evil spirit. One can't utilize it more than once a week. It's the exercise which has a great efficiency and it is difficult to replace it with something else. This exercise does not purify the emotional memory, but for a short time eliminates the spiritual result of this lack of purification. One should utilize it on the stage only to break the activity of the spirit in the moments of weakness and powerlessness.

As far as the voices are concerned, one should act according to its suggestions. In the spirituality there is a hierarchy of the observation of the commandments, later one should hear the indications of the confessor and in the end hear the internal inspirations of the voices and one should categorically respect such order.

To ignore the mortal sins and to hear the inspiration given by the voices is a great spiritual fault, also dividing the voices into nice and unpleasant without the possibility of the verification of them can open to the false cognition which they very often claim.

The first stage is a stage relatively simple and joyful. Simple – because own effort is usually correlated with the progress in a grace. Joyful – because discovering everyday the new reality – the reality of the faith – is joyful.

There also appear new problems in this spiritual life, which result from the development, for example, because of the pride in the cognition. The ill person will be instructed by the environment and these instructions are not corresponding to their spiritual situation. One should be prepared for the appearance of these new external spiritual problems, as they prove the spiritual progress.

This stage is well-described by the manuals of the spirituality. One should go through it – not to make it shorter or faster – so as not to be ahead of the grace. This stage is completed by the appearance of contemplative prayers which guides this spirituality of the ill person in the totally new direction.

CHAPTER 12

FROM THE FIRST CONTEMPLATIVE PRAYERS TO THE CRISIS

The appearance of the contemplative prayers is the turning point in the spirituality. It is a great surprise. Practically nobody expects the nativity of God in their own spiritual heart. To every man this is a new image of God which changes in the fundamental manner the understanding of God. From the image of God taken from the catechism, the creator of rules to God alive who enters with his love to the heart of a man.

The first observation of the perspective of time is that a contemplative prayer has appeared in the life of the ill person relatively quickly. God has mercy on the weak, ill man - He fortifies, He rises and He heals them, He maintains them. He does not become discouraged because of their troubled cognition. What is visible here is the different logic of God than the logic of world and the logic of some spiritual leaders to whom the ill person is not the value to be directed or even to speak to. This is also the first painful opening of eyes to the problems and relations of the world and of the spiritual circles.

That the ill person is gratified so quickly with the gift of contemplation is granted as if on credit. God wants to rise them so that s/he will not go back under the influence of the evil. It is the first important step on the long way and the ill person should be conscious of it, and s/he will be not cleverer that the parish priest, s/he will not start to proclaim their own teachings. They should march consequently on the spiritual way and patiently wait for what this way will bring them.

It is the period of great spiritual joy, a spiritual surprise, a period similar to the first love which does not repeat.

The contemplation is takeing out from the natural order. The appearance of the contemplative prayers provokes to look in two ways at one's own life - at the future and the past. The natural way which dominated in the past has finished. What was important in it, what marked its canons has lost the importance definitively. Starting the time of contemplative prayers is also a time of spiritual mistakes which accompany the spiritual progress.

The first is **the spiritual greediness.** The ill person is very often a solitary person, beaten, who needs the feeling. The contemplation gives them a great sentimental satisfaction, but one should not induce God by force - one should be not spiritually greedy. Tauler comments it shortly, "Not to try to drink more that somebody can do it".

Saint John of the Cross learns that the feeling of God is not God - and one should not stop long time on God's consolations and such consolation doesn't testify about the state of the soul - and one should not make the conclusions because of it. It is good when God comes, one should not be despaired when he is absent and not to induce his presence by force. God purifies the soul by presence, and one should receive him with dignity and in the noble way. The spiritual greediness is one of the "illnesses of childhood" and one should pass by it as quickly as possible.

The second mistake is **the perception of every spiritual presence as the presence of God.** The evil spirit comes also with his presence. The example of the beautiful dragon from the life history of Saint Ignatius of Loyola which fascinated the saint is the classic example.

The third thing is as Tanqerey writes to tell **the sanctimonious nonsenses** in the style of Saint Peter as – 'God how much I love you and I will never leave you'. It is the first time of such meeting in sentiment. Infatuation full of great and noble plans. The time of deep intimate declarations and the great extraordinary grace. **This state is named in the spirituality as the spiritual intoxication.** The deep experience of God's love in spiritual hearth which can be taken out of the natural rhythms. **It is the second stage of the imperfect union.** The first was the beginning of contemplative prayers named in the theology of the internal life as **the prayer of quiet**. Now this is the second stage named **the spiritual intoxication.** The example of such intimate declaration from this period looks like this:

Lord Jesus, my dearest God, ruler and master of my soul, my only love, after the days of trouble, of struggle against the devil, against the world and against myself You gave me the time of rest, of joy, in which you are pouring on my soul the abundant streams of your God's pleasures, as beloved to be loved in the deepest secretiveness we can declare the love to each other. Being happy we can maintain in happiness and reciprocity, which the world can't give. Your heart fulfilled by the grace, the infinite source of love permits me, a sinner and perfidious man, to take part in celestial feast prepared to your elect. I implore you not to lose this time when you are speaking to me personally. I want all to become a dessert on which only You and I live. Only You should be a teacher of my soul and only to You my soul should listen. May the virtue of prudence advice me how to admit You with dignity, to place you in the first place, to sit at Your feet and hear You, hear without end. To glorify and adore You, to leave the whole external world and to look at You without end. To thank You, to admire only You, to look at Your loving eyes at the time of Your visitation. Let Your stamp be engraved in my heart forever. That I should not waste this time by distractions or unnecessary activities, that I would not reverse my soul to the vanity in this blessed time. That I would deeply draw from the well of life, that if it suffices forever, I will never be thirsty, that the words illusions would go away like husks and your heart would be the only guide to the eternity. That the bad thoughts and whispers of the devil would not reverse me from the aim and Your presence in the Eucharist would make me stronger and when the times of dryness, weakness and difficult experiences come, I will ask you to guide me, to give me a force deriving from Your cross. To look for the force and the light in it and as after the storm the sun rises please make this experience bring me closer to You. That I would love you in the joyful admiration and stay in such state forever.

In this union God enters to the feeling and satiates it to the depth in a sweet, subtle and delicate way. This union lasts some (4-6 weeks), because of this fulfillment by sweet love and the satiation of the feeling to maximal possibilities - this union is characteristic. So great and subtle satiation of feeling will not repeat at other stages. The ill person will think that s/he obtained the depth of the spirituality.

Alas the crisis, which will come soon, will invert this arrangement state after this union in such a way that there will be no trace of these noble declarations or of this state which will stay only in the memory. **This union will complete its aim - to extract from the preceding state, but the spirituality will go in another direction.** The state of the spiritual intoxication will not be continued.

What can one advice to the ill person? That s/he will find the conditions to survive this period deeply and with dignity (and the next if this state will repeat), that s/he will detach themselves from the fixed schemes of prayer and that s/he will be conscious and recognise this extraordinary visitation of God.

But also at this stage the ill person should not take any pledge, any declaration, because s/he is too weak in recognizing the will of God and the time to undertake the will of God will appear much later by the union of the will. If it turns out that will of God is different than it appears from the first noble declarations, the ill person can later have great scruples, and the case of Saint Peter is the best example of this.

A little later in the spiritual way, in the fourth mansion (using the language of Saint Teresa) **the temptation of the activity** can appear - to be a Church activist. The ill person recalls:

There was a moment when I started to perceive a weak organization in my parish church. I wanted to organize new loud-speakers to my church, to buy new benches, to order new song books. I finished the course for guides to organize the pilgrimages. Generally, I started to look for the field of activity in the church, in the beginning in my parish church.

It is well-known that at the certain stage the people with the disposition to contemplation are tempted by the activity. It is well-known also that this temptation appears on the level of the fourth mansion. It is one of the symptoms that this level of the fourth mansion is coming - and it only proves it. It is important to know that one should not collect the merits by the activity and there are many examples of such attitude - one can find them easily around.

The trait of the contemplation prayers is that by them God purifies the mixed elements. Separation of the spirituality from sensuality makes order in the cognition, enlightens and rises a person and this is how it happens for a healthy person. For the ill person the contemplative prayers purify only partially - they do not purify the emotional memory from the contents accumulated there. **Contemplation does not liberate from the past emotions.**

The natural cognition will be still limited, the supernatural cognition based on it will not be able to do the synthesis. The spiritual progress will take place, but soon it will be stopped. The spiritual progress will cause that the ill person will feel the most subtle knocks on the upper layers of their spirituality and s/he will be surprised that s/he feels them so much. They destroy the basis of their spirituality which as s/he thought was solid. Thus, the spiritual development will take place, but by the partially limited cognition (of which s/he is not conscious), increase of spiritual power, but after the numerous knocks made by the environment, it is surprising that the resistance is not greater. There are differences between the normal way, where the cognition, the knocks and the resistance go parallelly in the way of the ill person.

In the normal spiritual way, after the appearance of the contemplative prayers, the quantity of prayers should be limited, their nature should be changed. But in schizophrenia if one will limit the quantity of prayer, the ill person because of the distractions will start to be occupied by other not useful things. It is a real problem of this stage. The distractions emerge from the not yet purified emotional memory, which collects the events as before and are engaged by them and they are obstacles in the prayer.

Because of this (despite the grace of the contemplative prayers) the time of the prayer and reading should be rather long (up to 2-3 hours daily). Only such quantity guarantees that there will be distractions.

The distractions are the thoughts coming during the prayer detaching from it. The thoughts are: how the mother is feeling, what things I have to do today, what the neighbour said yesterday, what I must buy today in the shop, how was the scene in the film and so on. Such thoughts appear during the prayer and engage all spirituality for a lot of minutes. Because of this, the time of the prayer should be longer to finally be concentrated on the prayer.

On the other hand, too long prayers cause **the "rinsing on the prayer"**. The result of it is the loss of spirituality, joy, freshness, lively reaction during the prayer. Such problem exists and the ill person should take it under consideration and to realize it according to their possibilities.

Thus, the task of this period is to detach oneself from the world passing by the distractions, despite the troubled perception to deepen a relation with God by asceticism, to create the new spiritual behaviours, based on the spirituality, which needs time.

This is a very important task. Without separating from the world, there is no return to it with new perspective. This separation emerges in anxiety – although that the world hurts, the ill person is afraid to be separated from it. The ill person will criticize the world, complain about it, but will not allow to be separated from it. But s/he should remember that without such separation, s/he will not make any progress in spirituality.

This intensive deep spiritual life after the time will introduce the will to **the crisis.** It is a surprising phenomenon, extremely difficult experience, different than the expectations. The ill person, after the long way to God, after a relatively short period of admiration in contemplatives prayers, faces the terrible spiritual power which tries to overturn the spiritual way.

When the contemplative prayers obtain some depth, when the level of the prayer is up to two-three hours and there is no problem to maintain it, when the ill person starts to accord to the word of God, when the word of God starts to be alive, when the ill person starts visibly to accept the will of God and this is accompanied by the visible symptoms of separation from the hierarchy and perspective of the world, when the ill person starts to hear the first internal inspirations of God - at this moment **the great crisis of faith** appears. All this happens at the moment when the deeper union with God seems to only be a question of time and it should be the next stage in the spirituality of the ill person. When one can observe the first greater success (subjectively perceived) on the spiritual way, the beginning of which is evidently visible – at this moment the spiritual way is rapidly interrupted.

The ill person recalls:

Suddenly (it means during two-three weeks) the attacks on the purity started, difficult to define, because I was not able to relate them to any person. I did manage with them, because I increased the quantity of the prayer, which was great before. Somebody made remarks to my father (but to help him) and I started to go in his direction to "explain his behaviour". I felt that I would punch somebody with pleasure, but I didn't know whom and for what. I was surprised because of my aggressiveness. I was under great pressure of the great power, with which I did manage by the rest of my forces, but I was afraid of what will happen with me after some months.

The image of God has moved a little further. It was not God touching my heart as before by the subtle, tender touches. God was distant and he did not react. He was as if behind the transparent world – absent. God which has left me.

I was introduced to the huge spiritual space separated and distant from God, but also separated from the environment. A person who was not able to recognize oneself, as if his spiritually stuffed dummy, lifted to the unknown spaces. Currently, I was not able to perceive the external world – I was not feeling the necessity to open to it – I started to be afraid of it a little. The attacks were greater and greater. I felt that I will succumb to them and I will destroy all effort and grace.

What are the reasons for this crisis? To unify the will, one should purify the emotional memory and make order in emotions and feelings – just for this purified lower part this sanctified upper part will be submitted. In the normal spiritual way active and passive purifications do this. It goes on in the natural way – nearly automatically. These purifications go in parallel to the progress in the spirituality.

In the same way in the beginning it goes on in the case of schizophrenia (because there is no difference in this phase), **but the great part of contents from the emotional memory of the ill person are not liberated.** These not liberated contents are some kind of obstacles, bridgeheads which the evil spirit possesses in the ill person. In this spirituality there is a moment when the evil spirit attacks just in these places, with great power. The ill person has to face this enormous power. All this process of spiritual integration suddenly stops. If the upper part purified and pulled by God and the lower part, in which the spirit has its bridgeheads and which resists and this causes the crisis. In the spirituality of a health person the night of senses will take place there.

This crisis comes suddenly – it can appear during some weeks. It can attack in a sharp and violent way. Again one should recall the structure of the bad spirit which can help in explanation of the direction of this violent attacks.

There are generally:
- attacks on the purity
- attacks by aggressive thoughts and aggressive attitude towards the environment
- attacks on the God's teachings (especially on the theses of God's justice and God's providence) and accusing God of many problems.

This attack is so violent that the ill person in the short time faces a great power which negates the bases of the Catholic faith, by force tries to separate from this, what they used to proclaim and practice, ridicules this spiritual way and spiritual efforts, negates the possibility of life of faith. It tries to show that the life according to these rules is impossible.

This experience touches a person who already knows something about the faith and religion. S/he knows what is a contemplative prayer, has some experience in the prayer, asceticism and struggle against the devil – is a person who struggled against the mortal sins.

The problem of the crisis related to not liberated memory is an interesting problem with which the majority of the "reformers" of the Christianity have not been able to deal. They have drawn the conclusions from the crisis such as:

- the life in total purity is impossible,
- why one should wait for the God's justice when one can execute it by force immediately,
- the Christian religion needs a reform, because life according to its rules is impossible to be fulfilled.

From the fact of the crisis one should drawn the conclusions concerning the therapy of schizophrenia:

- that the crisis in schizophrenia will take place in every case, because **the emotional memory is a point of contact of two orders: the natural and supernatural order** and they are mutually distorted
- if more contents are situated in the emotional memory – the crisis can be more violent
- from the moment of the appearance of the crisis **one should change the assumptions of the spiritual way** and move on to the active purification

The exit from the crisis will not take place until the emotional memory is not actively purified. If it does not take place, the crisis as described above will appear, similar to the nights of spirit (and therefore one can mistake them for the night), from each the ill person is not able exit even for 20-30 years. The attacks of the spirit are regular – deeper and deeper, they cause a great damage to the spirituality of the ill person. S/he is helpless during them. Receiving knock after knock causes a great suffering, losing the confidence in God. Only the radical change of the spiritual assumptions different to those according to which the ill person moved till now can lead them out of this crisis.

CHAPTER 13

THE ASSUMPTIONS OF THE ILLUMINATIVE WAY (FROM THE CRISIS TO THE UNION OF THE WILL)

The assumptions of this period result from some basic factors and their combination. The important factors at these stages are: the structure of the spirit which invaded, the functioning of emotions and functioning of the emotional memory, the person's feelings in the history of their life and their inscription in the memory.

1. The first assumption is **the choice of the upper love (the love of God) before the lower love (love of a man to a woman and vice versa).** One can pose a question: why the sentimental life and also the sexual life do not cause progress in the life activity and healing of the schizophrenia sufferer. Why the way by sexuality (in spite of the success in the beginning) is so weakly correlated with the healing of schizophrenia, although many people think that this is the way to the exit from the illness.

There are deeper levels than this fulfilled in the human sentimental life. Even the happiest person is not able to reach this level of the sentimental life. Also **the ill person is hurt much deeper.** The meeting with God touches the top of the soul – and this relation fulfils a man in the deepest way, gives a man the deepest meaning. Only God is able to satiate this deep part, only God can integrate a man internally – despite the necessity of natural needs and the inner thirst of a man. It would be a great mistake to ignore God and follow these sentimental needs. If the schizophrenia sufferer does this, s/he will be never healthy. One should radically skip this lower part and its needs. Even though it seems illogical, one should start to construct the life based on the upper part. **This is the most radical, the most difficult step in the therapy.**

Very often in the marriages of ill people after some time both sides need help and are not able to manage with life obligations. There is a small difference whether it is a sacramental union or not. The entering in sins is always the reversed process to the healing, but even this second case is not able to heal.

The reasons of this phenomenon one can find in the complicated structure of the evil spirit which attacks the ill person. As I have written before in the structure of the evil spirit on the top there is the strongest element, representing the pride. Its essence is the constant negation of the will of God, revolting against Him, constant negation of theses which are in God. Subtle, covered negation which forces a man to do the same. These spirits are the strongest in the hierarchy. They are stronger than the evil spirits which force to crime, aggression and cause pain. They are also stronger than these spirits which provoke the sexual sphere, causing impurity.

Thus, evil spirits create a hierarchy – from the strongest to the weakest. All of them rebel against God, but there are some differences in this rebel. Every person who undertakes the spiritual life starts the spiritual struggle against the evil spirits, from the weakest to the strongest ones. In schizophrenia the struggle takes place in such a way, if one can accept that the life of the ill person in a sacramental marriage can partly heal the spiritual damages which caused the impurity – for the healing it is necessary to regain what in the upper level was caused by the spirit responsible for the pride or aggression or anxiety. Only the struggles with the results of their attacks give the healing and it is one-two spiritual levels higher that reaches sentimental and sexual life in a sacramental marriage. Additionally, one should notice that the sphere of feelings is very often so deeply wounded by the evil spirit that the prescription should be putting the "sentimental patch" which is created by another person. All this sphere should be given to God which will start to purify and rise it by the contemplative graces and later by the nights which will come after the active purifications, He will heal it totally.

I will repeat once again that the assumption is very difficult. Similar to the struggle against gravitation, but it looks only so in the beginning. One should support oneself by the God's grace – because nobody with their proper forces is able to force the nature.

Why such arrangement in the structure of evil spirit causes such trouble to a man?

Because in a man a natural arrangement is opposite. On the top there are problems of the transmission of the species, transmission of life (and also sexuality). Lower there are problems of anxiety, but rebels against God are very often ignored by a man and considered less important.

Therefore, to fight against the structure of evil spirits one should do something against their own nature.

The level related to the sentimentality and sexuality is the highest level in a man. In the hierarchy of the evil spirits it is one of the lower levels. After going through it, the removing of the effects of anxiety is difficult and complicated, but relatively easier than the struggle against own sexuality and sentimentality.

Recapitulating, one should choose the radical way to God, the way by the nights of spirit, because only such a way guarantees healing. If the ill person stays in the sacramental marriage, s/he should be aware of the necessity to undertake the spiritual way, the purification of the emotional memory and the necessity of the struggle against the evil spirit located on the upper levels and the effects of their knocks.

2. **The emotional memory has two fundamental recordings – time recording and spiritual recording.**

The time recording can be compared to the veins which are put on the tree year after year like layer on the layer. Because of the original injury these events, these painful events are many and they are multiple registered in the memory. The psychology tells to start the examination of them from the first layers to another. Every surface should be examined, none should be let passed by, because the emotional memory registers the events very exactly. The facts are mutually related. One recalls the other one. **All registered facts remain in the major part in the emotional memory of the ill person.**

The time record overlaps with the spiritual record. Here the problem is more complicated, because looking at the problem from the side of the spirit, one event can be located on different levels. The evil spirit attacks a man with his all complicated structure and for example, by the event in which s/he has limited the freedom (which is situated on the highest level, he also paralyses by anxiety which is spiritually perceived one level below. The spirit attacks a man as if simultaneously on many spiritual levels. These levels one can combine and notice that these levels which take out the freedom of a man cause the deepest wounds and the man reaches them in the end of the spiritual way. The existence of the spiritual levels is an important problem, a sort of a key to conducting the therapy.

Studying all events from the spiritual side one can create groups of them and situate them on these levels and the evil spirit knocks a man to sign in oneself in such a way as to make later the invasion to the spiritual heart after next punch – and to enter the heart with all this multiple structure.

It causes such practical problems that if the spirit is able to attack many levels in a man – a man during the struggle against him **can purify only one level – level of their current spiritual problems.** This does not go on faster because of the weak possibilities of a man in the spiritual cognition. A man doesn't perceive spiritual problems which are two or three levels higher. Because of this weakness in the struggling of a man against the evil spirit, one should fight level after level, not higher, because the spirit will use this and will upset the balance of the ill person and the ill person will be able to understand the depth of all knocks after many years of this spiritual way.

Because of the spiritual factor the capacity of the emotional memory is limited. This memory can't endlessly collect the events with spiritual factor – and this is one of the greatest limits of the human psyche.

3. **The assumption about the spiritual beginning of this neurological blockade.**

Thus, going back and liberating from the successive knocks and simultaneously unblocking these nervous connections, **one**

can go back to the root – to the original injury, to the first neuron spiritual blockade which caused the illness. Coming back one can liberate parallelly – from the spirit which caused the original injury and later inscribed himself by the knocks – one can unblock the blocked nervous connections in the limbic system and in the body. This assumption looks to be true, but because there are two different problems – spiritual and neurological – and because the emotions are governed the same as the body – two different overlapping rules will be used, governed by these orders.

Spirituality is governed by the rules of the spiritual life with its basic states of the soul. The manuals of the spirituality describe them.

But the body is submitted to different rules and the rule whose knowledge is useful in the therapy is the rule of super compensation. It consists in this that the impulse or charge causes the temporal decrease in the capabilities and after some time, because of training of the impulse, the capabilities surpass the starter level – it means that they rebuild with surplus – it is super compensation. The knowledge of this rule is utilized in the construction of plans for sport training. One can estimate exactly the size of the training factor, a period when the body will regenerate itself and when it will pass the beginning level and the length of super compensation. The awareness of these simple physiological rules is necessary for wise planning of active purifications and self-observation, which is related to them, necessary in the case of liberation of the emotional memory.

One should understand the general scheme of active purifications. First, one should express the anger in all relations or meditatively expressed unions with the feeling. This purification liberates this spiritual factor of the picture and touches the wounds in the nature related to the picture. Later, during the confession God cuts out the influence of evil spirit so that he does not return to his previous activity. Later, one should wait until the part of nature related to the wounded place heals. Next, God comes with the grace of contemplation on the new higher level and completes this purification and this is the most important moment. After a time one can observe again the activity of evil spirit whose appearance shows that this cycle has come to the end – and one should do the next active purification.

It means one should follow the scheme: active purification – super compensation and healing of the nature – the contemplation on the higher level, the grace which heals and purifies and again the greater activity of the evil spirit.

These cycles should move by themselves. One should not accelerate them. One can only divide the time – instead of one session of active purification, do 2-3 sessions within one week – and later allow this cycle to go on by itself. The scheme of the super compensation are generally like that, but the ill person should estimate by themselves the dose of purification.

The active purifications are not a dominating element in the Christianity. Generally, the Christianity does not use such exercises and training as leading. In the Christianity it is important to go through life bravely with faith, to keep the evangelic rules, **to reflect the evangelic truth with the heart and reason.** It is about life and taking its challenges. They are the training factors. **It is the observation of the Holy Gospel in the current life that gives the reflection of the image of God in the heart and in the reason of a man or does not give it when the rules of Gospel are ignored and broken.**

Using of such great active purifications is an exceptional situation in schizophrenia, but it is necessary. During the normal spiritual way there are elements of active purifications, but generally God purifies by difficult situations and difficult states.

The active purifications create the bottle neck of the healing process. One cannot go through this stage quicker, as it results from the rules of the super compensation. This is the main reason for this stage to be so long. From the spiritual side there is no reason for such long period, but the neurological and emotional sides are not able to submit to this process quicker. Thus, for the union of the will all processes will be directed by double rules – first resulting from the physiology and second resulting from the rules of the spiritual life. After the union of the will these first processes will start to disappear (finally they will disappear by ecstatic union). This double order with the great active purification will create the trait of the spirituality of the ill person on the illuminative way. As a result, this way will be quite different comparing to the normal spiritual way of a healthy person on this stage.

4. **The emotion which blocks the work of the limbic system (after some time destructing it) is anger – accumulated and impressed in the emotional memory.** Anger accompanies also other emotions. It is considered as **a fundamental and universal emotion.** This union of anger with other emotions enables the possibility to liberate of them all. By the expression of this emotion to God, one can heal the limbic system. Other emotions liberated from anger will return to their proper colours, which till now have not been able to be present. Where does this anger come from? The most general answer is: from the breaking of the natural will (after the original injury), and after the constant breaking of the will by the wills of other people. From the lack of the internal integration and perceiving the spirits present in other people due to the perforation of the system.

The healing starts after the liberation from this extraordinary accumulated anger linked additionally with anxiety, different kind of rebel – which all were accumulated in the emotional memory during for many years.

This anger is accumulated on different planes – at other people, oneself, devil and God. It is very often hidden, covered. **It is difficult to notice it, to observe and to find all people at whom anger is accumulated and directed and to notice it in the full perspective – the natural and the supernatural cognition for this is necessary.** Only in these two orders of cognition, one can see visibly all people (in one's own relationships) who contributed to the emotional state of the ill person.

The absence of the therapeutic success in many schools of the psychiatry is related to the absence of the full perspective, showing all people and all their relationships involved in the events in the life of the ill person.

The emotions of the ill person do not submit to the prayer. As a pounded splinter does not submit to smearing with the ointment. Therefore, the accumulated emotion will be not miraculously changed after the beginning of the spiritual life. It will remain as it was before – and it will fall down deeper in the memory. The arrangement of the will shall be changed, but the emotions will remain as before. Telling to God that such emotions exist will not liberate. **The emotions such as anger should be expressed to God with the same insensitivity, with the same tension as it was perceived before**. One should express the emotional and spiritual factor, but not tell God that such emotion exists. Because of this spiritual factor, the emotions in schizophrenia **are not subject to the process of forgetting.** Because of this the illuminative way will be different to the way in the normal case. The continuation of the spiritual way without the purification of the emotional memory will block the progress in spirituality. What relates to the will should be mortified, but what relates to the emotions and feelings should be expressed to God.

So on the first stage the most difficult thing, because of the presence of the perverse spirit, is to undertake the spiritual way. Now the most difficult is to start the expression of anger. The ill people are the champions of running away into absurdity and negation of anger in relation to anybody. They are perfect in the suppression of anger. Thinking that they are well educated people (and very often it is so) who should not be angry at anybody. They provoke quarrel after quarrel, they violently explode with anger and after that they apologise and so on. And this circulation can cut only the active purifications of the suppressed emotions – in this case of suppressed anger.

This expression of anger is related to the extraction of great hidden pain, because such were the past events in the life of the ill person – deeply hidden in their emotional memory – and one should be prepared for this.

5.   **A factor which has the liberating nature is a pardon**.

As the expression of anger touches the pure emotional factor of emotions and liberates from it – the spiritual factor of emotions and of hobbled will in liberating pardon. On the spiritual way one cannot stop only by the liberation of the pure emotional factor. The expression of anger and pardon linked to it are definitely liberating and making the settlement with the past. It eliminates the tearing and hobbling of the will. This liberation by the pardon is very important in the healing process. Without it healing will not take place.

Why only the pardon is not sufficient – why one should express anger in all relations and this removes the picture linked to emotions?

There are such schools which maintain that one should mostly pardon (by the subsequent steps of the pardon) and this is the most important element in the healing. And the rest after the time will be replaced by itself. That the act of pardon made by the will, it means by the highest and most important power is sufficient and the rest of contents derived from the pardoned problem will disappear by themselves.

But the practice shows that in the case of schizophrenia, this is a mistake – **and such advice in this case of the illness is wrong.** The thesis that pardon is the most important is truth, but a man is not an angel, where the only act of the will causes such results.

It can concern simple drastic events where there is not a lot of accumulated contents – accumulated by the years like in schizophrenia.

The human soul is composed of two parts – the upper and lower part. A part of the upper powers of the will is hobbled by the lower powers, especially by the corporeal sense linking the soul with the body and later the body with the surrounding reality, by emotions and feelings and the act of the pardon made by the will not liberate the will from this hobbling. These upper and lower parts in schizophrenia are separate and the lower parts can be additionally separated by the contents accumulated in emotions and by contents accumulated in the feeling. The illness explodes, when these two parts not only separate, but also when they go beyond their possibilities and stop to react. These two parts are governed by other rules. The upper part uniting with God can be touched by the methods elaborated by the spirituality. The lower part which unites with the world and the body can be touched by the methods which correspond to their nature. **Therefore, the influence of the will is not useful here.**

In the lower parts of the ill person there are thousands of pictures accumulated with these two factors, where one can meet the bad spirit and the pure emotional or pure sentimental elements. Only the breaking of this duality will make this spiritual process move on. The liberation of the emotional memory is necessary to the development of the spirituality. Without this liberation the spirituality will not move on.

The schools telling about the pardon also tell that one should do it in all relations.

In schizophrenia nearly every meeting ends up with the conflict, there are almost as many troubled relations as meetings between people. It means that there should be many thousand acts of the pardon. These pardons should be done exactly. Many years of life – after the expression of anger. Very often the ill person doesn't know who really wanted to knock them, and which event only looked like a knock. **Only the spiritual development will expose this spiritual perspective fully.** Only passing by the point 0 – it means by the union of the will unveil the arrangement of other wills. Until now the ill person reacted emotionally at other people and nothing more.

The schools of pardon tell that one should pardon the first cause and here again one should make the reservation that this is not visible in schizophrenia. This first cause exists, but it is visible after many years and one can find it after many expressions of anger.

In the case of schizophrenia even after the act of pardon the will is still hobbled and the lower part is still influenced by the evil spirit – and this fact alas one should accept. Even the confession does not liberate this lower part. The devil will have still the bridgeheads there, and he can utilize them in certain time.

The practice also shows that the ill person is not able to pardon without the liberation of the emotional memory and one should not force them to do it and to accuse them that they do not want to do it. For the ill person the time has stopped on the past events and only when they see after the active purifications that it will move, they will pardon more easily, because they will notice the liberating force of pardon.

One should mention here the cases where even the liberation of emotions and even the acts of pardon do not bring results and here one should repeat these acts once again after certain time and leave the rest to God and time. It can happen that some single drastic cases will not disappear from the emotional memory until the end.

The evil spirit hit a man not only by his presence, but also by leading the ill person to the extreme tension in emotions or feelings which reached the level of ecstasy – when s/he tries to extract the spirit from the body. The pardon can eventually reduce the spiritual presence, but it is also important **to liberate emotions and feelings from this extreme tension.** This tension one should recall, repeat, because it is written in the nervous system and this ecstatic tension alas can only call God during the violent ecstasy and here the acts of the will not do it. There aren't many such events, but one should remember about them too.

Also, only expression of anger (without the pardon) is not sufficient, because it does not liberate by the spirit which was present in these tensions. We have to do here with the evil spirit and the struggle with him must be led on many levels and plans (even by removing them by the act of the will which is pardon). As a consequence, the spiritual struggle will pass from the state to the state, eliminate the evil spirit from every reached spiritual level.

Without pardon and confession, only by the expression of anger, one can't liberate the spaces occupied by evil spirits.

6.   **The way to the healing leads through the crises and later the nights.** On this way there are the joys derived from contemplation, but there are also long periods of apathy, discouragement, the feeling of nonsense, spiritual breaking, loss of consolation resulting from the absence of God. Thus, the feeling is led by brave entering in the crises and nights and going through them – instead of the expected great spiritual success and joys.

CHAPTER 14

ACTIVE PURIFICATIONS – THE ANGER AT OTHER PEOPLE*

The first gifts of grace encounter totally blocked emotions and enslaved feeling. This causes a crisis and the spiritual progress suddenly stops. Thus, the purification must take place and order should be made in the emotional memory – it means in the emotional history of life. This must be done to find the exit from the crisis.

Anger is a fundamental emotion which accompanies other emotions. Because of this, by the examination of the anger in different spheres and by removing it, one can purify the emotional memory.

The entire illuminative way relating to emotions goes according to the following pattern:
- **the expression of anger**
- **confession**
- **pardon.**

This pattern should be repeated up to making the total order in the emotional memory. This can permit to liberate the condemned will and unite it with the will of God.

The problem of the expression of anger can be reduced to the problems:

- why to express anger at God but not at another person?
- how and how often one should do it?

---

* The scheme of the expression of anger is taken from the spiritual exercises "Healing of the memories" led by priest Andrzej Grefkowicz – the head of the spiritual centre "Wieczernik" from Magdalenka near Warsaw.

The total healing of the troubled relations between two people can be done only by God – and in front of Him one should present these relations. In God all relations are filling up, and without Him there are not able to reach the fullness. God clears the accounts of all closed past situations. Only He can liberate a person from the spirit, which was present in the past, in the passed emotions or in the passed feeling, and which wounded a person in the past. Also one should expose emotions to God, not to hurt the other person and not to totally break the relation with them.

Very often the ill person gives back by the same spirit by which s/he was wounded but that s/he will give back, s/he will revenge, doesn't mean that s/he will liberate themselves from the knock and the spirit.

One should not organise therapeutic meetings and invite for example a mother or father to present to them all the griefs and to express the anger at them – and expect the healing. This is a natural pattern: either me or them. This pattern will not liberate from the spirit which was present and which hurt a person. This scheme has also a false thesis that by the expression of the knock to other person, by pay-back you will receive the healing. The engagement of own will to hit back destroys the relation with God and leads the healing in an unknown direction. On the other hand, if the passed hurt emotions are not expressed, they will not be healed.

Thus, one should invite God to the healing process on the level of emotions, and express to Him the past emotion towards another person – to entrust all past complicated situation to Him.

What are the forms of anger expression?

It can be a form of writing a letter. One should write a letter to the person which wounded the ill person. In such letter the ill person should express the contents which s/he has not expressed before for different reasons – anxiety, because s/he didn't want to hurt somebody, s/he didn't feel strong enough to do it, etc. In this letter **it is important to liberate the emotion of anger from the past – to express this accumulated anger from the past.** It needs a courage and honesty towards oneself. Practically, it means to challenge this person and to present this expression to God – this letter should not be sent to this person. This letter should be read to God – in the Church, before the cross. These visits to the church in the beginning serve to force the consciousness to Whom one should express the anger.

The second form of the expression is to find a secret place and to express anger loudly – practically shouting.

The third form is to construct a dummy which symbolises a person who wounded – and to knock the dummy with a stick, a piece of rubber, etc. But this form should be utilised in the end and only to those cases which after 2-3 rounds of expression were not able to be liberated otherwise.

One should answer two questions:
– who wounded me in my history of life?
– when was it?

In the emotional memory the facts are spiritually linked – one recalls the next one. Because of this, one can reconstruct their whole own emotional life even with the alleged memory loss. It is good to construct one's own emotional life history – history of emotional hurts. It will be necessary for the following analysis and purifications.

Psychology teaches that the expression of anger should be start from the oldest situations – and one should do so. Also the beginning of the relations in human life are the relations to a mother and father. Any other relationships are base don these two relationships. Also one should start from the analysis of these two basic relationships – if the ill person is strong enough.

During the examination of relationships and the expression it is good to take under consideration one year. One year at school, one year during the studies. To recall the places, the people, the situations. To recall 30-50 situations when somebody hurt us emotionally. And to express anger at these people. And to make such analysis and expressions year after year.

How often should one express anger?

Anger at other people is the simplest kind of anger. It can be expressed practically every 3-5-7 days, if the number of people is not big. The first expression is usually a great shock and one should wait when all the functions will go back to the normal state. And in a such way one should behave in other cases – this results from the rule of the super compensation.

One should remember also about the discipline during the expression – not to jump from one period to another – because the emotional memory accumulates the events very specifically. One period should be purified as exactly as possible. During the expression the emotional unloading occurs. If it happens, it means that the session was well done. These 30 – 50 situations should be divided to the groups of 3-5 to be expressed together. After this there should be 15-20 minutes of break. Because the expression of anger is a spiritual struggle, one should not start it, if they are mentally tired.

I write about it in detail, but one should only use the rules of the Christian discernment.

After one or two expressions of anger, **one should go to the confession.** The confession includes the sins from the last period, but everything that was the object of the expression happened usually many years before this period. However, one can repeat to the confessor some more difficult situations. The result of every confession besides the absolution and the elimination of the results of the sins, is the cutting out of the spirit which influenced the person. Every confession creates a new spiritual quality, which is the basis of the spiritual health.

The next stage is a pardon. One should once more remind the situations expressed before – and to say – by the power of Christ I pardon (and here one should notice exactly what and to whom) – and in this way going through all previously expressed situations.

The pardon is the act of the will. I pardon – it means also that I renounce the devil which was present in this situation, which did hurt me and I pardon to a person who hurt me, and I pardon the evil by which this person has touched me. By this pardon I want to restore the troubled emotional balance and will-related relationship to God and to the person who hurt me. A pardon is liberating and internally unifying too, because it restores the relationship to God, and renounces the spirit – one removes him from the upper and lower part – from the will and from the emotional memory (from the past emotions and feelings).

There is no healing of emotions without their expression to God, without the confession and without the pardon (where the spiritual factor of emotions is finally liberated). All the schools which proclaim that a pardon is not necessary and one should only liberate the emotional factor – do not provide the spiritual progress. The pardon liberates from the spirit, which was present in the past emotion and which blocked the spiritual development. On the other hand – only pardon as such doesn't eliminate the emotional blockades – is an ineffective practice, beyond the capabilities of the ill person. A pardon itself doesn't liberate the emotional level which can be still occupied by the evil spirit.

Thus, only such triple acts – expression of anger, confession and pardon remove from the spirit and liberate from both – emotional and spiritual factors.

It is difficult to pardon. It is necessary to recall painful events from the past and to split with them spiritually, as they became the part of the history of the ill person.

What are the results of the expression of anger?

The emotional freshness returns, tension in the emotions is eliminated, the natural perception of the world appears. In the spirituality the prayer of languages begins. It is the contemplative prayer in which also emotions take part. This prayer can appear after the liberation of emotions, but not before – even if a person has known the contemplative prayer.

After the first expression of anger the ill person recalls: *In the morning, when I woke up and looked through the window at the green branches of tree, moved by calm wind, I had the impression that last time I had such feeling 20 years ago – and the following life was well illustrated by the picture of The Battle of Grunvald with all tension, chaos, disorder and struggle. I became extremely calm, silent, and softened. I wanted to come back to this primary order which I have lost in my life. From this morning the world started to look otherwise – calmer and milder. The tension which accompanied me for many years disappeared and I was not aware of its existence.*

What problems can accompany the expression of anger?

1. The ill person is extremely disintegrated, spiritually broken. In their emotional memory one can see visibly this disintegration. It is exposed by the hundreds and thousands of events perceived as painful. For the ill person it is difficult to see the basic problem – s/he is not able to pass through these numerous events, and s/he stays in the background of these events. There is not other way than to remove them as expression – one after another. The ill person will feel how the great layer of anger and tensions is below each event. And how much time one should spend on removing it.

2. One should remember that the anger towards a father, mother and especially the anger towards God has the specific weight – the recovery time after such expression should be longer.

3. The problem with the expression of anger is to face the false ideas which the ill person has. The first one is that a polite person doesn't feel anger towards anybody. It is very difficult to persuade such person to start the expression of anger. Such person can use a thousand of arguments against this. But s/he has the symptoms of accumulated anger. The repressed anger is visible in them.

4. The ill person notices that they enter the expression of anger with the impure, full of desire thoughts. It is the result of the structure of spirit. In the schizophrenia the aggression is linked with desire and rebel. One should know about it, and to keep discipline during the expression. The aggressive thoughts are linked with desire and rebel against God – and they should be expressed all at the end of the session.

5. It should be known **that anger can be hidden also in other relationships and in other planes – and it will be liberated later** – at the higher stages. If the ill person observes that the anger

exist, but s/he is not able to remove it – s/he shouldn't do it by force. This anger will be liberated later.

How long should one express anger at other people?

As long as the ill person feels that the anger is accumulated. And the second test – when the next little crisis comes.

The expression of anger at other people results in the visible progress in unloading of the emotional memory. The ill person starts to be active, their life is slowly changing. But it becomes such state when s/he feels that s/he has no accumulated anger towards anybody, but still other people hurt them by their wills – by their irritating opinions which load the memory for many days and from which s/he can't liberate. They paralyse, cut out the forces of life, hobble their will. The ill person notices that even though s/he expressed the anger – s/he is not able to enter the external world, s/he is afraid of the next knocks. The ill person will notice too that their resistance to the knocks is not much bigger than before. S/he is also not strong enough (spiritually and mentally) to undertake regular external activity. And here, s/he should pass to the next stage of the expression of anger – to the expression of **anger at oneself.**

CHAPTER 15

THE ANGER AT ONESELF

What does the ill person think about themselves is shown in the poem by William Cowper *On the reed*.

I was of late a barren plant,
Useless, insignificant,
Nor fig, nor grape, nor apple bore,
A native of the marshy shore;
But gather'd for poetic use,
And plunged into a sable juice,
Of which my modicum I sip
With narrow mouth and slender lip,
At once, although by nature dumb,
All eloquent I have become,
And speak with fluency untired,
As by Phœbus' self inspired.

In this description made by the ill poet, practically there are no positive traits. No good origin, no good look, no importance, no place in the society. Additionally, these negative traits are so exposed and written in such unexpected context that one can doubt whether somebody from outside would be so great a critic as "oneself". The unknown spiritual force pushed the ill person out from all planes of life and deprived them of any support in their own nature and society.

This is the first argument for starting the expression of anger towards oneself and starting to restore the true image of oneself and enter the real place from which the ill person was forcefully pushed out.

The second argument is that the ill person is pushed out by the spirit, but through the wills of other people, whom s/he met in their life. These ill wills pushed the ill person out to the place where s/he is now. Also the contents accumulated in the emotional memory after the original injury – as they become greater (and they become such as the others' wills were pushing out), caused such a state of the ill person.

And there is a paradox – **to take out the influence of these wills and leave the sphere of their activity and to liberate from them and purify the own emotional memory and liberate own will – one should start to express the anger at oneself.** This mechanism was already noticed by Dorotheus abbot – the monk from the 4th century.

After the original injury the ill person couldn't leave the sphere of senses, s/he couldn't enter the spirituality – s/he couldn't accept the other perspective than the perspective of the hostile world. This false perspective hurt their emotional memory and caused the hate towards oneself and prisoned their will. Now through the expression of anger one can cut out the influence of the wills of other people and purify the memory of emotions.

What the ill person will accuse oneself of?

Of that s/he has no success in life, of all failures in personal life, numerous mistakes committed throughout life and many particular things and behaviours. Generally, the ill person hates oneself for this how s/he is, and whom s/he is. But the way as s/he seems to be – the devil inscribed in them – and the ill person accepted this false picture of oneself and this false opinion.

And here, one should take year after year – express the anger at oneself by choosing 30-50 situations. The scheme is the same as described before: **expression of anger – confession – pardon.** The pardon to oneself by the words – By the power of Jesus Christ I pardon oneself (and here one should remind and say what exactly).

What is the state of the ill person who starts to express anger at oneself?

Even in the expression of anger at other people there is a hidden aggression directed to the surrounding world, to other people.

The ill person feels to be hunted down and thus, s/he is deeply unhappy and unfulfilled.

S/he has no physical and mental powers to undertake the activity and to enter active life.

S/he dreams to be a strong and great person. S/he has no faith in achieving this in life. S/he feels totally burned inside. The hobbled will makes them enter into the wills of other people and s/he accepts them or answers them aggressively. All the time s/he is disintegrated, doesn't accept any teaching or critics – s/he is hurt even by slight criticism. Despite the expression of anger at other people s/he is not able to enter the external world.

S/he does not take care of their appearance and healthy lifestyle.

S/he does not live in the present in the real life, but in the past or in the unreal imagined future. Trouble emotions separate them from other people.

Very often s/he has no contact with their generation.

Despite the grace of the contemplative prayer, s/he treats God as a subject.

S/he doesn't understand the love of God to people who do not undertake the will of God. S/he has pretensions to God that He tolerates them.

S/he has no symptoms of trust in God – s/he prays with the same internal tension, and tells God about their problems as if s/he was afraid of that God leaves him.

How long does the expression of anger at oneself last?

With the expression of anger at oneself the periods of the super compensation are longer – they can last up to 3 weeks. The look into oneself is more difficult than the look into another person. Thus, if the period of expression contains about 20 years – the whole expression of anger can last 1½ – 2 years.

It is also important to do it exactly – from the oldest to the present event. One can see here also that to stay in truth and accept truth one can only in the light and in the power of Holy Ghost. Only in the case of fortification by Holy Ghost and after the pray to Him, one can express and see clearly where the anger at oneself is.

One can see also how big part of anger is hidden in different relationships in the depth of the emotional memory.

One can also see how this anger burdens, and how degrading is being in the memory for many years. One can see also how great liberation the expression of anger at oneself gives.

The expression of anger at oneself results in the liberation of additional surfaces of anger at other people for example at the father, mother, ex-partner, teacher, all people who caused this anger. This additional anger one should also express at this stage.

The surprising observation is that in schizophrenia the anger to oneself is 2-3 times bigger that anger at other people – because of this anger it was impossible to fulfil duties, because the ill person struggled mainly against internal obstacles.

What changes in the spirituality appear at this stage?

The ill person starts to slowly understand the logic of God's love – the unconditional love also for sinners.

Looking at oneself in truth starts – their own sins, faults, hate towards other people.

The image of oneself becomes more real – the ill person starts to accept the truth about oneself, stops to prove to oneself and other people that s/he is better, stronger, cleverer than s/he is in reality.

The new quality, new subtlety appear during the prayer, a great desire to pray, to unite with God.

The better comprehension of Lord's Gospel – begins. Gospel reveals its meaning, starts to speak to the ill person.

A pardon to oneself and to other people gives a great liberating joy.

It starts to change the places – the opening to God, the comprehension that God is great and saint, that He is the Master of history – also of the personal history. Till now even in the spirituality the ill person has wanted to rise by the help of God – and God served them mostly for this.

That God is a Person is the greatest discovery at this stage. The expression of anger finishes by the integration of the ill person on the natural level. Only the integrated person is able to see in the light of grace that God is a person. Despite the grace of contemplative prayer the ill person is able to see it only now. S/he sees also the dignity of other people which follows the comprehension of the dignity of God.

The ill person starts to be conscious of the existence of different griefs and resentment to God in oneself. They appear and they are greater as the healing continues. The ill person is not free from the perception of the evil in their life and in social life. S/he does not understand the Christian perspective about Christ who is stronger than the sin and the evil till the end.

What mental changes follow after the expression of anger at oneself?

After each expression of anger the ill person feels the reduction of the tension in the mind and body.

The quality of sleep is better – the sleep is deeper – it returns to its natural rhythms. Before, even after 10-12 hours of sleep s/he felt tired in the morning.

The concentration appears, the dialogues to oneself are reduced, the rubbing of hands, the rhythmic swinging are reduced too. **The time which has stopped when the illness exploded – starts to run again.**

The ill person stops to train themselves, to torment themselves by the rigorous lifestyle or by refusing themselves any pleasure.

S/he stops to be rigorous, tough, requiring towards oneself and the environment.

The ill person is more open to people. S/he is not afraid of a failure in a contact with them. S/he is not afraid of human opinions as s/he was afraid till now. People look more naturally to them.

S/he starts to perceive and understand the emotions of other people. Till now s/he was not able to penetrate such emotions.

Their taste changes and the habits of nourishment too.

After the expression of anger to oneself shines in the consciousness appear. After some days the ill person starts the full consciousness of oneself, s/he starts to be active, starts to work, to organise their life. After this short period s/he starts to enter again stupefaction. Again s/he doesn't perceive clearly the environment, s/he loses again the spiritual and mental perspective – and it is like that until the next expression which restores the good functioning for some time again.

S/he starts to notice the reality in which s/he lives. In the church s/he will notice the arch to which s/he didn't pay attention, s/he will see the front of the building in which s/he lives, s/he will notice the architectonic idea of their district. S/he will notice a beauty and the changing of seasons of the year.

S/he starts to form their own "self". S/he starts to have their own opinion, s/he starts to really recognize their capabilities.

S/he has more mental powers – the joy of life appears.

S/he stops to struggle against oneself – s/he notices that this is what s/he has been mainly doing until now.

The real external spiritual obstacles become the most important. The new realities of life, not known to them, appear.

If the expression of anger at other people was necessary (as the first step of making order in the emotional memory), its therapeutic results in many cases were rather weak. The total reduction of medicaments has not been possible yet. But the expression of anger at oneself has greater importance in therapy. After finishing it, in many cases one can eliminate the medicines totally.

How does the expression of anger at oneself finish?

One can see that the accumulated anger still exists. It seems to be strange – because the ill person practically went through all situations and all people in their life which could provoke this anger – and it seems that there are no other planes to express this anger.

The anxiety still exists, one can see it in many situations of life. The existence of anger is in the foreground and the ill person starts to be conscious of this. Despite the internal integration on the natural level, the ill person has internal obstacles to undertake normal active life due to this anger.

Despite a great reduction, the impure thoughts still exist.

There are elements of mental weakness and stupefaction which reduce the activity. The tiredness during the day still exists. The spirit of the place influences the ill person. There are still places spiritually better and worse and there is no change, but the ill person starts to be conscious of this.

All the time the ill person enters the wills of other people, agrees with them, accepts them – s/he doesn't block them, doesn't return them – s/he doesn't hurt the other person by this – even if s/he is pressed by the tension of their wills. But s/he starts to be conscious of all this.

The ill person stops to struggle against oneself and this is what s/he has done until now. The spiritual external obstacles appear. S/he can't resist yet the great spiritual pressure.

In the internal spiritual obstacles, despite the integration at the natural level, the spiritual impotence remain and the ill person is not able to get rid of it, s/he doesn't know how to do it. It is a sort of partly spiritual possession by the mysterious spiritual presence difficult to define, which appears and disappears from time to time.

CHAPTER 16

THE ANGER AT DEVIL

The expression of anger at other people and oneself can be included to the active purification of senses – the expression of anger at devil and God one can name as the active purifications of the spirit.

What can be noticed when starting the analysis of the knocks received from the other people?

One can notice that **these knocks create a certain logical pattern** – there are not accidental knocks. They are very often received by the ill person in series – **even though they were made by different (as if arranged) people.** It is important to see this mysterious logic (even subjectively).

Later one can notice that **these knocks were given with a great precision.** This precision was **beyond the possibilities of the people who gave them.** Beyond their possibilities of cognition and beyond the possibilities to make evil to other person.

Based on these observations one can conclude that in the background of these people there is hidden also a person – a spiritual person – intelligent, brutal, perverse, with a great cognition, consistent in the attacks, smart. It is this person that uses physical people for knocks. **S/he inspired the attacks and s/he is the source of evil which touched the ill person.** This person is a devil. About this, that he exists, about the manner of his activity teaches the faith and the most important depositor of faith – the Roman Catholic Church.

Because one can't see the devil, his presence and his person can be perceived only in the spiritual way. According to the spiritual progress this presence can be seen in the reactions, in the behaviours and situations of other people – and of oneself too. **The Holy**

Ghost shows the devil in his activity but also in the logical constructions of thinking, which is used by the apostasy directed by devil.

To comprehend and analyse the devil the spiritual cognition is necessary. In the natural cognition the devil is not visible. The importance of the devil and his participation in causing the illness is so great that it cannot be ignored in the diagnosis and therapy.

And therefore the spiritual way is necessary in schizophrenia – to give the cognition of spiritual matters, to reinforce the ill person internally and to illuminate them by grace. And also that the ill person would perceive the activity of devil in situations where he was really present – not to perceive him everywhere.

The meeting with devil is not a subjective impersonal projection of the evil – but it is the meeting with the acting, living, existing person – the author, and the source of evil.

Since the devil is a person one can enter relationship to him. One can also – as in the case of other people – express anger at him.

What influence does the expression of anger have on the devil?

Of course none. The devil exists beyond the time, his will is fixed in evil and he will not reverse this separation of the will from God.

But the ill person expressing the anger at him purifies the emotional memory – disentangles themselves from the relation to devil. From this relation which the devil created by his knocks.

The expression of anger is a hard spiritual struggle with a great power, which can liberate the emotional memory. The devil stops the domination over the memory. In the case of schizophrenia there is no other possibility to make such purifications. It is difficult to replace such type of purifications even by the charismatic prayer. Therefore, all the spiritual way cumulate at this stage. The ill person should be spiritually strong enough to start the struggle against the evil spirit.

All the scheme of the expression of anger will be similar to the preceding – **expression of anger, confession, pardon.** But the pardon will look otherwise.

As I have written the devil has the will reversed from the theses which are in God – by his will he has reversed himself, separated himself from God. He will never change this badly arranged will. A pardon is the spiritual reconstruction of the relationship between two people. But in the case of devil – no reconstruction of the will is possible on his side – because of his extraordinary hostility against God and man, and because of the impossibility to change the arrangement of his will. Thus, the anger at the devil can be expressed, but an attempt at reconstructing the relationship makes no sense.

Also one shouldn't start to be in any relation with the devil, except for the expression of anger at him.

The evil spirit knocking the ill person accuses God, so a man is sure that God is a source of the evil – he accuses God of the evil. **This image of God who is the author of the evil is hardly inscribed in the consciousness of the ill person**. During the illness, due to the weak spiritual development the ill person doesn't perceive the whole complicated panorama of their relations. Thus, when expressing the anger at the devil, one should pardon God to start to reconstruct the correct relation to God, the relation which is troubled by the devil.

Thus, one should remind themselves an event, for example a slap on the face made by Smith and to pardon in three relations:
– God I pardon You that You knocked me by Smith.
– By the power of God I pardon you Smith that you knocked me.
– I pardon myself that this knock made so great impression on me, or that I permitted to be knocked, etc.

And in this way, to go through 30 – 50 events which where the subject of the expression of anger accumulated in the examined period.

Also one can do this in such way – to pardon God in all situations, to pardon other people in all situations, and to pardon oneself in all situations in the end.

By pardoning in three relations one cut out the activity of the devil not mentioning him directly, but trying by the pardon to reconstruct all relations which he has broken – to God, to other person, to oneself. It is done without going into any relation with the devil during the pardon.

Of course if the ill person knocked Smith during the pardon he should not say – God I pardon You that I knocked Smith – but he should say – God forgive me that I did this.

It is important to reconstruct the relation by pardon or by forgiveness. The same concerns all other people and relations.

The expression of anger at the devil is typical to the spiritual struggle. One should start it from the prayer, during the expression one should be very concentrated. During a few days after the expression one should behave considerately, not to be provoked to aggressive attitudes, because the perception of the reality can be troubled at this time. Despite the anxiety or scruples the ill person should know that such expression has the liberating nature for their emotional memory.

In this case of such expression the return to functions of life will take longer up to 3 – 6 weeks. The next expression should be done after this period when the functions will return or when the sleep starts to drop rapidly and there will be the pressure to express emotions. Also one should remember that the knocks given by the devil should be expressed exactly starting from the oldest ones. In the period were they are numerous, one should take one year as the basis and recall and express exactly the events from this period

To examine by which scheme one should express the anger at the devil one should return to the scheme of devil's structure presented before – by which he invaded the spiritual heart. In this book **I presented the scheme of three spirits linked together, symbolising the pride, murder and impurity.** Each of these spirits influences a little the will of the ill person, and their his emotional memory. As I have written, the spirit on the top of the structure by accusing God detaches from Him. The spirit symbolising murder paralysed by anxiety, provokes suicide. The third urges to impurity, also blocks the supernatural cognition – the same as the two others.

All of them additionally linked separate from God, make the union with Him impossible, hobble the natural will, close a man in the tragic sensible reality.

Examining the matter from the side of the structure of the evil spirit, theoretically **one should start from the weakest spirit which symbolises the impurity, later the one which provokes anxiety and in the end the one which symbolises the pride.**

But for the ill person anxiety is the most painful. The ill person can easily show the most brutal, most painful events from their life. Their anxiety have the spiritual factor – it comes from the spirit, from the knocks, from being under his influence.

Thus, taking under consideration also the spiritual horizon of the ill person (and a healthy person too), reaching only one level, **one should start generally** from the events which by anxiety, brutality, pain, humility touched the ill person very much. And to go through them and people who have taken part in them.

And in such way to go through the history of life and express the anger at the devil hidden in these events. And later, at the next stage, one should return to the structure of the spirit and express the anger accordingly.

As I have written, the spiritual capabilities of a man reach only one level – the present level of grace. The ill person doesn't see all complicated structure of the spirit. S/he will learn about it after finishing of active purifications.

Also one event can be spiritually situated at different levels. For example, the teacher who terrorises the class, the rude teacher – takes the freedom off, touching by anxiety and additionally by the rude behaviour, s/he destroys the emotionality and body and sexuality which are linked with emotionality. And additionally presents the image of God a tyrant – it means s/he accuses Him. This one event is situated on 2 -3 different spiritual levels. As the human cognition reaches only one level, one should return to them 2 – 3 times – every time on the another higher level of the spiritual and personal development.

What changes in the mentality of the ill person appear in this period of expression of anger?

After the expression of anger at the devil for the first time since the explosion of illness the moment appears when the ill person feels normally. S/he stops to feel the anxiety, s/he can undertake certain social activity.

The quality of sleep is much higher. S/he starts to sleep in a natural way without medicaments. Their face looks nicer and more natural.

The image of "oneself" starts to correspond to the objectively existing image. Slowly the spirit which caused this disharmony is eliminated. The mental balance not existing till now or on this level starts to appear.

The change of rhythms during day and night takes place. The silence appears in the thoughts – for the first time since the explosion of illness. The ill person stops to be lost in thoughts, sit without any move, with emptiness in the head – the ill person starts to be conscious that s/he did so.

The ill person feels the relaxation of natural tension in the whole body.

S/he has more natural power to fulfil their ideas.

S/he perceives other people better. They look better and more subtle. They start to behave milder – the ill person is conscious that sometimes s/he was too tough, too rude, too formal. S/he starts to reconstruct the relations to other people, as until now they have been dead. The sense of time is restored to a greater degree.

In this period hesitations and low mood appear and the ill should be prepared for this.

What changes in the spirituality happen at this stage?

The expression of anger at the devil is the next turning point – a great step in the spiritual way. Parallelly to the purification of emotional memory, the visible purification of the spiritual heart happens and it gives a new quality – purity, subtlety, joy, naturalness – on the level not existing till now.

The ill person starts to be spiritually stronger and more integrated. The spiritual factor of many emotions caused the spiritual weakness. The ill person has made a great effort to remove the spirit from their emotional memory. The effect was the exit from the spiritual disintegration and spiritual weakness.

The ill person notices that only the evangelic love and goodness are valuable in this life. S/he notices also that the evil, even attractive and catching theories and acts, even a great effort and domination in science and social life – in front of God they have no value, and the people relying on them not able move away from the spiritual zero mark – and this is their common denominator.

The lightness and softness during the prayer appears. The ill person starts to understand the mystical texts – all their delicate complexity and subtle beauty. S/he displays the traits of the spiritual mildness. The ill person starts to be thankful to God for all this.

Thus, after the first part of the expression of anger at the devil – where the ill person expresses this anger generally – when in the situations as s/he though that was knocked by the devil – one should return to the structure of the spirit, reminding the most representative and characteristic knocks in the history of own life. Thus, on the basis of the scheme explained before in this book, one should start from desire, go through anxiety again, finish with the events where the spirit has taken out the freedom, where he has broken the will touched by the rebel against God.

If the ill person feels to be strong enough, s/he can express the anger according to the scheme from the beginning. Or to express the anger at all three levels at the same time and to some of them come back later.

Thus, one should start to express anger at the spirit which caused **the desire.** Of course it concerns a sexual desire, other types of desire exist, but they have not such great importance in schizophrenia, one can take them under consideration later.

One should recall all the situations when the ill person sinned in this sphere by themselves or with other person in thoughts and in acts. To remind the person with whom s/he did it. And to express the anger at the devil that he incited these thoughts and acts. And in this way to go through all the life situations which were recorded and remained in the emotional memory of the ill person.

What gives the expression of anger relating to the desire?

The God's love to man and man's love to God is also the betrothal. Every sin, every falsification on the level of emotions and feelings by desire covers and falsifies the picture of God in the man and separates the man from God. The devil very often uses this situation, perverting this sphere and he makes a person dependent on him taking away the freedom in this sphere. Therefore, it is very important to make order also in this sphere.

To the pure all things are pure (Titus 1:15). (NIV) After the expression of such type of anger the world looks spiritually purer to the ill person. S/he feels separation from the spiritual dirt dominating around. S/he observes also how pure and saint is the love of God. This causes a great veneration and respect to Him and to this saint love, a great respect to the pure and saint God.

The expression of such anger gives also the internal peace and spiritual silence, it gives also a new sort of spiritual freedom. It also disconnects (it starts to do it) from the natural love, which prisoned the ill person till now – and from disorder, which was in it. A visible separation of the natural man from the spiritual man takes place.

The next stage is the expression of the anger causing **anxiety.**

This anger should be expressed by the same scheme as before – expression, confession, pardon. The ill person should recall people (for example – their father, mother, teachers, neighbours, hooligans, policeman, politicians), and all situations from their life (from the oldest). S/he should notice the presence of the evil spirit in them – and express the anger at him.

The expression of the anger at the devil which paralysed by the anxiety is one of the most important stage in the therapy and in the spiritual way. In the past the extraordinary knocks and the escalation of accumulated anxiety led to the explosion of illness, broke the mental and spiritual structure. The illness started from the escalation of anxiety (which resulted also from the disintegration), and after managing it, the illness will end. After the expression the ill person feels for the first time (from the spiritual side) internally integrated. This is not the integration on the highest level, but for the first time symptoms of achieving it can be visible. And this provides positive spiritual and mental consequences of this stage. For the first time (to a great extent) the limbic system is unblocked. The external result of this is that the ill person for the first time uses the sense of smell. S/he can also feel one's mood and the mood of other people. The feeling of springtime with its whole subtle beauty appears.

The mechanical slow moves, the rigidity go away.

The ill person starts to be conscious that the anxiety caused a distance to other people.

The new quality of sleep appears.

The ill person sleeps without interruption.

S/he wakes up calm, rested, concentrated.

The time is as if getting slower, the environment becomes more natural.

There are changes in the silhouette.

Many pictures from the emotional memory are removed just during the expression of anger related to the anxiety. The other contents of the emotional memory start to take its proper place. It makes impression of the return of the memory.

The ill person starts to occupy themselves with their own matters, not of the matters from the outside world. S/he stops to concentrate on oneself, to look at oneself, to observe oneself. S/he stops to take care of their own past. S/he starts to enter the life, s/he has real plans for the future and s/he starts slowly to fulfil them.

The expression of anger is unaccompanied by semi-psychoses and the ill person should be prepared for this. The anxiety caused extreme mental pain on the level of ecstasy. Therefore, the period of super compensation is longer – up to 6 weeks and such break should be kept between the expressions.

Also after the expression of such anger one can observe the changes in the spirituality.

The prayer of heart appears in a new quality. For the first time "a whole man" prays, the whole centre of emotions prays.

Till now the ill person felt as stranger in the Church and s/he hasn't felt the spiritual community.

The anxiety caused also the spiritual weakness. The ill person made the impression of a very tender, subtle person, but spiritually extremely weak because of internal disintegration. And this changes after the expression of anger related to the anxiety.

The period from the first contemplative prayers till now in the spirituality is named as **the period of the sweet love.** The aim of it was the detachment from the natural schemes and the attraction to God. It was a nice period, full of joy, sometimes without any complex problems.

Now the second part of the illuminative way starts which is **a period of the dark love.** It goes on from the first night to the union of the will.

The order which takes place, which touches the sphere of emotions and feelings is linked with going through the nights – the **night of senses and the night of spirit.** In man, the nature struggling against the spirit supported by the grace does not give in easily. The ill person should be prepared for this. The spiritual states are becoming clearer. Before they were put one on another, it was difficult to separate them. The numerous crises additionally complicated the spiritual state of the ill person.

Now, for the first time **the night of senses** appears clearly. One can observe it for the first time so clearly. Below is an example of such night. The ill person recalls:

One day I noticed that a normal prayer, which was always a pleasure for me, became a burden. It was difficult for me to start it. I was indisposed to it. I was sitting half an hour in front of the picture of Mother of God, and I couldn't take a rosary or a brewery to my hand. I was sitting in stupefaction – I had no internal power to break this state. I wanted to address God with these problems, but God was absent. It lasted some weeks and I started to think that I had lost my faith, and God took me the grace. I started to be terrified. I didn't want to go back to the world, because the world was throwing me out – and I couldn't stay in God's presence – because I was not feeling God's presence at all.

The joy of life disappeared totally, also the will to do anything disappeared. There was no joy coming from the activity. I felt the nonsense of any activity. In my thoughts the quotation from the book of Ecclesiastes resonated – vanity of vanities and all is vanity. I was dejected. I was not able to think anything. I was not able to concentrate myself. I was sitting by the desk, I was opening the book and during one hour or two, I was able to read only a few sentences.

Physically I felt very bad. I went to the internist, and I told him that I have no internal power and physical power to do anything. And I feel a sort of bitterness in my body, a great internal pain difficult to qualify – and I suppose I have a heavy unknown illness. The doctor examined me exactly, and he gave me the prescription to the drops of hawthorn and he told that he doesn't see any illness. Angry at this situation, I did blood tests and the X-ray. Another doctor confirmed that my results are good.

The image of the environment has changed for me. The sunrises and sunsets had no romantic charm as before. They started to remind the descriptions from the book of Apocalypse. Also the baroque places and the windings of the river didn't make any impression on me. They were as if deprived of their ancient beauty. I couldn't find the coloured, alive, odorous, full of sunshine world which made such a great impression on me before. I was not able to find that ancient mood in myself. I couldn't emanate from myself that way of perception which I had before.

My body started to rebel against me – like the animal which knows that after a moment it will be killed. I wanted to go somewhere where I have never been, to eat something that I have never eaten. In thoughts I had attacks of wild desire. I have led the spiritual life for 15 years and I did not suspect myself of such desire. I had known that I can't succumb to such thoughts and return to the world and its joys which will never satiate me.

This state lasted 3-4 months. I was as if in the trap and I couldn't leave this state. I was as if without my own will. When I finally started to pray by force, my prayer was as if dead, without any echo. I was extracted from the world, but I was not able to find God. I was totally deprived of the supernaturalism. The memory of numerous graces has disappeared. I was afraid that the dark-

ness will open a new space in the spirituality in which I will be not able to find myself.

The nights of senses and the night of spirit are experiences in which God is introduced by the grace, and from which He leads also by the grace. One should be conscious that this is a night and passively undertake it. God touches by them such spheres which cannot be purified by active purifications. The nights appear after years of leading the life in grace. The nights serve the purifications before the next stage of union.

Here the most important is the fact that the night has appeared, not the next crisis, but the first night. It means that **the spirituality has moved on and entered to the well known patterns.** It means that God started to fill up these active purifications which the ill person has started.

By the end of the expression of anger at the devil two interesting phenomena happen – **the liberation of emotions and feeling** and restoring of the real proportions between them, and the **reconstruction of the natural will.**

The anxiety not only blocked the emotions and feelings, but it also disorganised the activity of the limbic system, and parallelly blocked emotions and feelings.

During the expression of this anger they both exploded suddenly with a great force showing the old colours, already forgotten.

What can it cause? That the spiritual heart already formed with a great effort will start to turn – the will starts to fall off from God and will return to all pleasures which could not be fulfilled till now.

The liberation from anxiety unblocks also the feelings – and one should remember about it. The suddenly liberated feelings should also be expressed to God. **One should do it by telling about them to God during the free expression.**

In this way they will not dominate the will, they will not trouble the activity of the will. A person with disorder in feelings was distracted, chaotic, easily confused, sometimes s/he begged for the feeling, and was superficial. S/he couldn't obtain the spiritual depth.

Near the end of the expression of the anger at devil **the recon-struction of the natural will occurs.** During the healing, these two ways – the reconstruction of the will and the undertaking of the will of God go in one direction. A great problem in the therapy is to persuade the ill person to do this. For the person who a limited will because of the illness, dreams about the unlimited freedom it is very difficult to understand why after the limitations resulting from the religion, the hobbled will can be liberated.

The people who have undertaken the will of God (as they thought), but without the reconstruction of the natural will break down under the burden of it, or they think that to undertake the will of God the cross is extraordinarily heavy, unbearable, and the religion is a sort of a prison, of yoke, of burden, and limits very much. Such thinking of the passage from the prison of the illness to the prison of faith is common in the case of undertaking im-proper vocation, or undertaking the vocation in the incorrect time. It is a typical spiritual error very often committed in this stage of healing. The great progress in the spiritual cognition causes that the ill person observes the spiritual circumstances in which they live, tries to manage them, even if s/he was no called upon to do it, thinking that God requires this from them. The ill person is very often terrifies and makes bad decisions.

The natural will acts according to the thesis "I want". It is hob-bled in the illness. The schizophrenia sufferer has an extraordi-nary subtlety in the will. Because of this s/he must give way to other stronger wills.

There is a time when other people drive their strong and falsely arranged wills into the will of the ill person, break and hobble their will. They do this with a great brutality. The ill person was not able to go through these wills and very often s/he didn't want to break them by force, as it was done with their will. S/he couldn't also pass by their wills, because s/he was disintegrated and united with the environment – and every false arrangement of somebody's will af-fected them very much.

The breaking of the will very often takes place in the childhood, and there are families (of soldiers, policemen, officers of the mer-chant marine, workers of the prison management), where this all is visible because of bringing the professional habits to home. Other people with the similar behaviours met by the ill person break again their will, adding their punches.

The symptoms of the broken and hobbled will are faintness, helplessness, powerlessness, submission, passivity. This all gives also the lack of mental forces to pursue any activity, the submission to the external events and total subjection of them. In contacts with other people their wills enter and are accepted. The ill person does not live their own life, but by the life of other people – s/he observes their life, considers their life. Later, it gives the absence of joy of life, absence of invention, apathy. The mental symptoms of it are a permanent tiredness, lack of the concentration – sometimes so great that any activity is impossible.

A broken and hobbled will prevents any development. A personal development – because such person does not live their own life, and spiritual development related to it.

In the education it is very important that the parents, teachers would be characterised **by mildness of the will**. In the Sermon on the Mount Jesus suggests the mildness as a program for the Christian. Why mildness? Because such is God. The point is not to break the will of the other person – not to hurt their emotional memory in the long and difficult process of teaching and formation.

Putting into practice these remarks to the scheme of active purifications, one can additionally sometimes express the anger at the devil **in situations where he limited or deprived them of freedom, where he has broken the will of the future ill person.** One should remind the situations from the history of life and express the anger and later to pardon in three relations.

Why the ill person couldn't unite this natural will earlier?

Because one can do it only after the expression of anger at the devil, which caused anxiety. Only after the managing the anxiety the natural will shall slowly return to its natural disposition.

The expression of anger is a turning point in the therapy, which is also a spiritual way. The spirit which has written himself by the knocks in the emotional memory is removed from it step by step.

The immobilised limbic system returns to its proper functions. The emotional memory is liberated from the pictures, especially strongly at this stage. The feelings are clarified. The natural will is reset. The spiritual development, because of the liberation from the anxiety, becomes very dynamic. It is also a period, when the ill person returns to the social life. But this period (even if the first nights have started), ends also with the crisis like every stage of the internal healing.

What this crisis is about?

The ill person can't pray as before. S/he can't tell to God about their problems. S/he feels that the relation to God is blocked.

S/he is emotionally tired, mentally and spiritually rigid and stiff. Blocked only in the relation to God. S/he feels that s/he has the anger in some relations to express.

S/he also feels that a sort of the barrier, the spiritual apathy, discouragement, absence of the spiritual powers are created and this all creates the emotional wall between them and God.

The ill person expected that after the expression of anger at the devil, s/he will approach God. And it happened, but some kind of a barrier between them and God remains and it cannot be removed. S/he feels also that from the certain time s/he does make any progress in contemplative prayer. Despite the effort during the prayer this emotional distance to God is not possible to be reduced. It is a subjective feeling, but it visibly exists.

In some part this state is a consequence of entering in the relation with the devil during the expression of the anger at him. But the main reason is the absence of healing in the emotions, the last relation which remained to be healed, the emotional relation to God. This relation should be healed by active purifications – by the expression of **the anger at God.**

CHAPTER 17

THE ANGER AT GOD

The devil symbolising the pride (on the top of the hierarchy) – it is the main ideologist of apostasy. He is the strongest, the most revolted against God. It is him who dissuades a man from the place prepared for them by God – and he does it consistently. It is mostly him who introduces the false image of God as the enemy of a man. But with how deeply he enters between God and a man one can see how graces and spiritual gifts he could have had if he would have not revolted. The proverb "the pride touches the heart of God" can be understood in this spiritual stage. The matter is the nearest and deepest relation which can be taken by the spirit. It is one of the revelations of this stage for the ill person.

The schizophrenia is an illness marked by extraordinary suffering. It crosses the plans of life, causes great humiliation, sometimes the spiritual pain impossible to be taken. These states in schizophrenia last a very long time, they have been accumulating for years in the emotional memory before the explosion of illness. Sometimes their illness is related to the illness of their own children what one can observe with despair.

The pictures of schizophrenia are the pictures taken from the Book of Job, contrasting with the colourful, joyful life without problems which is full of trivialities. **The schizophrenia is a subjective feeling of the abandonment by God, but it is also the permission given by God for such great suffering – suffering which results in the resentment to God.** Alas they are present in schizophrenia. This resentment also has the form of accumulated anger at God.

Where does this anger come from?

The devil accuses a man before God, a man before another man – he inscribes in the man the hate to oneself, he accuses God before the man. He is a perverse intriguer acting in all relations – ruining them. By each successive knock given to the man he inscribes the hate to God. He creates God as the author of all human tragedies. The ill person after the years of such knocks, misfortunes related to them accepts more or less such devil's catechise.

The devil knocks in a very smart way. Very often he does this by through the people loved or liked by the ill person e.g. by the father, mother, teacher, priest, in the situation of the extraordinary opening to these people – full of love and trust. There are the people who represent God or the nature directs the love to them. Thus, there are the knocks which destroy the original image of God, unified with the nature. There are the relations in which the devil enters, using the personal sin of such people or their temporary false spiritual opening.

The devil uses also the weak cognition of the man after the original sin and builds the false image of God thereon. He knocks and hides himself behind God, presenting to the ill person a bad opinion about Him. If the existence of devil can be known by the natural cognition – this – in which situations he knocks the man – can be observed and analysed only with the help of grace. The devil is at some point spiritually invisible to the man and therefore he can accuse God before the man with impunity.

Also the logic of God is different to the natural logic of a man. These two logics meet on the spiritual way – and this human logic must submit to God's logic. If on the level of the will it is possible to be accepted by man after their troubles, but on the level of emotions in difficult cases one can find the traces of human rebel and resentment towards God. On the level of emotions, all difficult cases are perceived as the knocks given by God.

Thus, where does this anger come from?

The terrible experiences to which God admitted the illness, the moral crisis – the ill person accuses also God of them.

Also this, that He gave them such a father, such a mother, such a teacher, such a priest, such a prime minister who have destroyed them emotionally, who provoked the emotional wounds, but this was not their vocation given by God. Also the logic of the cross which is magnificent, but on the level of emotions very often not easy to accept – for example God's care and protection concerning people who publicly lie and treat Him with disregard – and of whom He takes care.

The examples are numerous, but it is important to present a general thesis **that one perceives differently on the level of the will and differently on the level of disintegrating emotions** – one doesn't accept not only the knocks of devil, but also many decisions of God's providence.

Which periods of life are mostly linked with the anger at God?

Generally, with the periods where the contact with the devil was more intensive. Thus, it was the period when the devil entered to the spiritual heart and stayed there, or the period after the explosion of illness, or this is a period of the biggest sin in life. Alas, after years the ill person will also accuse God of this period.

Thus, during the analysis one should take into consideration these periods and the people who had the greater influence on the formation of the spiritual heart as a father, mother, teacher, priest, girlfriend and so on. These people should form the spiritual heart according to God's intention – but very often they hurt brutally instead.

What are the results of this accumulated anger at God?

The ill person even though s/he is spiritually advanced, can't feel the closeness of God. The whole time s/he treats God instrumentally. From the certain time their contemplative prayer stops to develop. The ill person feels the barrier between them and God. This barrier is visible in some aspects of the spirituality.

For the ill person, it is very difficult to hear the subtle, internal inspirations, to perceive them, to react to them, to perceive all subtle spiritual atmosphere accompanied by them. The ill person feels that the proper subtlety in contact with God is too low.

There is no intimacy with God. The ill person does not talk to God about their joys, sorrows, problems, plans, expectations. God is a distant person to them at all times. The ill person talks about their problems with the family, friends, but not to God, on whom these problems depend.

Also there is no confidence in relation – the ill person does not consult with God their life problems – with God who by the person of Jesus entered to the human life.

God of course exists, but at the further plan – He is not perceived as He should be.

The ill person doesn't see the beauty of the world, which is the reflection of God's beauty. S/he commits small sins in language, s/he has no subtlety, delicacy in opinions. S/he is not conscious in the presence of whom s/he utters these words.

The complains, nagging, permanent discontent also prove the hidden anger at God – practically it kills the inspirations given by the Holy Ghost at oneself.

The spirituality is habitual – there is no deepest and most sincere joy resulting from the full healed relationship between two people.

The problem of the anger at God is a very difficult one. To be in truth demands to pose a fundamental question – if the anger at God exists in my own will and emotions – or not. One may not pose the question if it is correct that the anger exists – because one knows that it is not.

Also one should not present to oneself the backbreaking theological reflections – if God is good – in that case one should not have the accumulated anger at Him.

Here one should ask oneself a very simple and a very difficult question – **if this anger exists in me or not?** And – if I have this resentment towards God for something in the history of my life – or I don't have it. And to give to oneself the sincere answer taking into consideration that to God the more valuable is the attitude to be in truth, but not the simulation of the nobility, but in fact the distortion of the problem. The anger not expressed will be the bridgehead of the evil spirit, the source of the perversity which is so much present in the spiritual life now.

The next question is – if such anger exists – how one should express it?

They are the authors who claim that if the anger at God exists – one should tell God about it. Alas, the science on emotions shows that it is not possible to get out anger from the emotional memory. The accumulated anger will stay there – as it was there before.

The ill person should express the anger at God by the same method as s/he used before. It is very difficult for the ill person. To express the anger at own father is difficult – and what about the anger at God. These difficulties alas is used by the devil, hiding himself behind the relations protected by the nature and by God's commandments which are not well understood.

One should remember that God knows and understand the intentions of the arrangement of the will, the life history of man expressing the anger at Him. God knows also what is the aim of the expression. God knows that the ill person does not do this to insult Him in impudent and blasphemous way – but to liberate the will and the emotional memory from the accumulated spiritual contents, which were placed there years before the devil, and which had additionally hobbled the will.

This ascetic exercise is extremely difficult – simply drastic to the ill person – the most difficult thing the ill person has faced until now – as if against their own nature and all spiritual way which s/he has led. However, this exercise completes and finishes the whole process of active purifications of emotions and there is no possibility to replace it with another spiritual exercise.

The anger at God should be expressed every 6-12 weeks. The periods of return of functions is the longest here. The disintegration after the expression (mostly after the expression of the anxiety) is reduced – one should find the most fundamental facts from the life of the ill person who s/he feels the accumulated anger to God.

What changes one can observe after the expression of the anger at God?

The stronger union with God appears. The wish to pray comes back to stay in the presence of God, but to stay otherwise than before – in the silence and depth. One realises the mystery of the meeting which is saint, mysterious fulfilled by depth and subtlety of the two persons interacting. The ill person understands for the first time what it means to meet God in silence. **Such silence is the result of**

the emotions healed by the grace. This type of silence doesn't exist at the level of nature. Such silence allows seeing the sanctity of God. That God is saint can be perceived only in the silence of emotions healed by the grace. The ill person remarks that the mystery of God can be transmitted by keeping silence, taking care of words but not by rebuilding coloured descriptions full of pathos – that all of them disturb the transmission of the mystery of God.

The life starts to be the adoration of eternally existing and saint God. Together with this the moderation and respect to the words said, avoiding even the smallest sins in the speech appear.

It starts to enter to oneself. It is opening to God perceived by the prism of the own spiritual heart. Till now a person after the original injury couldn't fully perceive the presence of God in their own spiritual heart. Because of the knocks of devil s/he was thrown out from their spiritual heart. S/he couldn't meet fully God there even in the grace of contemplative prayer. Therefore, such person was partly prisoned in the external world.

The ill person lived only externally, s/he couldn't enter fully their own heart. S/he was brutally thrown out from it by devil. Now after the active purifications their spiritual heart has become a centre of meeting with God. All internal life is focused on the spiritual heart. The entrance to oneself starts to leave all the external world outside. It stops to enter to the interior as it did till now. The entrance to oneself liberates from the external world which from the centuries is the same because of its schemes, false hierarchies, attachments and it will not change. The ill person was united with it, because s/he couldn't detach themselves from it and s/he couldn't fully meet God – one can meet them fully only in own purified spiritual heart. The ill person couldn't meet God fully even in the grace of contemplative prayers.

The problem associated with **the entrance to oneself** is the real image of other people. Till now the other person was perceived as a superman. The ill person lived by their life and by their success, entered their will. Now after the entrance to oneself, after fully meeting their own heart, the relation to the external world (and also the relation to other people) is totally reconstructed. The real man appears with good sides, but also with faults, defects, sins, an imperfect man who should be helped, but not a superman who hurt and persecuted.

The stage of the anger at God finishes the active purification of emotions. The relation God – man is the last relation expressed which the devil distorted in the emotions.

During the expression of the anger at God (as the last) **a deep reconciliation of the ill person with people and with situations occurs.**

In this period during the sleep or during the day, **the past situations** (their pictures) from the different periods of life go through the memory – **as if they tried to find their final place in the memory** – as if till now they were not in the correct place – and just now they found their place. The place with the responsible spiritual factor – liberated from the factor which accompanied them before. **The arrangement of the pictures** is a phenomenon which can last for whole weeks and it starts the final order of big memory chaos which dominated the memory of the ill person till now.

This phenomenon proves that the purifications (active or passive) go to the end, that it runs out of the possibilities and served its purpose – to cut out from the spirit which hobbled the ill person. The ill person will meet such arrangements also at the next stages – after the active purifications of the pictures related with feelings and during the nights of the spirit – and one should understand it and interpret it always in the same way.

The arrangements of the pictures appear always when the psychotic element ends. In this case – when the part of schizophrenia (it means the psychosis) based on the memory related to emotions ends. The purely emotional element which entered into the composition of emotions separated itself from the spiritual element and started to look for its own place in the memory. The arrangement of the images always proves this. When the memory related to feelings will finish liberating itself, when during the night of the spirit the psychotic element finishes, even after the singular element is absorbed, then always **the arrangements of pictures** will appear.

Throughout the time of active purifications one should remember that this stage is God's – human work. **The expression of the**

emotions or feelings is the task of a man. The frequency depends on the ill person, on their capabilities – and also on the physiology, which rules must not be ignored and accelerated.

But the healing of the relations is the work of grace – when, and to what degree it will happen – it depends on God. The ill person will discover a fact that after some time, after the expression of the relation, the ill person will feel a deep spiritual peace and when recalling a given person and if s/he starts to look for the anger at them – s/he will not find it. God healed this relation in the time known only to Him. It is joyful and revealing experience, forcing the reflection about the role of the human effort and the mysterious activity of God.

Thus, the active purifications of senses and spirit are based on the active effort of a man completed by the grace of healing of the relation given by God.

CHAPTER 18

ACTIVE PURIFICATIONS OF THE FEELING

A turning point of the expression of the anger at God is when the ill person for the first time meets God fully. For the first time s/he comes back to their own heart, of which s/he was thrown out by the devil during the original injury. It happens not only because of the progress in the spirituality but also because of active purifications which have liberated the spiritual heart and qualified it to perceive God's presence in a new way.

Now **the presence is constant, invariable,** the presence of the Person who always exists. This image of God is well presented by the literary comparison to the drop of rain which has fallen to the ocean. Especially the comparison of God to the ocean – a great power which commands respect. But simultaneously to the loving, patient, solicitous, supporting and protecting Person when He leads a man. Such God meets a spiritual heart purified from the knocks, resentments, proper plans, imaginations and claims.

But here becomes the last step of the active purifications – **the active purifications of feeling.** This stage is also preceded by the crisis.

A great inflow of the sentimentality, even the desire appears, when the ill person was sure that s/he managed with it. **They are accompanied by pictures** for example of a friend whom s/he liked in the second grade, of the singer whom s/he admired in the elementary school, a girlfriend from the college and also the pictures of women about whom he was thinking and dreaming in the thoughts pure and impure, with which he was planning to unify his life, sometimes of women whom he met occasionally, pictures of women who because of unknown reason has fallen down to his memory and accumulated there durably. Sometimes there are the pictures of women whom the ill person would never suppose that they would remain, and would be accumulated in the memory of the sentiment.

The ill person notices that s/he loves and s/he wants to love God by will and by the feeling, but their spiritual heart is partly occupied and divided. Occupied by the spirits coming just from these imaginations by its all complicated nets, which were discovered just in this moment – in the moment of the new approach to God. The heart divided between the feeling to women (mostly of the perceived pictures of women) and God.

It will be the third, the last crisis in the sphere of feelings. The first crisis occurred before the start of the active purifications (and partly caused them). The second one appeared after the expression of the anger at devil, which caused the anxiety (because the sphere of the sentiment and anxiety were partly linked), and the third crisis – takes place just now.

The spiritual heart falling off from God and divided – it is a characteristic trait of the spirituality of the schizophrenia sufferer.

The active purifications of memory concerning the feelings can be started after the expression of emotions. Thus, for example in relation to the ex-girlfriend (for example Mary) – earlier, at the stage of the active purifications of emotions one should express the anger to Mary – that she didn't respond to the feeling of the ill person, then the ill person should express the anger at themselves, that he didn't come up to expectations of Mary, then to express the anger at devil, for example because of the words, which Mary said to him during the moment of the split, and finally – to express the anger at God that He led the ill person to meet Mary and be spiritually hurt by her.

Thus, one should notice later that even the expression of all emotions concerning Mary – the pictures related to her remained. The pictures of her, of the environment, pictures of the places related to her. The active purifications of emotions have removed a lot of these traces of the pictures of Mary, but not completely. After using the methods of expression described before the pictures related to the feeling remained as if on the sieve. Now, to eliminate them completely one should change the method – one should use **the method based on the meditation.**

The meditation is also a sort of prayer. It consists in repeating the short sentence or simple word – mantra. As a mantra one can use 2-3-5 words from the Gospel or from the Bible and repeat them 10 – 20 times to pass after one hour meditatively 8 – 12 verses. One can use also another words for example – *Heart of Jesus have mercy on us* – or similar.

Such form of the meditation doesn't consist in the consideration but repetitions of a short mantra. It is a prayer of the spiritual heart. Indirectly in this prayer the feeling is touched, because in the spiritual heart God meets the emotions and feelings of a man.

The schizophrenia sufferer is not able to have such meditative prayer. Such prayer makes them quickly tired and burdens them. The ill person is also much distracted during it. S/he can't actually practice it. The spirit, which is not a Holy Ghost enters during such prayer and starts to fight against them and it takes a lot of time and effort during the meditation. It is because of the state of the memory of feelings of the ill person – s/he has the spiritual heart divided and occupied and very often falling off from God. **Meditation is a zealous attention of mind, a prayer which focuses the powers of soul.** And this is its greater advantage.

Unfortunately in the schizophrenia the spiritual contents accumulated in the pictures, which are hidden in the memory make such concentration of powers impossible. In the illness one should remove the pictures, and introduce the meditation of such type later, when the pictures will disappear.

The meditation is a good test, which shows the state of the emotional memory – the existence of pictures, to show the degree of the spiritual disintegration which the feelings caused. I will repeat again that such meditative prayer used by the ill person will not give any spiritual progress – its development is restrained by the barrier of a divided and partly occupied spiritual heart.

Thus, **the meditation is a prayer of heart and mind.** By repetition, one forms the spiritual heart and according to it the contents from the mind (and from the memory of the sentiment).

But here its application will have the opposite effect. The emotional memory (the memory of feelings) is occupied, the mind is partly touched by the stupefaction, but the spiritual heart is partly purified by the contemplative prayers. One uses here this disposition for contemplation – as if one induced it – and according to it, on the basis of the partly formed and purified spiritual heart, one make order in the mind and memory of feelings. **By the force of the meditation one removes the pictures together with the contents occupied by the spirit.**

Repeating by this pure heart partly occupied by God the spiritual contents which were accumulated the evil spirit (or which the memory of the sentiment has registered), **one leads to the tension between them.** In the effect, they are removed by force from the spiritual heart and also from the mind and the memory of the sentiment. **It is as if the reversal of meditative method.** One doesn't repeat the contents to make accord with them, but to induce the tension on the line God – evil spirit and to remove them by force through the heart from the mind and memory. Practically it is the only method to reach these contents and one should be conscious of this – because this is not an easy method and one cannot use it before this stage. Because before it was not possible to create this tension between God and the evil spirit.

How to do these active purifications of feeling which should be done now?

One should recall in the memory the people important in the sentimental life to the ill person or such people whose images remained in the memory of feelings – starting from the oldest ones. And to recall for example this Mary – to imagine her and think about her and repeat – *Mary, Mary, Mary*....

And in such way repeat 5 – 10 – 20 minutes – as much as it will be necessary to pass by the pictures related to her.

In this way one recall the situations from 20 – 40 years. The spirit which was present in this situation will return again. S/he will show the pictures, s/he will recall them, once again s/he will pass by the deeply hidden places and situations, which the ill person thought that has been forgotten, but which remain in the memory, and which still disintegrate their person. The spirit will call them all once again – longing, joy, desire – to the hurting presence in the situations from the past.

One should go through all these places and situations by meditation. The spirit will lead through these situations once again. He will open seemingly healed wounds, he will recall forgotten but accumulated in the memory pictures, he will refill the ill person by his blessing as before presence – **and he will go out with the pictures forever.** In the contact with the spiritual heart possessed by God it will look like all this sentimental past situations have fallen down to the ocean of God's love. **It will be a liberating and healing experience.** Meditation is a prayer of the unity. The pictures appear and disappear (together with the spirits united with them), because **they are not able to resist the confrontation with God – with His incredible spiritual sanctity and unity.**

The active purifications of feeling are possible when God comes with his presence to the spiritual heart so deep that the heart of the ill person will not fall off from him during such meditation. The spiritual heart of the ill person will be formed taking the example from the heart of Jesus – the heart pure, not divided, sink in God, and give to others the evangelical love.

The active purifications one should repeat also according to the rules of the super compensation – it means when the functions of the ill person will return to the normal after the expression.

The active purifications of feeling is the stage more difficult than the active purifications of emotions. The pictures related to the feeling cause the psychosis to a greater degree than the pictures related to the emotions. Because of this one should pay more attention to them. During this stage the ill person went through the semi-psychoses (as during the purifications of emotions). One should be conscious of it – and make such doses of expressing pictures so as not to fall down to the psychosis. Also the periods of the of the super compensation should be longer, even up to 3-4 months. Because of this, the number of the meditations during the year can be 4 – 8. The second number when the psychosis will appear by the second meditation (1-2 weeks after the first).

The psychosis states are like a greater excitation, telling a lot of words, a sleep running out, rubbing the hands, and other similar. The ill person as before should observe themselves and wait when these troubled factors will return to the normal. And later after the visible activity of the evil spirit which will provoke them – to do the next meditation. And this cycle of the active purifications should be finished, when the psychotic states will not take place after the expression.

The unfulfilled feeling (after the original injury it couldn't be fulfilled) after years causes a dripping pain – a spiritual one but also a physical one. The meditative expression liberates from this. The extraordinary phenomenon occurs – removing of this pain from the memory connected with the liberation from the spirit which caused this pain and burdened during the years. From this moment this feeling of pain disappears forever and it will not come back – so one cannot recall it.

Also, cutting off from this sphere of feelings, from the hurts made by the external world occurs. Somebody's unfaithfulness, bad behaviour, putting too low the ideals in the sphere of sentiment – so present in the world – there are the events which a short time ago shocked, paralysed, took up the hope, prisoned by years – now do not make any impression on the ill person – as if they did not exist or as if they remained in the other space.

This is the greater advantage of this meditative expression – **the extraction from the prison of the sentimentality.** It is the separation from the spirit which prisoned for years and caused the pain. It is the replacement of the lower love with the upper love, with conviction that this love in the previous bad shape will not return again.

The main goal of the active purifications of feeling by the meditative expression of pictures is to start the process of the purifications, which till now practically hasn't moved on.

The most important real success of the ill person is **the elimination of the stupefaction.** But the process of unification with God goes through the nights of spirit which are the natural consequence of the spiritual way after the active purifications of the feelings. The ill person at this stage is introduced into the night of spirit – not to the next crisis – but to the first night.

It is good to examine the night of spirit on the example. The ill person recalls:

After a joyful, sunny springtime and after a great hope to pass the successful summer, suddenly I started to feel bad. During 1 – 2 days the spiritual darkness has appeared – as if somebody has put a dark filter on my life. I felt like in the depression. I was full of stinging spiritual pain. I couldn't find in myself this previous mood. I felt that I went out to another spiritual space, different than the one in which I was till now.

I had to force myself to pray and I reduced it. I was feeling as if I was had been to myself and that I lost my faith that God is offended with me and He lost me. I have known that it was impossible but the real impression was just like above. Any activity didn't give me the happiness and I haven't seen the sense of any activity.

I almost completely lost my strength. I felt the physical powers went out from me. I was like made from wax – weak and delicate. During the 12 kilometres bicycle excursion I had to rest 4 – 5 times and go back home by bus – although one year ago I was able to cycle 50 – 80 kilometres daily.

I couldn't concentrate on reading or thinking, because I was immediately mentally tired. I noticed that I couldn't associate and recover things from the memory, in which as I was feeling – everything was melt. In the game consisting of construction of words from letters I lost with a 8-year-old child. I was not able to leave this state and I thought that I would stay in it forever.

I felt that my head is floating. I was not able to read nothing more than the newspaper. The more serious texts made me immediately tired. My memory didn't function – as if it was made from cotton – I was not able to retrieve anything from it. It was not possible even I concentrated myself only on the essential life functions so as not to neglect them. I lost the contact with my environment – with my friends, neighbours – they had ignored me (I perceived them in this way) – as if I was out of the sphere of their interests.

My mother with whom I lived started to accuse and attack me for no reason – she said that she would disinherit me. A doctor in the clinic during the visit started to shout at me for no reason so brutally that I had to change her to another one. I worked 1 month but I received only half of the salary without any explanation and in such way that I lost hope. During 2 months I received 7 great knocks, about which I was thinking for many days. Nearly each external contact finished with such a big conflict as if all people were unified against me. From one side I felt that these attacks were great, caused the pain – up to my possibilities – but no more. On the other hand, I felt encircled by devil and I was no able to push out this devil's siege and to change my situation.

In springtime I planed to spend my holidays on the bicycle trip. During the free time I planned the itinerary. Meanwhile the pain of foot started, so great that I was not able to put the leg on the ground. Later, I lost the strength. Later, there was a heatwave, during which I had a sun stroke and I felt very bad. After the heat, it was raining for many days and there was no sense to move from home. When in the Autumn there were 2 weeks left to go anywhere, there was a failure of the sewage system.

Very surprised I observed this sequence of events which looked as if the mysterious powers introduced me to the magic labyrinth, from which I was not able to get out.

The night of spirit consist of 4 essential elements: **the element of darkness, psychotic element, devil's element and providential element.**

The element of darkness. Saint John of the Cross explains that the night is the reaction to the light of grace so great that at the first moment after the entrance all becomes dark to a man. Emotions and feelings liberated from the spirit followed by the will are shocked. The spiritual development on the stage goes through such shocks. To change the human perception God disappears, He is absent. He is not active as before.

The psychotic element is the most difficult element of the night. The pictures accumulated for years consist spiritual elements foreign to God, and they are removed to the end during the night. These pictures became the property of a man, but in this spiritual moment they are the obstacles in the further progress. Removing them reminds taking out hundreds or thousands strange to God elements from the organism. Looking from the perspective of the possession it reminds the taking off the property – because the pictures became the property of the ill person – in this way he perceived God and all environment.

Unfortunately, in case of such removing even a healthy person reacts with the psychosis. These pictures linked the survived reality with the body and the spirit of the person. With the body, because as they reflected unscripted events, they were not only unscripted but also according to the time of the inscription were translated to the body and also linked with it.

The night of the adoption of the human spirit to the Holy Ghost does not go without any pain. Every passage from the sensual level to the spiritual level takes place with the psychotic element. During the spiritual way, because of the existence of a huge quantity of pictures this element is additionally present. The evil spirit removed from the pictures (which deprived of the spiritual factor are quickly forgotten), causes **a temporary perturbation in perception of the reality – psychosis.** The spirit of person on the same phenomenon reacted by darkness.

Psychosis is a disturbance from the side of nature, which must have the time to adopt itself to the spirit of a new quality, which was not present till now. This temporal disturbance results from the adaptation of the body and spirit of a man to Holy Ghost, which touched the spiritual heart and mind. In the illness, when the evil spirit invaded the spiritual heart, he pulled the soul to himself, constrains the nature linked with the soul. The ill person describing the psychosis very often uses the words that it is "floating" in their head. The feeling of "floating" is subjectively perceived as if the brain was composed of the tank of the liquid, or as if it was changed from the solid state to the liquid state (the patients often compare the dulled brain in the illness to the piece of wood in the liquid). There are characteristic subjective symptoms of the psychosis. Of course there are other symptoms – drop of the physical and mental forces, temporal loss of the deep memory, the loss of the life perspective and others. In the spirituality of the Saint John of the Cross writes about the soul shielded and hidden in the "dark water" near God. This dark water is just the psychotic element.

In the advanced spirituality this psychotic element of God's activity is called as **the dark contemplation.** In the dark contemplation there is no element of light and love, there is an element of God's presence, but only as unidentified spiritual presence (without light and sweet colour). God can't at this stage fill up the soul with light and love, because the nature, from which the pictures were removed by force is not ready to meet God perceived as light and love. God will wait when the nature will be healed and adapted and in that time the ill person will be filled up with the light contemplations, which the soul has not met until now.

This psychotic element does not degrade like in the illness but very much ennobles and raises, because it is God (not the evil spirit) who appears in the spiritual heart with the new magnificent quality. **The general opinion is such that the dark contemplations give a greater comprehension than the light contemplations.** It is also so, because the dark contemplations take place in the period, which is characterised by the growth of the spiritual comprehension – in the period of such "leap of the comprehension".

Thus, one should keep calm and without hurry to go through all this cycle. The looking for the clear presence of God by force is a great fault, by which one can stop the spiritual progress. It is difficult to understand specially to the person emotionally and sentimentally wounded, which would satiate with the God's love endlessly. But the first period which lasted till now – the period of the sweet love has finished definitively. The night which became just now prove this.

Thus, the dark contemplations is a characteristic psychotic element of the night.

The devil's element during the nights is also specific. Devil during the night will not have any sentiments about the knocks from outside and he will not save the ill person. The attacks will be brutal and on the fundamental level. They remind of what some time ago caused the illness.

But what about his internal influence – here one can meet a characteristic element. As a result, the psychotic element in the contact by the sensual part with the environment is broken – to the evil spirit also. He can't enter to the interior of the ill person through it. And this causes a great fury from him. He guesses that something goes on between the ill person and God, but he can't penetrate this (because of his too weak possibilities in comprehension) and to reach this place (because of the psychotic element Saint John of the Cross writes about the cave, in which the soul has taken refuge, and to which the devil can't enter. Meantime, God by the dark contemplations gives the soul the spiritual growth – which the evil spirit is not able to disturb – and only suspecting something – beats the ill person by the brutal knocks from outside.

The providential element. The night of spirit is a state inscribed to the realities of life. The night is not the spiritual exercise which one can undertake in any time. The night is a form of the trap to which God introduced, and from which moved out. The manuals of the spirituality try to give the advise how to behave during the night of spirit – but the only one piece of advice is important – one should undertake the night and submit it, even though its trouble as the night will fulfil this task and God will finish it.

A person after the experience of the night will perceive all events in them life like a gift – with distance – interested what else the life will bring them.

The first stage of the active purifications were aimed to liberate the emotional memory from the pictures. It was conducted according to the scheme – meditative expression – half psychosis – absorption of the psychosis – return to the contemplative prayers – crisis and the next expression.

These expressions one should do as long as this scheme repeats. The expression of the pictures in some cases should be completed by **the expression of the feeling to the person to which the picture was related and to express to God the expectations which are linked with the examined feeling.**

The majority of the pictures is removed as by the battering ram during these meditative techniques. But very often if it was accompanied by the feeling – some traces of it stay in the emotional memory. The wound of the original injury causes a great hunger in feelings – a dream about the great feeling and the plan to fulfil it. Because it is the last not removed thing in the emotional memory, the evil spirit will utilise it and will start to be influenced by these old dreams. These are the feelings which were not undertaken for different reasons, but also such which a person was not conscious of at that time. The fact that they exist (the consciousness that in the relation was also a feeling) appears much later – in a moment of making order in feelings.

How one should make such expression of feeling?

One should recall a person and the feeling linked with them and tell about all this to God. One should express these contents which were not expressed before – even those more intimate. The dreams linked with the person which were not fulfilled. The point of this expression is to express to God the spirit which was present in this past feeling. Unfortunately, one should do it as in the case of the emotions, but with mildness.

One should recall once more the situations from 20-40 years ago, and express to God all contents related with it. It will become evident that the spirit which was placed in the memory of the sentiment was also the evil spirit. He wounded the memory, charged it, disintegrated, caused the tensions. It caused many consequences as the physical weakness, sleepiness, breaking of the mood, distraction, sensibility to the other spirit in the environment, internal tension in simple situations.

Because the feeling in schizophrenia contains two basic elements – I love and I desire – one should express it according to this key. This expression should be made as the meditative expression of the pictures. Thus, one time (or 2 times within one week), every 3-4 months. One should repeat it as much as is needed to express all situations and God will fill up it by the grace of healing. It will be a supplementary method to the meditative expression.

The feelings are also linked with **the expectations** of love and desire and expecting something from the other person. One should also take under the consideration the expression of the expectations.

What gives God the exact expression of these old sentimental longings and expectations?

God will take them out from the memory where they are situated, will liberate the will from them, they will be no longer attached to them. God will be perceived by the places possessed before by the spirit. God will start also to integrate a man internally and to satiate him by His love. He will eliminate the internal tear in the soul and in the body which was the consequence of the original injury.

If the spirit is not expressed, the contemplation will stop and the unfulfilled feeling will return. One should not be afraid of this expression. Practically it is the last step of the active purifications. Devil already has no power to invade the spiritual heart again. He can destabilise the ill person by the crisis, but if the ill person does not turn definitely to the way of sin, and if s/he does not reverse themselves from God – the evil spirit can't harm them – he does not dominate over the spiritual heart any more. But after the expression of the successive situations linked with the sentiment to more people one should consequently eliminate the presence of the spirit from the memory.

Unfortunately, this expression is also difficult. It consists in the opening of the old wounds which is painful. Reaction to it is the next night. If there is no presence of God in the spiritual heart – it would be the depression with anxiety. This suffering full of the excruciating pain with the tension is called **dryness** in the spirituality. This tension appeared earlier – after the meditative expression of the pictures – usually in the moment when the ill person prepared for rest (before sleep) or when s/he was resting (before the sunrise). It would be classic anxiety if it was not for the presence of God in the spiritual heart. One should go through these difficult states and know that only in such way one can purify the emotional memory related with the feeling. This is as if **the second face of the night of the spirit.** In this first night, the dark contemplation prevailed – it means the psychotic element related with the feeling of bareness and abandonment by God. Now the contemplations are lighter, the psychotic states exist, but **the dominating element is dryness.** The ill person recalls:

Throughout the winter I dreamed about the excursion to France. I bought a flight ticket in advance and I was waiting. In my opinion France was one of the most beautiful countries in the world. I was very glad that I would see once again its subtle beauty.

In the meantime, God introduced me to the night. As I couldn't give back the tickets I went on the excursion.

But instead of enjoying the beauty of France, all the time I was posing myself a question – what I am doing here? – why I came here?

To the medieval castles and renaissance palaces I reacted only by the first gasp of admiration which didn't last more than one second. Later it hid in the depth of my mentality and did not move me. It did not associated with any impressions from the past. The beauty of the architecture and the landscape did not touch me like it was in the past. I was not able to find out the old feeling of beauty – I was not able to reach out to it.

Before the journey we lost the case in the court. The municipality in a very smartly under the law has robbed us by planning the road to the neighbouring residential quarter half on our ground. The thoughts on the judge and on the mayor were coming. I was not able to liberate myself from them. And also I was analysing the interview with the "progressive" bishop – I was not able to liberate myself from this text for 3 weeks.

I was not able to find a place myself, because of the internal anxiety and distraction, nothing could calm me down, nothing could give me joy.

When I returned home it was the same. I had to force myself to any activity. In the morning I woke up early – I couldn't sleep longer. In the evenings I was glad that the day has passed.

I wanted to give my life as if external frames, because I have not seen any sense in my activity. A garden in which I was working and cycles of the nature created my activity – and nothing more.

I started to receive the knocks from different people – from the priest who cruelly replied to me, from another priest who refused to give the holy communion on my hand. The woman whom I helped in the past made a critical and painful remarks about me, two policeman stood on the hook of my trailer and started to jump on it and with a great joy were looking whether the hook would not break down.

And this all occurred as if the people had no human feelings. The devil attacked me through them brutally and ruthlessly.

The interpersonal contacts were full of gruffness and scoffing causing pain. Devil influenced even the clergymen to knock me by words, gestures, disrespect.

The summer was strange – cold, rainy, later there was a short heatwave – and the rain again. I was feeling tired and over-worked (even though I was not working much), and apart from that, I received knocks. God experienced me and He had no mer-cy on me.

I saw all my faults: how I complain, how I abuse, how moody, how unsteady I am. My faults were magnified to the monstrous di-mensions. I saw them all exactly – they were compromising – God has shown me all of them as if in the distorting mirror.

All spiritual side run away from me – as if it had never existed. As if all my spirituality had no depth – as if it existed now only at the natural level. I was not able to get out of these natural schemes.

I felt absolutely defeated – spiritually I didn't behave well dur-ing this night.

The image of God had not disappeared, but it was so weak that it could only maintain my faith with the rest of my grace.

In the mentality my consciousness was burning, was full of pain – and it was like that almost everyday. I had only known that God would take me out of this experience one day – as He placed it on me. But to survive this state was not easy.

Even in the Church I couldn't find the support. One of the priests brutally scoffed and derided me. God had shown me all sinfulness of the clergy. Not the layer of their sanctity, which I saw before, but the layer of their sins and its great sizes. God had taken from me all the possibilities of support which I before had in such people.

These states lasted 5 months. As violently and unexpectedly as they started – they finished. God took them out and gave me a rest by the grace of the light contemplations and gave me a new more perfect comprehension of the spiritual matters.

What does the night with the dryness prove? It proves that **the spirituality crosses the border.**

Till now the emotions, feelings, will and comprehension were linked together.

The will was directed by the inspirations coming from nature. They fed the will, but at the same time they didn't go beyond the body's needs. Even the spirituality was based on this rule. The will didn't make any drastic choices, which could be unpleasant for the body.

The "pleasure principle" protected the body from destruction. This principle was applied even to the spiritual life.

Now a total change occurred. The painful change in which the will pulled and purified by God is detached by force from the union with the body and what caused pleasure.

One can compare it to the plant which had its natural root – root of the natural pleasure. Later after the contemplative prayers, God caused the growth of the second root – the root of acting according to the will of God. The plant took saps from its two roots and what is more – this supernatural root supported the natural one.

Now during this night God removes this natural root – and this is a shock, because the plant should move to another system of feeding. It is a shock for the emotions and feelings – they don't know how to behave when God takes out this natural and protecting spirit. They don't know how to behave – or they react with dryness. To them it is a sort of dying, and therefore it is so painful.

They will get alive, but they will start to act according to other rules. The pleasure will bring them focus. The joy and pleasure come to them by the will unified with the will of God. The vanity will be eliminated – the external impulses will not satiate them any more. The old impulses linked with pleasure will not feed them any more. Only a distant recollection that it was like that and that it was possible in the past remains.

The night with dryness is a sign of crossing the border between the body and the spirit. It proves that the will separates itself from the whims of the body, it becomes free – it liberates from the influence of emotions and feelings.

The second characteristic phenomenon **of the disorientation of the will proves the occurring changes.** It lasts for some weeks. Till now the will very strictly controlled what was going on in the natural cognition. The will was concentrated on this and controlled it all very strictly. Now the will loses its orientation. It allows everything – every good or bad act, and gives permission to the sins. One should know about existence of such phenomenon at this stage of the spirituality.

One should wait until the states of the night pass by themselves. Despite the suffering and struggle these states will fill the ill person with great hope. When these states come, in the beginning they are refused as something painful. But the night unifies with God – every night ends with a deeper union. The night is the experience for which one can long, because one knows how magnificent the image of God and the image of the world after the night will look. Therefore, the spiritual pain is mixed here with joy, because of the fact that the following night starts.

Here also is the period when the psychotic element finishes and **the pictures start to appear many times during a day** – of people, situations, places, from different periods of life – they appear according to the key known only to themselves – and they disappear. It makes the impression of making order of a great memorial chaos, which has started just now. It makes the impression that the emotions found their final place, which they have been looking for in vain till now.

As the books of the spirituality write – the night of spirit and the union, which takes place during it liberate the soul from its own sensibility. **The soul obtains liberty and freedom from the evil spirit.** As if by occasion, by the change which passes in it, the soul is liberated from the illness, which resides on the lower part of soul – by this its desires, passions get sleepy, are mortified and extinguished.

Removing the pictures related to the feeling and later achieving unity and simplicity does not pass without pain. This is a difficult stage, because the liberation is linked with the appearance of psychotic elements. The ill person should be conscious that these psychoses appear and disappear by themselves definitively.

The phenomenon of the psychosis is well-known to the ill person and it shouldn't be something new to them.

What else do the active purifications related to the feeling cause?

They eliminate the results of the original injury in the sphere of feelings. **They liberate from the disintegration** and sentimental complications in the personal history which were caused by this injury.

It liberates from great tensions, anxiety, which accompany the feelings from childhood which were accumulated in the memory.

The ill person starts to be calm, natural. S/he starts to perceive the external world quietly and in the natural way.

The internal order and harmony and efficiency come back. **The permanent tiredness** which was related with the wound in the feeling disappear.

The pictures of people in the memory become pure – without the sensual contents which they contain.

The ill person is liberated from the necessity of the great feeling not by the sentimental satisfaction, which s/he was looking all their life, but by **the elimination of the necessity of feeling by God.** The ill person understand that it was not the natural feeling by satiation and the scale of their possibilities was limited because of it.

The ill person is also taken out from the isolation which was related to such sentimentality.

The active purification done correctly should be finished by the characteristic phenomenon indicating the healing of the emotions and feelings. It is **the widening of the spiritual heart and the internal silence.**

The spiritual heart and the spirit which flows from it remind the stream of the river – once flowing rapidly, once near dry. What permits this river to flow are the spiritual contents accumulated in the memory and descending to the spiritual heart.

And it becomes a moment near the end of active purifications when the spirit flowing through spiritual heart reminds the impetus of the river flowing through the overloaded river-bad, where this river takes all that was placed on its way.

And this is what happens with **the enlargement of the heart.** A person who prays feels that the spirit refills all capacity of their spiritual heart. All blockades which had not permitted this before – now has disappeared. The spiritual dams which existed before are definitively broken.

A new spiritual quality is created. It is strictly linked with the state of emotional memory. The stone of sensuality (emotionality and sentimentality), which descended to the heart and which the heart has blocked until now, is pushed away.

But the most important result and factor indicating the healing of the sphere of emotions and feelings is **the feeling of the deep internal silence. This silence has the supernatural origin.** The spiritual external movements entering through emotions stopped to influence the ill person. The silence also proves the beginning of harmony between upper and lower powers.

This silence is a sort of sanctuary which one should take care of and protect. Emotions and feelings calm down, because the spirit which was present in them separated itself from the evil spirit, which also dominated around and synchronised with the Holy Ghost.

The answer to this feeling of internal silence should be **the life in silence**. The healed sphere of the emotionality and sentimentality calms down – it becomes silent. **Becoming silent means that it is harmonised and does not transmit the activity of the evil spirit from the outside as before.**

Only now one can see how many troubled thoughts, internal inspirations were transmitted by this sphere and how such person was linked through with the environment.

By the "gate of silence" the border to the internal world passes. The dialogues with the evil spirit stop – before the spirit engaged the ill person for a long time – served the thoughts – the ill person answered to them. Such thoughts disappear now – the answers also disappear. All great spiritual background disappear. It becomes totally silent. Only now one can observe how great this sphere was and how many times the evil spirit engaged the ill person with it.

The sins committed by the language start to disappear, because now every opening of mouth is preceded by the reflection – by inspiration of whom the thought appears. This purification of the background causes that every dialogue with the evil spirit, which before served the thoughts unpunished now immediately sounds false. Now the ill person takes care of the words and makes the reflection over them – even provoked s/he doesn't answer, because the evil spirit has no any bridgehead in the memory of the ill person. Now the evil spirit is immediately recognized and exposed. The internal world perceived by such emotions and feelings **starts to be natural.**

Just now the life accelerated by the spirit slows down to the natural speed. The feeling of internal silence is a grace which lasted for a certain time and comes back – forms a person for life in silence. The result of this grace is important – the elimination of the sin committed by language – talkativeness, calumny, slander, mischievousness, roughly or ironic comments, explosions of anger in responses. Elimination of all this, where the person reacted like a table tennis player – where the knock returned on the side of the opponent by the same spirit as s/he has received it. It happened so in this way because in the consciousness a spiritual prompter functioned which gave quick, immediate answers to all outside inspirations. When the grace of the internal silence appears, this prompter is definitively eliminated – it is silenced. The consciousness which was violently touched by it – now lays down in silence. Now a person stays only with their internal inspirations.

This external which was in majority before – now are cut out. The external world occupied by the evil spirit, which together with the original sin and the original injury influenced so much – now definitively this influence ended.

The active purifications finish in a great part. They were necessary. They will be continued in the same cases when the pictures are not removed yet and stop the spiritual progress. Now the person is conscious that s/he stays in front of God – great, saint, with the perfect comprehension – and in the perfect unity. S/he knows that even s/he would train themselves s/he will go to the wall of their own possibilities. S/he will notice also that the spiritual cognition is a gift and the active purifications were created only by the conditions to receive this gift later. Now one should give back the initiative to God and open on Him in a new more passive way.

The ill person (even though it is difficult to say about them in such way) after many years reflects the mood dominating in the environment. S/he does not run after (really and in thoughts), someone else's or not real problems. S/he sleeps well – the moving of the dream phases has finished. The ill person is deeply fulfilled, reconciled with themselves to God and the environment. Now the next stage in the spirituality occurs which is **the unification of the will.**

CHAPTER 19

THE SIMPLE UNION
– THE UNION OF THE WILL

In the Holy Gospel according to Mark in the end of the dramatic description of the liberation of the possessed schizophrenia sufferer one can find the description – I will cite the evangelist: *As Jesus was getting into the boat, the man who had been demon-possessed begged to go with him. Jesus did not let him, but said, "Go home to your own people and tell them how much the Lord has done for you, and how he has had merdy on you. So the man went away and began to to tell in the Decapolis how much Jesus had done for him.* (Marc 5:18-20). (NIV)

It is also the description of the stage in the spirituality which is named a **simple union (union of the will).** One can observe in this description all characteristic traits of it – throwing the devil out from the interior of a man, inversion of all order of life, change of the relation to the people, finding in Jesus a Master and the will to follow Him (in the therapy it is a little earlier), vocation given by Jesus (but not such which the ill person wished to himself), acceptance of this vocation and beginning of its fulfilment.

In the illness what blocked the unification of the will from the beginning was the existence of two different spiritual ingredients. The Holy Ghost in the will and the evil spirit in the contents accumulated in the emotional memory. To succeed the union of the will, it must liberate itself from the influence of the past accumulated emotions and feelings. It will assure freedom to the will and will not induce the will to other strange spiritually movements.

The simple union is beautifully described by Tauler in *Sermon 56*. He shows how prophet Elias observed the wind which was breaking the rocks, the earthquake and the fire – ascertaining that

God is not coming in the form of any of these phenomena. Only when a whistling of the gentle air happens (1 Kings 19:12), does he discover that God is present in this phenomenon.

The simple union is the first different experience than what has been experienced till now. This previous existing one can qualify as the joy in the heart, something blazing in the heart, switching the light in the spiritual heart.

And now for the first time it is different. It is much deeper and more subtle experience – as the feeling of the heaven in the heart. **And when God touches the heart – He touches only it. This touch does not move the lower parts. It is different – mild and distinct**. It lasts for some weeks and changes. It calls the consciousness that one should serve God otherwise – with greater care and elegance. One should serve like the man chosen by God, to which God gave a title of nobleman – a title which is an obligation.

Why is this union named "simple"? As a contrast to the unions which existed before, and which could be called not coordinated or not harmonised.

In the example described in this book the unification on the simple way was preceded by the four nights of spirit. On the first night, the will adopted the spirit linked with the emotions, on the second, what influenced the centre of pleasure, on the third, what was present in the intellect and in the feeling, during the fourth night the will was finally arranged.

In the Holy Gospel one can read about Jesus resurrect who went to meet his pupils even though the doors were closed. For somebody who experienced it – the simple union is immediately associated with this description. The doors symbolise the emotions and feelings of a sensual man – through whom every contact with the external world goes. The doors open every time when one should open oneself to outside. Also the contact with God happens with the movement of feelings and emotions, when God comes with his presence to the spiritual heart.

Now God enters for the first time through the doors closed – directly to the spiritual heart – to the heart pure and not divided. He enters without any movement in the emotions and feelings. It can happen when a person undergoes the way to serve to Holy

Gospel, when s/he will go through the death, or the night of spirit and will come to the reality of the resurrection. Then God, like in the Holy Gospel, will enter his interior through the doors closed to the world.

God enters and says – *Peace be with you* (John 20:19). (NIV) Peace because He focuses the internal senses (memory and imagination) on himself, and all the external reality which invaded the spiritual heart together with the spirit regains its proper place – outside of this meeting. With this meeting the permanent tiredness, deconcentrating, distraction, disassociation disappear. It happens in the normal life and in the spiritual life too.

It happens so because the internal senses (memory and imagination) embedded in the spiritual heart occupied by God who is currently present in the heart not in the external world. They are not torn between the heart and the external world which caused this tiredness and distraction. The external world is not spiritually introduced to the heart any more. It stays outside. But to lead oneself to such state one should purify the spiritual heart by active purifications – to detach it spiritually, to separate it from the external world. To close the doors to the external world and to the evil spirit. Now the internal senses are occupied by the guest in the heart – God – focusing and concentrating the senses on Him. And this concentration on the One causes that the ill person is internally integrated, not broken and divided like before.

All trainings, improvements, exercises gave something only if they led to purifications. **But only the nights and simple union resolve the problem of disintegration.**

One can pose a question – what important happens for the first time in the simple union that one can recognize it as the end of the illness?

And so by the simple union the phenomenon described by Saint John of the Cross in the book *The Spiritual Canticle* in the 18th stanza took place. The upper part of the soul is occupied by God who fills its powers – the will and reason, and emanates to the virtues of the soul. During this for the first time He cuts out the activity of the lower part of the soul. The movements which come from the outside for the first time do not penetrate the upper part.

Saint John describes in a pictorial way that these movements – *only they are than said merely to touch the threshold, or to cry at the gate.* And really such phenomenon exists on this stage.

Describing all this by the language of the Saint – till now the external impulse goes through the suburbs of the soul (it means by the external and internal senses), it forced the walls, and entered to the interior and attacked the tower of the castle – it means it entered the will.

When before – the spiritual impulse entered from outside, found similar spiritual contents in the emotional memory which together moved the will and the reason.

Now the will trembles, registers this spiritual movement, but it will not succumb and will be not broken as before. For the first time these movements will stay outside – they will not enter the upper part. For this phenomenon to take place, the spiritual development is needed – up to the level of the simple union and the purification of the emotional memory by the active purifications. The spiritual impulse will not break through, because it met the empty and healed archives of the memory and the upper powers occupied by God. The formerly ill person is spiritually separated from the external world, which had attacked them through the emotions and feelings till now. **And this ends the illness.**

By the simple union God occupying the spiritual heart in a new way for the first time cuts this devil's circulation which had taken place till now. After the invasion to the spiritual heart the evil spirit harassed the ill person in a terrible way and after removing him during the long time going against the will of the ill person by the whole series of thoughts. He used these spaces in the heart and in the memory occupied by him as the bridgeheads and by them he influenced the will. He excited the abnormal states such as scruples, racing thoughts, revolted, aggressive, impure thoughts and thoughts with a changing tension during a day. He speeded up and slowed down these thoughts.

Now, when God touched the spiritual heart in a new way all this circulation was definitively cut out. During the years it had been disappearing, but it was definitively cut out by the simple union. After it had passed, it gets healthy and nothing new accumulates in it. The peace and the stable balance start to dominate. The devil does not influence the heart, because he has no control over it. The circulation of his activity was definitively cut by God.

The schizophrenia sufferer is internally broken, disintegrated. It is very difficult to explain it to someone who has not gone through the same thing.

From the childhood I remember a story about a bee, when she lets out the sting – she as if opened internally and later she is not able to close back. In schizophrenia this impossibility to harmonise oneself spiritually after the invasion of the spirit, and because of the overloaded memory last for years. The internal tear is real. There are internal breaks along the border marked by the evil spirit. The internal tear breaks into many pieces and in the middle of the tear there are traces of the spirit which block the possibility of unification.

In the simple union, these separated planes after the removal of the traces of the spirit during the dark contemplations can finally unify themselves at the simplest level for the first time.

By the simple union the ill person for the first time discovers the phenomenon of incredible fidelity and love given by God. Before s/he thought that the sin caused that God takes back the grace and turns away from a person. But God does not remove the grace – He gives more and more of it. He will account the sins, but He will not limit the grace. For the ill person this moment is a kind of obligation.

It is a moment when the radical fidelity and love of God cross with the sinfulness of man. One can add that this is about the subjective feeling of this phenomenon which appears by the simple union.

The schizophrenia sufferer doesn't want any changes. Any changes in their life, any changes in the external world. All should remain in its place, all things should be in the place where s/he had placed them, all situations should be the same, because the ill person is not prepared for the perception of the new matters.

When the healing progresses, the ill person starts to plan everything exactly. The future must change, but according to the strictly precise plan – nearly like in a script. Now after the simple union, because of a total change all these planning criteria fall off. Only one remains – to stay in the will of God – to fill up the will of God to the end.

Now the ill person takes every event in their life with joy, as a gift, as a surprise, which God prepared for them. The ill person observes all this with distance, thinking what new God prepared for them and how He will lead them in life. The ill person is finally liberated from their own plans, projects, anticipations.

The simple union is a time of receiving the vocation. Vocation is a fulfilment of the function in Church, or fulfilment of the task set by God. The ill person perceives it now when s/he fully developed spiritually.

The vocation is the understanding of the task which prepared God to the fulfilment. The appointed man is happy, because s/he has found the aim of the life. Why the vocation has not come earlier? – **because the ill person was not detached from the world and s/he did not have the evangelic love** – the absolute condition of the effective fulfilment of the vocation – s/he was not "God's man".

Now s/he is united with God in the internal harmony, s/he is sure about their opinions. S/he is also conscious of their situation that it is God who bowed to him and rose them. It is the man who passed to the side of God. Now s/he must pass on all the evangelical love to other people.

S/he couldn't have done it earlier, because s/he did not react correctly to a mistaken or sinful man. S/he forced them to take other attitude, was aggressive against thinking otherwise. S/he couldn't pray for them, s/he would willingly convert them by force. Without the evangelic love s/he could be only the religious agitator or even a member of the fighting hit squad.

S/he had also no unified spiritual cognition – s/he had the divided cognition, because of the divided spiritual heart, and because of the manner of the cognition with the sensual movements.

On the one hand, the background to the emotions and feelings is created by the memory and imagination healed and occupied by God, on the other hand the will is pulled by Him. Therefore, the emotions and feelings have entered certain frames and borders which they will not cross.

After the healing **the spiritual influence of the environment disappears.** The evil spirit does not cause movements as before. It does not penetrate the will through the emotions healed and instilled in the spiritual heart occupied by God.

Later **the emotions are not hobbled by devil.** They are free and they can have the full expression. The world, which hurt before – now stays as if in another dimension. It still exists, it is ruled by the primitive flat logic, but it does not influence the person like before. The relation to God is so fundamental that the apostasy surprises by its false primitive logic, but can't attack like before. This sensuality moved only to the highest, noble, beautiful world of God – has the traits of development and nobleness.

The healed emotional memory cuts out all baggage of the past. The spirit which lived in it **bounded, loaded, fatigued a lot.** By the unification with the external world, with other people, by the disintegrated internal presence. Now **this extraordinary fatigue disappears** – fatigue which was present even in the simplest acts.

Till now the ill person was attacked also by the wills of other people. The spirit which was in their will, and which was not a Holy Ghost, attacked their will, introduced the trouble to their will detached from God by its power, throwing out on other positions. There was practically no place for the ill person's will, as s/he met the strong wills of other people. After the undertaking of the will of God and after going through the nights of spirit, which removed to the end all of the pictures the will becomes free. Free, because it can unite with the will of God – God who providentially leads the world. Free, because it is no longer influenced by the emotions and by the feelings, from which it gets more and more liberated. Free, because the other wills which were influenced by the emotions and feelings can't do nothing wrong to it as before and can't trouble it. If the other wills didn't go through the nights of spirit and usually they didn't do this, they have no access to the purified and unified will of the ill person. **This is a moment of the liberation from the influence of the environment.** The terrible world eliminating God which doesn't perceive other man, world which before has caused the illness still exists. But it exists somewhere below and it is less and less common part of it. It has existed, exists and will exist, but the world of people united with God and free exists too – and this all is discovered by the ill person at this stage.

The purification of the emotions causes also **the emanation of colours of the world and full behaviours of other people.** Before the world was perceived by the emotions occupied by the evil spirit. It looked as if it was mat. Now it becomes coloured and full of beauty. This beauty emanates. The beauty moves now the sensibility and emanates even in the normal life. Other people are also perceived differently – without any falsifications which caused a strange spiritual presence. Before the texts proclaimed by other people were over-interpreted or not understood completely.

The healing of emotions causes also that **the emotions are not the main driving force,** are not the main impulse of the activity as before. The ill person starts to take breaks in prayers – to hear the echo of the text. S/he does not spend all the day in a hurry. S/he starts to act with the emotional distance, with reflection. S/he starts to understand their own emotions and emotions of other people.

Also in the case of feelings – **the spiritual heart does not move in the direction of a nearly every met person as before**. The ill person does not beg one's feeling, doesn't flirt, doesn't provoke, doesn't dream about romances. S/he perceives the beauty in other person, but beauty without any desire. In God s/he found their fulfilment – also the sentimental one.

A period comes when the ill person starts to feel a very deep and subtle joy of faith. The faith is for them pure and very easy. Pure and easy because in a clear way s/he starts to understand the roles of the faith in the normal life. Till now the faith and the life were two different spheres. The ill person, once was occupied to make the faith deeper, and once s/he simply lived. Now the faith starts to penetrate every activity, every relation with other person. The life starts to be in the natural way penetrated by the faith. The life in faith starts to be very simple.

From the two kinds of man – sensual and spiritual – one is created – a spiritual man. S/he is liberated from the influence of emotions and feelings, which when occupied by the spirit determined their life. Now the ill person understands how great burden they were, how they hobbled the will, how much of the force and energy s/he wasted for leading such life determined by the emotions and feelings, and how much time s/he lost for leading such life.

The simple union is followed by an important and characteristic stage in the spirituality. Figuratively one can compare it to the inverted tree with the roots in heaven. The medieval pictures of the inverted tree symbolise the reversal of the order – from the natural to the supernatural – and this takes place in a man by the simple union (by the union of the will).

Thus, **more and more perfect alignment of the human will to the will of God takes place and giving oneself up to the will of God's providence.**

How does the image of a man after the union of the will look?

One of the changes in the man is **the facility of the contemplation.** Till now this facility was blocked by the sins or their reminders, or not healed emotionality causing the difficulties and loss of the spiritual lightness in the contemplative prayer. The condition for the progress in contemplation is the purification of the will and emotions and feelings.

After the first contemplative prayers the contemplation stops. After the beginning of active purifications, the contemplation in emotions starts, it means the charismatic prayer in languages. But this prayer is also limited after a short period.

Here a very interesting phenomenon takes place – **the contemplation in schizophrenia (as every prayer) does not purify the emotional memory.** One can survive great movements in the contemplative prayer and not get rid of the blockades coming from the wounded emotions. When the active purifications finish, these blockades are removed. The contemplative prayer will receive the full expression.

The beginning of the internal harmony and perfect order occurs.

It is also a characteristic phenomenon, for which the ill person longed from the beginning of the illness, and which s/he was not able to imagine themselves. It is the internal and external order in the man made by God. Till now, it was a struggle between a spiritual and sensual man, between upper and lower powers. Now God unified with the man with their will and reason by love and faith pulls Himself in the extraordinary way giving the lower powers their proper place. It is similar to constructing and ordering of the mixed layers where God made the final order – from the highest to the lowest. This loss of synchronisation in the powers of soul was the result of the original sin and also of the original injury like in schizophrenia. After a long spiritual way the order was made. A new spiritual quality appears which introduces a new logic, different than the logic which dominated till now. A great spiritual peace is introduced which the ill person had never felt in their life. The order in all activities replaces the chaos which dominated till now.

In a sensual man the separate spirit moved emotions, another one moved feelings, another one touched the will, another one influenced the cognition. Now one spirit influences the integrated person – the one which is in the will. And others synchronize with it. These moves and their results caused by other spirits are taken out. Only by this (which happens during the nights), a person becomes internally integrated. Going through these states is painful. God through the painful nights synchronizes things which made this internal unity impossible before.

Finally, God introduces his hierarchy, his order, and his perspective. Also the new coordination instead of previous disintegration is visible in a man from outside. **The order and harmony of powers emerge for the first time since the simple union.**

By the union of the will **devil is thrown out from the healed emotional memory.** In this way he irrecoverably loses a sort of bridgeheads which he possessed there for all these years (from the original injury). He can't now break and destabilise the personality by this internal influence. The emotions become ordered. Now the ill person can observe the attacks of the devil on their person – how brutal they are now, how frequent – and also who the author of them is. Unfortunately, these attacks do not disappear. Nothing changes here. Neither brutality nor their frequency. But thanks to the integrated healed internal structure the ill person can observe them quietly on themselves. S/he can observe how they pass

214

now, reflect on how devil had attacked them before. These attacks were not the illusion, not the persecution mania. They were real, so strong that they caused the psychosis – and they did it more than once.

And so strong are they also now. But before the ill person perceived them by the internally broken structure which the devil broke again by smartly provoking and pulling in the space of evil and later brutally knocking.

Now the ill person healed and internally integrated perceives and understands the activity of the spirit, but s/he doesn't pull themselves into this activity and s/he doesn't allow being provoked. The devil who has lost the internal bridgeheads can only brutally attack from inside – and he does this. One can observe in such situations all his limited cognition – he doesn't see the changes, it is impossible for him to penetrate a new relation man – God. He assumes only that such relation can exist. He also thinks that these primitive and brutal attacks will give the result as before.

The effects of the new spiritual quality in a man are the radical observance of the commandment of love and the consciousness of gratification of God's grace.

What image of God does appear after the union of the will?

The image of God which exists – a deep, unshaken consciousness of God who exists and acts. The consciousness which gives great peace, cutting all these doubts and speculations concerning the future and salvation (so common in this illness). Despite the difficulties, despite the struggles, the consciousness of the presence of God dominates like the life in the sun which never sets. The swinging disappeared – the joy remained, because of God's presence, or anxiety when the ill person doesn't feel this presence.

There is an extremely deep consciousness that it is God who rules and leads the world and dominates it. But this consciousness of the existence of the evil and of the test: the most dramatic, the heaviest and most important one, to decide on which side one should place oneself.

Before the ill person was afraid, observing the successes of the evil people (who ignored the theses consisted in God). S/he didn't want to live in such world. Now it is the beginning of the new way based on the struggle in which s/he can observe the visible and real success.

It is also the image of God which directs a human life – leads a man. It is a deep consciousness of existence of the Person who providentially directs the life of whole social groups, but also the life of an individual. The ill person discovers such aspect of God's presence, because s/he did not think that the entering of God into a man's life is so deep.

It is the consciousness of God which does not break the freedom of man. It is difficult to understand to the ill person because s/he was deprived of the freedom by devil and their will had been broken many times. The ill person observes the bad will and sins of other people and that s/he was mysteriously united with this evil. This evil deprived them of the freedom, made the further life impossible. Till the moment of the healing the ill person looked for the prescription of this state as the introducing of the morality by force or by execution of the morality by force.

After the union of the will, the ill person will find their own place in the world. The relation to God will take the first place and the people will be perceived in this new perspective of this basic relation. The previous great solitude gives a place to the certitude in cognition and to the identity derived from finding God – similar to finding of the homeland and Master.

Thus, the image of God appears which gratifies a man with freedom and respects the free choice of a man. The image which had not been acceptable to the ill person until now. The ill person starts to accept the paradox, where God doesn't infringe the freedom even of such person, who doesn't respect the freedom of others – and the ill person starts to behave in such a way.

The union of the will is **the end of plans of a natural man and the end of the natural perspective.** This natural perspective during the long time couldn't be left behind, because the ill person was prisoned by emotions and feeling. It is the end of the natural man with their plans of life, projects and inventions, own image,

216

images of oneself as a champion, aspirations to such image and accounting of oneself for achieving this aim.

Now with joy, gratitude, curiosity and admiration because of God's leading, s/he accepts all dispensations of God's providence concerning their person. Their life starts to be as if the spiritual adventure, a surprise – not the settled plan of aspirations to perfection. The ill person knows that s/he depends on God. In the spirituality s/he will go as far as God will lead him by His grace. S/he is grateful for every God's dispensation. S/he knows that God is the constructor of their interior and s/he should permit Him to form themselves as He wishes. Also s/he knows that s/he should serve God in such place where God has placed them. The ill person stopped to climb up, stopped to assign the aims to themselves, stopped to pursue them. Before s/he only protected themselves against the knocks, avoided next injuries. Now s/he starts to enter a more difficult situation. S/he is conscious that the life takes place in the internal plan.

Also the ideals of the spiritual perfection with which the ill person has started their spiritual way are now totally different than what the ill person thinks about the spirituality now. The union of the will is the period where **the radical declaration for the sanctity not for the perfection occurs –** even in the spirituality. The aspiration to the sanctity relies on the transformation of one's own will to the will of God. One can do it without the gift of contemplation. And people who are not gifted with contemplation do it in this way. The union of the will relies on the acceptance of the theses which are in God and living according to them and submission in everything to God's Providence.

On the spiritual way of the ill person, **God leads them by the extraordinary graces, not only because s/he has the disposition for contemplation but also to compensate the states which were caused by the devil and to heal the effects of them.** The ill person should remember that the spiritual way by the contemplation is a difficult way. It requires self-denial, grounding in virtues – especially in humility and evangelic love. The ill person must remember that the progress in humility and evangelic love is the main indicator of the progress of the spiritual way.

But the supernatural words, visions, ravishing, spiritual delights, being in God's presence – there are all secondary symptoms of the spiritual life. One should accept them but not be fascinated by them, because they are not God.

The choice between the sanctity and perfection is a great dilemma to the ill person on the spiritual way. The sanctity and perfection are in opposition. The perfection is related with the body, nature – it is their attribute. And as it was difficult for the ill person to leave the sphere of nature – it is difficult also to leave the aspiration to perfectionism. **This inversion of the order by the union of the will, permits to radically declare for the sanctity without the feeling of any loss.** As a result, the ill person stops to compare themselves to others, stops to compete. S/he starts to be happy because of their own life. S/he perceives a beauty of the gift which is life. The life is no longer a burden, a yoke which binds. S/he starts to be grateful to God for the gift of life and for all situations which the life brings.

S/he starts to respect this gift in other people. S/he starts to be happy with small joys and successes. S/he is curious of what the life will bring. S/he stood as if outside – s/he is the observer of their own life, reflects on it – and also takes part in it. But s/he has the emotional distance to events and to their own experiences which s/he had not had till now. **The opening to God takes place.** Till now the ill person had not perceived the inspirations of God, s/he hadn't read the situations which appeared in their life. S/he was obstinate. Now s/he starts to understand God's inspirations, starts to understand the situation. S/he is not a slave but the child who starts to understand his Father's logic, different than the natural logic.

By finding the Father and Master in God whom s/he addresses, and whom s/he asks what his will is – **the simple union from the spiritual side ends the illness.**

CHAPTER 20

THE BEGINNING OF THE UNITIVE WAY

Formally the unitive way starts a little later, after the night of spirit linked with the union of the will, but as in the theory of the conjuncture, where some indicators are ahead of the cycle and announce some states – the same happens on the spiritual way when the symptoms showing the progress of the union appear.

Thus, the unitive way starts from some kind of an announcement telling what one can expect in the future. The ill person recalls:

I feel that I was standing on the shore of the ocean of silence. On the mild shore. The waves are so small that they barely touch the shore.

I love this silence. I am afraid to breath deeper so as not to frighten it away. The colours are mild and little pale – as after the resurrection – as on the paintings of Giotto – willow-green against green, the yellow sun which does not burn the little pale sky. The colours as if a drama had happened. I feel well in these colours – in their mildness they do not enter sharply to the depth of my soul.

The problems went out – as after the tempest. I have forgotten them, Although not long time ago they knocked me with a great power and had been tearing me as a pack of dogs.

The silence has been conceived in me. It started something that will never finish. The old ended.

The world without end, without the horizon was born. But it is strange that I know how to move in it.

I want to go deeper and deeper to this world. I don't want to frighten this world by the false world, false gesture, false move of the will. I will observe it. I will absorb it with every breath.

I found my homeland – mild, pure, where the eternal peace lasts, where the pictures do not race in the mad speed.

I would like to plant roots in it and last in it like the thousand years old tree and never leave it.

As usual during the spiritual way in the beginning an announcement of a given state is made to give direction and separate from the preceding state, so that the ill person will not get accustomed to the given state. Such habit would introduce the philosophy of the evangelic wealthy man and would stop every spiritual progress.

As usual after such an extraordinary state the crisis follows against which one should fight also through active purification. Also the preparation for its appearance was the task of previously elevated states. The ill person recalls:

I can't find the place for myself – it is a tension which cannot be released. This is not only the dryness and the elements of psychosis, but also the tension. It makes it difficult to sleep. It doesn't permit to find the place. I am posing the question to myself – what I am doing here? – in the places where I have been living for twenty years.

I started to be frightened. I see on the television the pictures of lawlessness – the insolent breaking of God's law and the arguments – even from the people who are spirituality engaged, that this is correct and one can, or one should do this. I am afraid of this people and feel lonely, because I have nothing in common with them.

I noticed that even the religion serves many people to build their own meaning, even their career. That God is nearly totally absent in all this, that I have no support in such people. That every contact with them is painful to me. That I crush myself with their falsely arranged wills and as a concrete pole.

It is the last crisis of this type. This crisis appear always there, where the spiritual development takes place, but in the memory the spiritually strange contents still remain (coming from the evil spirit) and here the remedy are also the active purifications – expression of anger in all relations simultaneously, and also the meditative expression of the pictures linked with the feeling – if such pictures will appear and there will be the necessity to express them.

The ill person will recall that for example during the examination of the twenty years of their life that the anger at other people related to 60 problems, at oneself – 54, to devil – 35 and at God s/he expressed the anger in 47 problems. As I already wrote, because of not the best spiritual development and because of the limited possibilities of such expression, the ill person had to express each kind of anger separately and between expressions there was a break of 2-4 years.

It appeared that now after years the small part of the problems expressed before remained in the memory of ill person and new problems will be added, which had not been seen before – because of the new perspective of the ill person.

And so analysing now the 20th year the ill person will notice that s/he would express anger at other people in 14 problems (because such number of problems remained in their memory, at oneself s/he would say something in 25 problems, at the devil in 6 problems and at God s/he would express 2 problems).

Taking by example the 23th year of his/her life – these proportions will be as 50, 59, 48, 42 and adequately 10, 26, 17, 9 problems.

All the time one can observe the great dose of remorse to oneself and the increase in the anger to the devil and to God as it was close to the explosion to the illness.

Thus, now one should combine this anger in four relations together and express it during one seance of expression. Such expression done simultaneously will remove the devil from all space of emotional memory concerning the given period.

One should once more go through all the important periods in such a way that during 1-2 years (doing the expressions every 3-6 weeks) to finally remove these contents from the emotional memory.

And here one can observe a very characteristic and interesting phenomenon of the final liberation from the structure of the evil spirit, which loses the points of support in the memory.

The ill person recalls:

Already on the next day after the expression of anger I started to feel the extraordinary spiritual trouble. On the third day in the morning after the awaking when I saw myself in the mirror,

I noticed surprised that my face looks as if I came back from the house of the ill fame.

Two days later the terrible aggression at almost all people, whom I have met – people in the shop, in the bus started. Neighbours from the block were very polite to me – but I was thrilled because of the aggression. It lasted 2-3 days. When it finished the extraordinary indifference to the religion, spiritual problems started – as if they had never existed in my life. The relation with God was full of pretensions. I was nearly revolted.

During all these states (I observe myself full of anxiety), I was changing myself like the spiritual chameleon and I had absolutely no influence on it. I was passively observing what was going on with me. After seven days suddenly everything calmed down, as if it had never taken place.

In the next expression this state repeated in almost the same way.

Thus, **the final liberation of the structure of the evil spirit takes place –** in this case by the influencing impurity, aggression and revolt. The spirit, with such structure invaded some years ago to the spiritual heart and now finally lost its bridgeheads.

Here also **the liberation from the spiritual and physical pain takes place.** This pain was related with the presence of the spirit. It stayed for years, it caused the total lack of joy of life. The ill person was filled with pain, although s/he was not conscious of this.

Then these liberations started something which can be called **the assistance of the Holy Ghost.** The awareness of guidance and care of the Holy Ghost even in the smallest things, mildness of the will, internal unction, silence and harmony, facility of the prayer and feeling of its sanctity.

But the greatest advantage of this period to the ill person is **the internal satiety.**

It is the first experience of such type. **God satiates by himself. A person satiated is a person fulfilled.** S/he doesn't pursue many false aims which were supposed to give them the aim of life – the aims that s/he set before. S/he does not make efforts which were to give them the eternal satisfaction. **S/he gets calm in the aspi-**

rations. Similarly like the possessed from the Gospel who stopped to climb the mountains and beat himself by the stones, because of non-fulfilment. He sits in the feet of Jesus and this will be enough for him.

Many authors of books concerning schizophrenia analyse what the possibilities of the development for the ill person are. Well – these possibilities if the ill person does not purify the emotional memory are not big. Second – **the essence of the illness is the insatiability** and even great development will not eliminate it. Hospitalized people with the titles of professors are good illustrations of this.

This satiation can be achieved only by a person with purified emotional memory. The satiation happens when the active purifications come to an end.

The subjectively felt grace of satiation is God touching all places in the body and soul which had been ill till now. It is the touch which heals and calms down these places. This grace lasts 3-5 weeks. It transforms and calms down.

A person who experienced it doesn't need to train themselves, assign a task, s/he doesn't need to beat a record, s/he doesn't need to develop themselves or aspire to great results – because s/he is a satiated person. God satiated them, got them calm, fulfilled and transformed them, even though ss/he has not achieved any visible success.

The satiation of the sphere related with the feeling causes that her purity rises to the high level, the impure looks and thoughts disappear. When looking at another person of opposite sex s/he sees their spiritual and physical beauty – sees them without any desire. The look at another person is purified, gets noble.

The satiation purifies the will from the vanity. The ill person stops to lose time for the things which were till now the therapy for insatiability.

The ill person regards also distinctly their past sins **especially those committed by language.** The sins disappear now before the ill person reacted impulsively to almost every external situation. It touched them visibly, it caused pain and forced the ill person to make comments. Now s/he is integrated and satiated. S/he doesn't feel the necessity to comment every situation. With little effort of their will, s/he stops to commit the sins made by the language – complaining, slander, judging – and other similar sins also disappear.

Therefore, as the simple union which becomes deeper and deeper after every night – **ends the spiritual disintegration – the beginning of the unifying way satiates.** There are two great enduring advantages in the struggle against the illness.

The spiritual states clarify – the crisis ends, because the emotional memory is in a great part purified. The unification with God happens through the nights – the nights change their nature – near the well-known states the new states appear. This situation is not characteristic to a natural man, when if /she achieves something – possesses it forever – and such state constructs their self-worth.

The nights when they come give back what somebody would consider to be their property and such is just the intention of God – to focus all attention on Him, not by the experienced states, which pass. The nights are the proof that the spirituality develops. The ill person recalls:

I noticed that during some days my physical powers started to wear out. I was fragile, delicate – without internal powers.

I was not able to pray. I was concentrated without thinking about anything, with emptiness in my head.

I was not able to find the place for myself. I felt that something finished in my life and something had not started yet. I was suspended and I was waiting for the new quality to appear.

I woke up early with a headache.

Three times (every few days) there were attacks of the sentimentality and desire, but I observed them like from outside – surprised that something was going on in my lower part. The spirit attacked me – caused the resentment due to the sentimental non-fulfilment. It also caused the burning pain.

I did not remember to buy a bread, to validate the ticket on the bus. I was frightened, because of it, but I knew that it would end one day.

I almost didn't feel the presence of God. God existed, but He was absent as if hidden somewhere.

The external world stopped to interest me. The banal programs from the radio and television and trivial problems, I couldn't listen to them any more.

After 2 months I got much weaker. My body has gotten soft as the warm wax. Psychotic dark contemplation has not passed, only they have becomea little lighter. I have lost the sense of time. I didn't know what the day of week or month is.

After next 6 weeks the intellectual emptiness started. I stopped to think, I couldn't get out any knowledge from the memory. The concentration had already been poor.

Later (after 4 weeks) the pictures from different periods of my life started to move in my memory. They came suddenly – a few during the day. I didn't know why I recalled only these events. They were coming, appearing in the memory, recalling the events and then disappeared.

After next 4 weeks I noticed that my physical power and forces started to come back, but simultaneously the attacks from the devil has appeared. First, the dogs of my neighbour attacked and bated my dogs. Later, the workers that were renting a room from me ran away without payment. They were very insolent during the conversation. During one month I had a few examples of human meanness. It was the last accord of the night – when the darkness started to disappear, this insolent attacks started.

After next 4 weeks I noticed that I started slowly to integrate myself. The night lasted the 5 and a half months.

In this night one can observe the characteristic stages:
1. The stage of spiritual disintegration.
2. The stage of lack of physical forces and attacks of devil (1 stage).
3. The stage of the intellectual emptiness.
4. The stage of ordering the pictures in the memory.
5. The stage of the end of night – attacks from the side of devil (2 stage).

The first stage is most characteristic and already well-known. The darkness, the psychotic element, dryness appear in full. They change the spiritual life. They take out all points of support

– subjectively perceived it remains falling down to the spiritual abyss without any bottom. In the described case, this stage lasted for about two months.

Simultaneously to this stage the physical powers go away. The ill person during these dark contemplations start to slowly integrate, but s/he loses the physical forces and internal power.

Here also the attacks of devil take place (1st step) and this is logical. The devil attacks a person who loses the powers, when a man is the weakest. These attacks do not reach inside because of the psychotic element, but the devil can cause the pain attacking also the people closely related to the ill person.

The third stage is a stage of **intellectual emptiness.** The cognition and the spirit in which it appears – they are two inseparable matters. The ill person has opened to the spirit of new quality. The lowest part adapts to this, but the purification touches also the reason. This exchange of the spirit is felt like the intellectual emptiness. The reason loses its spiritual base – loses the orientation and the old cognition in the same period of time. It will give back its properties – it will receive the cognition with the new spiritual quality, when the stage will finish. Now it is disorientated and this state lasts practically for the second part of the night – and in this most characteristic stage – for 2-6 weeks.

On the 4th stage the elements of darkness, dryness, psychotic occur in a small degree, but the order with the pictures dominates. The pictures appear in the consciousness and disappear. The appearance of this stage shows that two thirds of the night has already passed.

The last stage (2nd period of it) is the disappearance of the psychotic factor, the increase in the physical powers, but also greater attacks of the devil. So after such brutal attacks (4-6 weeks before the end) it can be assumed that a new spiritual quality is created and the night reached its last phase. After this night the small vulgarities in language by other people start to offend very much. **The ill person starts to hear themselves –** and this is a discovery stage for them. The tiredness during the day finally disappears. The ill person starts to understand their past relations with other people.

The last act of the unification in a simple way is **the unification of the will.** The will, as the upper part, gets rid of the influences of the lower part – liberates itself from them (it will finally liberate itself in the ecstatic union when will the bottom of the will be purified. The reconstructed natural will regains freedom. The split of the will disappears – only one natural will submitted to God exists which fulfils the theses in God. The final liberation of the natural will and unification of it occur also during the night. The ill person recalls:

I noticed that I didn't want to do anything. Nothing attracted me in the world and I was not able to find support in anything. God disappeared – and He was far away as if in the darkness. Again I prayed for the grace of the faith, because I saw that I have lost it. It was very difficult to start the prayer – with the rest of my forces I went to the church.

I noticed that my nature is not attracted by anything. Nothing will satiate it, nothing will please it, nothing will satisfy it, nothing will calm it down. I noticed that I am undergoing a great reconstruction of myself.

As the mantra two quotations went through my head. The first one that foxes have dens and birds nests (Matthew 8:20) and the second one Vanity, vanity of vanities, all is vanity (Ecclesiastes 1:2).

And really all lives of many people that I have met (also the clergy) consisted in digging dens or constructing nests – it means in constructing intellectual or material shelters inaccessible to others. And I saw a total nonsense of such act, especially to the growth of the spiritual life. It took away any willingness to act and I was immersed in such futility.

My life has turned into stone – nothing could please me, nothing could move me. My sensuality was dying. I didn't believe that such a man turned into stone can have any spiritual future. I remained in such state for many weeks.

It was difficult to think, I had no perspicacity. I was disconcerted – it was difficult for me to concentrate on anything. My concentration was running away in all possible directions. I had gaps in my memory. I couldn't take out anything from it. I didn't feel any mood.

I didn't want to do anything. Simply the will of doing died in me. I was totally apathetic and then in turn a struggle of the will which wanted to undertake some activity.

I was able to compare these states to the impression of a tourist who went out of the area showed by the map and who noticed that he was never there and he doesn't know how to move on this totally unknown land and how to get back to the map from this unknown territory. I stayed in such emptiness (2-3 months) and I only thought that these state would finish one day.

I started to limp – I had liquid in both knees, but I started to accept this. I didn't rebel against this.

Two months before the end of the night, the incredible attack of devil occurred. He extracted all unhealed situations and started to attack me with them. These attacks provoked me to leave the spirituality and God's commandments and to account by myself these unaccounted situations These attacks lasted for a few days – I was not able to recognize myself in them. Their force was so great that I was almost ready to abandon the spiritual way, and make revenge on some people. These thoughts were so importunate that I couldn't think about anything else.

I was just passing near the sanctuary of the Sacred Heart of Jesus and after the mass all these attacks finished as suddenly as they started. I was feeling that the devil was going out, and God was finally healing the places attacked by the devil in me.

Three weeks later similar states were repeated and related to the attacks on the purity. They lasted (2-3 days) and I observed myself very frightened that I may get some sexual deviation. Fortunately, everything passed as it started.

The night lasted 6 months and when it had finished I felt as an extraordinarily free and cheerful person.

Thus, the unification of the will, as the last act of the unification on the simple way ends in a classic way – **by the attack of the evil spirit.** He tries to detach this unified will from God by the brutal and insolent attack. One should know that this attack takes place on this stage – and the task of the will is to survive such attack.

Also the characteristic trait of this night is a difficult **passage through emptiness and nonentity.** The pictures accumulated for years create the strange situation – even if they hurt – they become the property of the ill person. Empty memory, empty imagination can cause anxiety, especially before the sleep when the ill person is closing their eyes and no pictures appear and none of the pictures can't be recalled from the memory. What causes the feeling of alienation? The ill person has no support in what happened in their past. No support in the memory. As if s/he would be a man without history, without present, because s/he is not able to recall also the current pictures. The memory has no support – as if it never existed. It stopped to work during the passage from the support in the natural spirit to the activity moved by the Holy Ghost. **This phenomenon of emptiness is onerous – it lasts some months and takes place before the unification of the will** – and there it should be situated.

Additionally, the will must stop in its natural movements and must go through the state of paralysis for some months. It must liberate from the old movements and start to act by the new other rules – without such great influence of the lower part. In this part it lays down in total apathy and in the nonsense of activity. Pushing it into activity by force would not change anything. One should simply go through this period.

What is the greatest achievement of this period?

The spiritual separation from the world occurs. The world stops to have a negative influence. It does not cause pain any more, because it has no common points with the will. The apostasy and its limited cognition are visible, that bad choices of the will such people will never leave the level of nature.

This separation does not result in the feeling of any loss – just the opposite – it is related with the feeling of subtle joy that it has finally taken place. It is connected with the feeling of a great relief.

In this example, the unification of the simple way was undergone in 4 rounds – each of them was preceded by the night – and lasts 4-5 years. In this third night and after it the elements of the unitive way – the next stage were visible. After every night one could observe greater harmony of powers, separation of the upper part from the lower taking the memory and the imagination to the possession of God (beginning) and other characteristic symptoms of simple union described before.

How many nights will precede the simple union depends on the ill person. I described in detail of unification that the ill person is fully conscious of what s/he can expect on this stage and how spiritual life on this stage looks. I described the states in detail so that the ill person can recognize these states and be able to diagnose them and to go through them.

The disposition for contemplation allows the ill person to change the illness and its states in the evil spirit to spirituality, which s/he will develop later in life.

CHAPTER 21

THE UNIFYING WAY –
UP TO THE ECSTATIC UNION

One can pose a question what happened in the simple union that the next stage is named the unifying way?

The concentration of the soul happened. The soul acts through its powers, joining God through the upper powers – the will and the intellect. It joins with the body and with the environment by the lower powers – by the sense of body and the imagination. Then the body by sensuality, emotions and feelings reacts to the environment. There are many classifications of the powers and their functions. They were constructed from the early Middle Ages. Certain matters are important for our analysis.

After the original sin a man is an internally broken creature and there is the possibility and very often it happens that the separate spirit can enter each of the powers. In such person the real internal tear is visible.

The second problem is that as a result of this tear every next external spiritual impulse (for example every spiritual knock) is perceived by the few powers simultaneously. **In this case this knock is amortized.** It does not come directly to the depth of the soul, but it goes through many powers and only a small part of it comes to the depth of the soul. Such system at the same time protects the internally broken person.

What are the conditions to complete the concentration of the soul?

Thus, the condition is that in every power the Holy Ghost should dominate and that there are not leftovers of other spirits. It is practically the only one possibility to create harmony in the soul and for the soul to be fully unified with God. For this purpose the ill person did the active purifications – to purify the emotional memory and so that the past emotions and feelings would not hobble the will. The nights (as the passive purifications) also served this purpose.

The soul achieves the unity and simplicity. The lower part is submitted to the upper part and everything is concentrated on God. The ascetic way serves this purpose – **to achieve concentration** so that a man is not internally torn throughout their life and right now this kind of attitude is promoted.

Why the concentration of the soul which on the fundamental level is made by the simple union can be considered as the end of the illness?

Because **the most important symptom of schizophrenia, the blurring of the boundaries between "myself" and the environment disappears.** With the simple union this boundary is explicitly fixed. The soul lives alone with God and all environment stays outside. And it has no access to the soul. The soul is defended by the will liberated from the influence of the lower part and the environment.

It does not change the fact that certain symptoms in some cases disappear finally on the unifying way.

The simple union and the concentration are the time of rest on the heavy spiritual way. It is the time of the retrospective perception of own past life and also a look forward when one can have an especially great perspective. It is a clear loos at the future, when the concentrated soul can perceive something more that it had perceived till now and it has a time for reflection because of this greater perception.

The greatest advantage of the concentration is that after it God – if He touches the soul He does it by **directly touching the will – without moving the lower powers of the soul.**

During the plunging into the schizophrenic depression, one can find the similar period corresponding to the concentration of the powers by the simple union – **which one can name as the quasi-concentration and it is made by the hobbling of the will.**

It is characterised by:

The change of the perception of the knocks made by devil which are not amortized any more.

The explosion of the great nearly ecstatic feeling, which happens in this period.

The awareness of the spiritual breakout – feeling that something has irrecoverably finished.

The reflection about the future, after this period the spiritual fall is rapidly accelerating.

It is not a tragic consciousness, which happens after the invasion of the devil to the spiritual heart, but the reflection which appears for the first time that there will be no exit from this situation.

The devil knocking man directly or through other people mobilizes them, focuses them. And this is the only positive element of the spiritual side made in the devil. No one can mobilise and train a man than the evil spirit knocking them in their weak points and having a great insight into their external situation and some insight into their internal situation.

Of course, the devil does not knock a man to raise them up the higher spiritual level, but to dismantle the internal system of the defence, to ruin a man and kill him. As a result of the knocks the emotional memory is overloaded and the emotions don't react correctly. **Emotions do not amortize the knocks any more.**

They hobble the will which totally surrenders to what is going on outside – and the knocks go to the upper parts to the soul (and they are not amortized). The knocks start to be very painful. One can observe the sequences of knocks. They touch the depth of the soul. It is a new phenomenon, which had not taken place till now.

This phenomenon is preceded by the period of reflection about the fact that something has finished and will not return.

This period of the reflection last 2-4 months and it is clear. The past is visible better as if in the deeper perspective.

One can see the future, one can observe it also more clearly. There an insight into the future, but connected with the tragic reflection that there will be no exit from some situations.

During this state (quasi-concentration) the explosion of the feeling, of huge, nearly ecstatic feeling can occur. It comes unexpectedly (very often it is the old feeling which returned with the new unexpected power) – it is violent, takes out of the old well-known schemes. It is adequate to what happens in the spirituality after the simple union.

But what is going on in the spirituality on the later stage, which preceded by the satiation and the internal silence, which prove the healing of the emotional memory?

The real spiritual way starts by **the wounded love** which is given by God. Tauler names this period as **the period of the wounded love**. He called the preceding periods **the periods of sweet love sweet and period of the dark love.**

The answer to the question why God in this period wounds a man with His love is clear – to attract the man more to Himself.

So why a man can be so much, so deeply and so visibly touched by God? Because **the concentration of the soul took place.** Because these touches are experienced directly by the upper parts of the souls, purified from the influences of the lower part. These touches are no longer amortized by the lower part. They are so strong and subtle that the natural man with the dispersed powers can't perceive them. Only a man with concentrated powers can experience them.

This subtlety and depth cause the feeling of hurt. Saint John of the Cross describes this phenomenon in the first stanza of the Spiritual Canticle.

Where have You hidden Yourself,
And abandoned me in my groaning, O my Beloved?
You have fled like the hart,
Having wounded me,
I ran after You, crying; but You were gone.

This is a characteristic phenomenon of the spiritual way, from which the unifying way begins. That Saint John of the Cross place it in the beginning of the spiritual way is a great inaccuracy. This phenomenon takes place (and here the description is exact), but not in the beginning stage. Only the concentrated soul is able to experience this deep and subtle touch as a wound. Earlier it is not possible. The unconcentrated soul doesn't permit to wound itself so deeply.

Therefore, this stanza should begin the stage of the unifying way. Unfortunately, this is not the only one displacement in this valuable work.

The next stage, which appears in the spiritual life after some months is **ecstasy.** Ecstasy is described by Saint Teresa of Avila (*The Interior Castle* – The sixth mansions chapter 5 *Life* chapter 20), by Saint John of the Cross (*The Spiritual Canticle* stanza 13), by Tauler *Sermons,* 66), by Saint Francis of Sales *Treatise of the Love of God* book VII chapters 4-6).

Meister Eckhart noticed that **the upper part of the soul possesses such ability that it can exit beyond itself.** This is the ability that God uses during ecstasy.

In the Polish literature there are beautiful descriptions of ecstasy in the poetry by Adam Mickiewicz and Juliusz Słowacki. Both poets experienced violent ecstasy.

Adam Mickiewicz describes the ecstasy in the poem *A vision.*

The sound struck – suddenly my flesh
Like a field flower in the dust,
Burst, broken by the angel's blast,
Leaving only my soul's seed. I seemed
Suddenly to come awake from dark dreams
And as a man, waking, will wipe his brow,
I wiped away my future deeds
Like so many dried-out fruitskins.
I saw the earth, the whole
Dark-passaged world whose course
I had despaired. I saw it clear
Beneath me, as in water's depths
Where light falls.

Juliusz Słowacki describes ecstasy in the poem *The King – Ghost.* (rhapsody I song III XXXVI-XXXVII, rhapsody IV song II XXIV-XXV, rhapsody IV song II XLIV – XLVI, rhapsody IV song

IV XXX-XXXII. This experience and its consequences in cognition form the basis of this poem. In the free translation one can present it as follows:

Suddenly my bones started to tousle.
Through the leaden hood one hundred thousand
Sparks has gone...wire and tin have fused on me.
I wanted to keep the proud shape of prince,
But was melting as clay in the fire.
My eyes were covered by the dark cloud,
And my spirit has concentrated itself in one grain.
Nothing more – terrible eclipse and dead silence!
On the heart God's hand was placed;
The last pressure under which my soul
Has cracked in flaws and the sight entered into the consciousness.
Thus as a worm which is moving in the fire
the soul – until it could breathe -
was laying in the depth of the heart stain...
When God opened to it the gates of eternity.

Causing so much over my frightening soul,
That eye of my sleep has broken as a crystal
And my spirit said – I will open my lips.

Till now I don't know... if the soul submitted
To the greater power of love – all trembled,
And from my body for a moment run away,
To perceive all by her eyes...
But if the hand of the priest did not protect me
The soul flying out from the mouth,
Would be – I say – exhilarated by the glory
Went out and never came back to the body.
In this flash of lightening and in this wind
I thought that I hear the voice of hundred angels,
One hundred harps were calling my name
By the silent crystal and blue silence...
In the fires – in the rustles – in ravishing – in songs

I felt a great frightening in my heart,
Because Holy Ghost forced me in the anger,
And inflamed on us the eternal light;
As the rustle in the tree before the tempest,
In my spirit the elements of sun were boiling,
When God marching with fire on souls
In my eyes has lightened and whistled in my ears.

God who started to take out my soul from my body,
Glazed my hair and opened my mouth,
But did not put any voice to my chest.
They were only trembling opened – and the face
it was getting dark, my spirit was shaking as the light was flashing.
Then not the pearls but the source of tears
Were in my eyes...I carried heavily my head,
Because I was feeling that this silent death would conquer me,
Already my sleepy head was getting heavy.
Suddenly from the whole of my body, from all my bones
As the wind from my opened mouths;
Went out the shout so magnificent,
That the structure is cracked and the banners are torn.

During the ecstasy God pulls this upper part of soul. It is violent experience, unexpected and quite new. It affects the spiritual heart and the intellect pulled by God with such great force that it makes the impression that God wants to extract them from the body. **By this act God separates the spiritual part from the body**. This separation is exact. This extraction is connected with a sort of the awakening – the perception of oneself and of the world in a totally new way. Reception of the own life in the new liberating perspective absent till now. Reception of own faults, faults of the world, reception of the own false arrangement of the will in the past, of proper false past aspirations and efforts in the incorrect direction. This awakening causes the rise over the natural schemes which were present till now. Finding finally the deepest sense of life, the elimination of false arrangements of the will deriving from the nature and liberation from them.

In the texts of the great Polish poets one can observe the elements common to every ecstasy: the sudden concentration of the soul, the separation of the spiritual part from the body, the sudden touch by God, the extraction of the soul to Him with the insured keeping. As the result – there is a new cognition which awakes from the previous life, the transformation by the touch consists in falling off the old schemes – comparable to the creation of a new man who says goodbye to the old life, the joy connected with the extraordinary lightness because of the new situation, silence in the emotions, because this touch causes that the emotions and the feelings are some kind of a shock (and they are suspended), because they can't unite with God, and because of this they react by silence.

Due to its huge and violent character, the ecstasy lasts very short – maximum 3-5-10 seconds.

What is important to the mentally ill people is the ecstatic character of this experience. One poses the question – what cases one can heal on this stage?

All the cases when somebody during the entrance in the illness felt the sort of "awaking" from the old life to the new. All these ecstatic elements, which now are repeated during the ecstasy.

Also all the cases causing the sentiment, where the quasi-concentration and the ecstatic character of the feeling occurred. For example – in the man the pictures of 100 women were durably inscribed in the emotional memory (which he was able to find in his memory), by the expression of anger in different relations he removed 80 of them, by the meditative expression he removed next 16-18. But 1-2 of them where the ecstatic element of the feeling occurred are removed after the experience of ecstasy. This experience repeated this ecstatic element and caused that now by the normal expression of anger one can remove these 1-2 pictures. Without ecstasy it was impossible to remove them.

What is the result of ecstasy?

The result is of course **the classic night of spirit** with the elements of it – especially with the psychotic element and the element of darkness.

One can examine such night on the basis of the account of the ill person:

After the ecstasy I was totally without internal powers. They went out. I get quickly tired at work. After a moment I was exhausted – and the powers were not coming back. I slept bad. I awoke 10 times, I had a headache and the pain in my heart. I observed the world in the half-psychosis.

But all the time I was occupied by God, because the experience of the ecstasy made such great impression on me.

After 3 weeks the deeper sleep came back, but the dark filter was put on all reality.

I noticed that my intellect got a total shock. It was out of order. I had no power to undertake any intellectual effort. I was not able to concentrate on any subject. I was not able to perceive many things. I was able to associate only the simplest problems. After next 1 – 2 weeks the devil started to knock me by the environment, by the direct insolent attacks. Simultaneously he started to insolently attack my mother and my brother. The extraordinary tensions which these attacks caused – provoked also the rebel against God, the element of aggression against Him.

After next 3 weeks my matters started to be arranged totally differently than I had planned.

I started to perceive the reality with the new sight. I lost my memory, but the perfect silence has dominated in my head. I wanted to stay in this silence as much as possible – to be only with myself.

After next 3 weeks I started to wake up early and I couldn't sleep longer. I had a headache. The half psychosis still lasted.

After 3 months from the ecstasy some reconstruction in my intellect started. I was not able to articulate anything correctly. I was very surprised because of what I said to other people.

The dark contemplations started. These clear contemplations which lasted together with the internal silence and the elements of the admiration and dealing only with God – after 3 months from the ecstasy – disappeared.

God disappeared. I couldn't find Him. After next one month I fell down to the level of a natural man. The life and problems had covered me. I was helpless against them.

After next month my mother noticed that I have become sharp, impulsive, categorical and quick – but in the bad way. The extreme tension dominated in my emotions.

The next month was the continuation of the level of a natural man. Dryness, tiredness, subjectively perceived absence of any graces and presence of God. The total return to nature and its schemes. Additionally, the hunger of desire but – like in the emptiness – rootless and senseless. There was also the sentimental pain mixed with the dryness.

During the next two months the anger against the devil started to appear and the pretensions to God. I started to assume that the night finishes. It was God who by the ecstasy extracted me from the reality, and after 6 – 7 months started to answer by revolts.

The night lasted 8 months. The new possibilities of the intellect came back in the new upper form. The night finished with an extraordinary event – by the healing of the relation with my father. During the sleep I experienced a great inflow of the feeling to my father in my spiritual heart. The inflow was very deeply satiating and healing.

The night finished by the feeling of subtle happiness, by the internal silence, by the feeling of internal fulfilment and harmony. The feeling of no necessity to look for the happiness beyond God.

One can visibly observe two parts at this night. For the first 3 months the light contemplations provoked by the ecstasy mix with the elements – psychotic, of darkness, devil's, and providential. Later, during the dark contemplations, during the fourth month the ill person goes through extreme sharpness of emotions. In the fifth month the sentiment stabilises by the attack of devil. During the seventh and eight month the new relation to God was arranged. The state from which the ecstasy was extracted changes to the new state.

In the spiritual literature the classification as the nights of senses and the nights of spirit is used. The matter is to divide the nights before the union of the will and after it.

In the schizophrenia because of unification of the upper part with the lower, nearly all nights will be the nights of spirit.

One can pose a question – what is the difference between the night before the union of the will and after it?

To the nights before the union of the will God introduced providentially by the appearance of darkness. The will was affected by weakness, the physical forces went out and didn't come back. During the night God purified the will from the influence of emotions and from the past feelings.

The night finished by the greater liberation of the will, by the greater union with God.

The nights after the union of the will are not more horrible – they are simply other. Very often they start with the ecstasy, which is so great experience that provokes the nights as the logical consequence of it. God touches this already purified will in such strong way that the night occurs. And for these states the metaphor about the light too strong which a man is not able to bear is suitable – and because of this s/he reacts by the night. After this spiritual extraction the spirituality and the nature come back to themselves for some months – when a person is able to reach the next level of the union which will permit to obtain a sort of stabilisation. Of course on this stage also the nights not provoked by the ecstasy exist.

What is the greatest spiritual problem of this period?

The greatest problem is the solitude connected with the great spiritual evil which throws out God and a spiritual underdevelopment which dominates in the environment.

No longer does this naive conviction which the schizophrenia sufferer had in the beginning of their life exist that all people are good and they all look for goodness and truth, and they voluntarily carry to others the light of the spiritual progress.

But there is no such feeling of entrapment which one can observe in the illness.

But there is a greater spiritual clarity and conviction that the majority of people have their wills fixed in the evil. This is not only such tale about the sin – because there is something deeper – it is not visible by these people the will to opt for better. But there is a conviction about how good and clever we are and forcing others to to live according to their own lifestyle. The man who has undertaken the spiritual way observes this great sphere of evil dominating around. S/he is again conscious that s/he had to be ill in these spiritual conditions. S/he perceives the real sphere of the conditions in which s/he lives. The conditions which are not discussed by psychiatry. And here one should take care not to try to repair this reality by force – not to utilise other methods than the evangelic one.

Another big problem on this stage is to create the spiritual conditions for oneself. The factor which ruins the spirituality is a great activity characteristic to sensual people and to the vocation to the active life. It does not result only from the satisfaction of the natural needs, but from the reduction of life only to the sensual level and to natural problems. A person who aspires to the union with God, can't accept such logic dominating around. This logic will be forced by the environment, because the world is arranged according to it.

The greater challenge in this period are lack of internal acceptance to such arrangement, the defence of what God by his grace has done in a man, the choice of the own way against the schemes coming from the outside.

Later, the life will go on by the normal rhythm – after the certain stabilisation the night of different natures comes – finally separating the will from the natural schemes. The ill person recalls:

This night started naturally. I noticed one day that I am not able to force myself to do anything. I couldn't mobilise myself to do anything. I had no internal power to accelerate any action, and I was staying internally moveless. Intellectually, I was rather efficient – I had silence in my head. I had little forces but the natural needs of doing something went out.

After six weeks I started to feel bad with myself. I was feeling bad even in the church. God was absent and I felt divided into two. I couldn't diagnose this phenomenon. I couldn't define it. As if I started to compose myself from two parts – from myself which was mine and from other "self" which was strange. This situation got

*me tired and was disturbing me. I couldn't compose and unify my-
self from this division. My mood was low. I started to feel solitude.
In the well-known place I started to ask myself – what I am doing
here? In the morning I woke up at 5 o'clock and I couldn't sleep any
more. I was feeling tired during the day. I didn't have any initiative. I only did what was minimum.*

*In the third month I was thrown out from the prayer. My reason
started to be inactive. With thoughtlessly I watched the television.
I was full of internal impotence. I got very nervous, because of the
meaningless situations. I was surprised because of my reaction –
that it touched me so deeply. Internally I felt deeply disharmonised.
Aggressive thoughts appeared and impure thoughts after a month.
They were absurd. I did manage with them without any problem, because they were rootless. And they did not reach to the deeper levels.*

*In the fourth month of the night I noticed that I am so dominated
by the life of others and by the external world and I have no own
will. Internally I was cracked, dry and broken into pieces. I felt
that I perceive the world like by the broken instrument.*

*The resentment towards God appeared that he defends scoun-
drels, to whom I can't do anything. That he is on their side and they
are drawn in the evil. I felt that by their wills they broke me with
the evil to the pieces. I was crushed by this situation. I was not able
to get myself out of this.*

*During the fifth month I still had no internal power. The psy-
chotic element, tiredness, lapses in concentration appeared. I slept
badly, I woke up very early. I noticed that my plans cross, that I am
detached from my habits. I was still encircled by the sin, hatred,
boorishness, thievery.*

*It started the chaos and swinging in my will. Every moment dif-
ferent thoughts came. The thoughts excited me – later others came.
I was not able to calm down – the will was clinging to them. And
so on. There was no decision and many false inspirations. The will
as if wanted to find the aim, but it received only false inspirations.
It tried to follow them, but they didn't calm down. It struggled and
hesitated. This situation destroyed me.*

*In the sixth month my reason has caught little light – I started to
associate a little. But my will threw me out from everything. From*

the spirituality, work, rest, amusement, cognition, relations to others – even though I wanted to do this all.

I stayed in the state of total aversion to all desires and pleasures which appeared. All the time the same scheme repeated – I desire something, I am thrown away of this. I also felt powerless in the will to undertake anything. I had no internal powers. I had the wall of the powerlessness in my body and spirit. Nothing made me happy, nothing gave me any pleasure. This powerlessness and darkness came from inside. I felt that my faith starts to disappear. I wanted to come back to the first zeal, but I couldn't. God was absent and the great sphere of the evil covered me. Again the resentment to God appeared, that He protects with his commandments boors and scoundrels, and one can't give them back by their methods. I was paralysed by the evil.

During the 6th month the pictures started to order. They were coming 10 times daily and disappearing. I assumed that a of the night had passed. My mother said to me that from 3 months I am tough, sharp, even rude and vulgar. It means – I had to be so.

In the 8th month I was feeling totally denuded by the active life. God was absent and I was occupied by the work. I had no time to make any deeper spiritual reflection. The spiritual life didn't exist – it was killed by the active life. The will was also blocked and dominated by the wills of other people. My will was not able to get out of others' wills.

The night lasted 8 months. It finished with the willingness to pray and to stay in the presence of God.

What was characteristic in this night?

Generally it was the night of the will. The reason was almost unaffected during this night.

The characteristic elements of the night appeared (the element of darkness, of devil's, psychotic and providential). They were visible, but their role was different, they did not focus on what was important in this night.

There were attacks on the purity and aggression, but it was easy to handle them. They did not reach the depth, because the life perspective has changed – from the sensitive to the spiritual.

The natural will was purified and transformed to the bottom during this night. But **on the bottom of the natural will the pleasure is situated.** Such purification cannot be done by any of the ascetic exercises. It can be purified only by God who acts in the interior of a man. It is Him who touches the bottom of the natural will – that it will not be fed any longer by what is natural – by pleasure, success, effort, satisfaction – and is separated from all this. And here God acts in the characteristic way. **The bottom of the will by His touch, it suddenly gets dark.** It gives the feeling of internal perplexity, when the ill person said that s/he feels bad with themselves and s/he feels something strange inside. **This will with the dark bottom loses orientation.** All manners with the old choices stopped suddenly to function. The numerous choices of the will which tries to struggle against this perplexity in this way **do not give fulfilment,** because the bottom of the will is dark and **the will works as if in the emptiness.** The disoriented will tries to function according to the previous roles but such night is to just get rid of them.

And so the will went through the night with faintness, perplexity, disharmony, domination of other wills, loss of the internal powers, the crossing of the plans, by chaos and swinging, throwing away from everything that it has chosen, by the domination by the active life. Through all these stages God leads the will to separate it from the natural desires, to purify the bottom of it Such division of the will and regrouping of the elements which took place during the night is painful, and takes a long time. Therefore, the external world affects too much. Little impulses are perceived as big ones, because a person with such transformed will is temporally with no protection.

A similar but **reverse mechanism** can be observes also during the schizophrenic depression on the stage of the invasion of the spirit to the spiritual heart. The ill person feels bad with themselves, s/he experiences internal perplexity. The will tries to liberate itself, **but it is hobbled by the evil spirit.** It makes decisions, but the numerous choices **do not give satisfaction, because they do not liberate the hobbled will,** and no choice will liberate it from perplexity.

Looking from the perspective of this night and its results one can draw such conclusions:

The life only by the pleasure and for the pleasure is something opposite to the theses and aims of the spiritual life aspiring to God. Also the arrangements and hierarchies proposed by the world disappear during this night. People who had accepted them consciously or unconsciously now get rid of them.

There are the borders to human asceticism – they finish before the nights and one should arrive at this end. Later, God purifies by passive purifications – a man is not able to do this.

For the ecstatic union to happen, the concentration of powers is needed – only or as much as this. All the schemes of the "spiritual leeway" and the schemes where "all is the grace" and "all comes from God" will not reach there. Finally, everything comes from God, but everybody should undertake the active effort. But the schools that suggest great asceticism – instead of the active purifications – will neither reach the ecstatic union.

After this night the world does not shocked with its evil. It is evil, because it has no will arranged as in God. The ill person starts to perceive it visibly. S/he also understands that s/he expected too much from the world, and because of the gift of contemplation s/he idealised the world. **The purification of the natural bottom of the will which takes place at this stage was the most important task of the ecstatic union.**

On the stage of the ecstatic union a very interesting phenomenon named the **"the wounds of love"** can appear. These are experiences qualified in the spiritual manuals as **the contemplative gifts multiplying the sanctity of the soul.** They were described by Saint Teresa (*Live* chapter 20) and Saint John of the Cross (*The Living Flame of Love* stanza 2 line 2). They are the experiences which cause the pain in the spiritual heart and simultaneously inflame it by the God's love. The ill person recalls:

Suddenly the phenomenon which I haven't known till now, appeared As if God plunged the pricker in my spiritual heart and has torn the wounds left of my past feelings. These wounds were touched, torn. In the moment of tearing the feeling of the spiritual pain appeared which accompanied these wounds in the past. These touched wounds at the moment were full of pain, but at the same time they were calmed by God with touch full of love. It was a nice experience, but I was afraid of getting depressed, because it was a strong, liberating experience. It happened after the awake, but also during the day, during normal activity – on the bus, in the church, at work, during the walk.

These experiences lasted for 3 days and repeated 2 – 4 times daily. I returned after 3 weeks to the normal state.

Previously, I have written that the memory of emotions and feelings is transformed to the body. This transformation starts in the limbic system, goes through the spiritual heart, touches it, and later goes down, transmitting to the body in its own way.

Now the healing of this transmission connected with feelings coming from the spiritual heart takes place. God touches them, takes it out from a man and heals. This phenomenon on the spiritual level is automatically associated with the parable of the Samaritan, who ... *went to him* and *bandaged his wounds, pouring on oil and wine.* (Luke 10:34). (NIV) And similarly, it occurs with the phenomenon of wounds of love. It is a painful event, but at the same time a soothing one. It is one of the last stages in the healing of the memory associated with feelings.

How does the ecstatic union finish?

It finishes by **the touch of the spiritual heart with the purest Divinity.** The insensitivity of this touch is the greatest possible – quite new.

This union was made by the scheme: injury made by God – ecstasy – nights of spirit which arranged and purified the will – union by this extraordinary touch.

The soul has to be extracted from the natural schemes to have the possibility to touch the Divinity without the interference of emotions and especially feelings. **She obtained God's peace.** Before this union – the feelings are finally purified.

And to finish this book with the strong appeal, like the preachers in all eras finished, I will cite the instruction which I received from the confessor at the beginning of the spiritual way, when

I was afraid of the future, plunged in chaos and I didn't know much about the spiritual life. He said – citing the sentence of Saint Paul from the letter to the Philippians – ...*who began a good work in you will carry it to completion* ... (Philippians 1:6) (NIV)

Today, after many years the truth of these words still resonates in me. That God leads this way to the end despite the dramatic situations, violent turning points, hesitations and doubts, despite the incertitude – all these states, which accompany the spiritual life, and which are also present in this illness.

And this way to the happy final – to the healing – to the union with God and finding life in God – I wish every reader of my book – with all my heart.

CHAPTER 22

THE CONCLUSION

The key to understand and heal schizophrenia **is in the spirituality,** but not in neurology or biochemistry. There is no proof that biochemistry can describe all human cognitive structures and there will be not. The biochemistry will never describe and never exhaust what happens in the reasonable human soul. Once more I will repeat – **the summits of the intellect and spiritual cognition are not available to the biochemistry** – it will never describe them.

What are the main theses of this book?

The main thesis is a statement that schizophrenia is a spiritual state caused by the evil spirit, which because of the original injury and later through emotions and feelings affects the will charges the emotional memory and later invades the spiritual heart.

And here one can pose a question: whether the spiritual power which can rise the ill person from such state exists? The answer is that such power exists and this power is God.

If such power exists, and if such power is God, one should start the way to Him, and one should start to unify with Him.

And here one should ask for the second part of the thesis, when somebody starts to unify with Him – will there be a moment when God will liberate the hobbled will and pull it to Himself, and will liberate and heal the emotional memory and imagination?

The answer is: Yes, there will be such moment, it happens in the simple union.

And one should use this spiritual phenomenon in the treatment of schizophrenia.

What happens in the spirituality of a man has some transmissions on the body. And here it is necessary to know the neurology or biochemistry.

The medicaments used in the psychiatry are an important invention. They do not affect the spiritual problems, but relatively quickly they fix the broken spiritual structure, on which the physical and spiritual life is based. They are not able to heal the spiritual problems of the ill person (because they can't have it), but they are an important help. One should take them as long as their help is necessary.

Schizophrenia is a spiritual and physical illness. **After the simple union the ill person is spiritually healthy.** But will the body return to normal functions? – this question is partially open.

After the beginning of the spiritual way the physical, mental and intellectual efficiency is much higher. But very often it does not return to the level of a healthy person. The degradation of the functions is stopped and the reverse process starts. The work and functions in the family are worse than in the case of a healthy man. The mental resistance is much higher, but a person after the illness can't withstand the extreme tensions, because of **the broken structure** in the past (if it has happened). This broken structure, this broken physical scaffolding, on which the physical and spiritual life is based is the most serious reminder of the illness.

The explosion of the illness **also damages the biochemistry and of the body.** One should be careful with the alcohol, mineral waters, bathing in the sea, activity in the fumes of solvents, during the anaesthesia. **Also in situations with a greater tension such person will not menage.**

Generally, the fitness results determine the opinion about the method. The spirituality does not translate into fitness. The illness partially damages the physical functions (although they return in a great part). Also the passing of the time – for the physical sphere is killing. **To the physical sphere the time of the illness is the time lost.** And one should simply accept this fact.

What the spiritual way gives to the ill person despite these reservations?

It gives the supernatural cognition which was absent before, the trouble in cognition disappears, the order in life starts.

The spiritual discernment, which the ill person had not known before appears.

The ill person experiences the purifying meaning of suffering and the positive consequences of it.

The meaning of life returns, hope directed to the supernaturalism and eternity returns.

Anxiety which paralysed all activities and caused isolation disappear.

The ill person starts to internally integrate. S/he starts to be inside, not outside the current events. And although the external events can touch the formerly ill person, they are different events than before, they affect differently than before – they do not disintegrate all spirituality of the ill person as before.

The negative results of taking the medicines are eliminated.

The ill person is healthy from the spiritual perspective.

Schizophrenia is an illness (because of the presence of the evil spirit) which has to be fought against, otherwise it would overcome an ill person. There are no neutral states.

The whole spiritual way is based on one simple assumption: one should follow the direction to God, to whom one should express the past emotions and feelings, and who is the satiation and fulfilment of the human feeling. Of course, this way has difficult points.

It is difficult to undertake it and the struggle connected with the purity is difficult. Its long beginning stage of separating from the schemes of the world – the pursuit of another lifestyle – different than the life of others – are also difficult.

The grace of the contemplative prayer is a turning point changing the perception of the spirituality. Later, the crisis which tries to destroy the faith is difficult. Later, the active purifications are difficult – because they cause great pain – by touching the wounds from the past. These wounds become the experienced property, which one should get rid of. The nights of senses are difficult, when they start to finally appear. The psychosis which appear during the meditative expression of the feeling is difficult too. The nights of the spirit which appear suddenly with their elements are difficult too. The choice of the upper love – the love of God – made in the beginning – are difficult because of the great sentimental needs of the ill person.

The characteristic of this method (and of the spirituality generally) is the struggle with the evil spirit, with the world, and with oneself – with the help of the grace. This spiritual way is based on the long, consistent struggle.

It should be clearly underlined that it is a sensual man that was brutally attacked by the evil spirit.. S/he was robbed of their sensuality without return – s/he was by force transferred to another spiritual sphere. In such situation there will be no return to sensuality. Only a new man, a **spiritual man can be healthy.** A sensual man is lost forever together with the illness. S/he lost forever their sensuality and s/he should accept this fact with all newness of such way. It is no possible to heal only this sensual part separately. During the night of spirit the healing of both parts: upper and lower together takes place – and only in this way it can be done.

The spiritual way – the way to God – is still open to the ill person. Other ways of life are rather closed and there will be no return to them. Here one should lose all illusions. **The spiritual way is practically the only way, which despite the illness, is still fully open.**

As I have written, people with the disposition for contemplation **even after the healing will be not the masters of the active life.** One can improve them, one can exercise them, one can train them – but the active life will be strange and distant to them. **The internal life will be their strong attribute.** They will understand some mechanisms of it without reading the manuals of the spirituality. But one should require from such people only the minimum active life which would be necessary only for their existence and survival in the society.

Here some questions appear concerning the relation to schizophrenia.

Isn't it better to get accustomed to the illness – to accept it?

Schizophrenia is surely the only illness where it is impossible. The devil has such different nature from the human nature and he is such a great enemy of a man that a man with the susceptible consciousness and nature can't get accustomed to his presence in the will or in the emotional memory.

Christ came to the world just to liberate people from all forms of the possession of devil and one should use it. And here schizophrenia is quite different than other illnesses.

Is it necessary to "dig" so deep in the past, when many schools of spirituality claim that one should not do this?

Yes, it is necessary, because after the original injury such great contents accumulated in the emotional memory exist, that in the consciousness of the ill person only the past exists, and this blocks any progress in the spirituality.

Will the illness pass by itself? Will the time cure the wounds and one should only wait until the mental health is better?

Such opinions are hold by many patients. They wait for this for years. They get weaker spiritually and physically year after year. Their will gets week too. But the interpersonal relations will not be arranged and changed by themselves. One should make an effort to arrange them every day.

In schizophrenia the time is the enemy of the ill person This results from the temporal inscription in the emotional memory. If somebody does not radically remove this inscription and does not reverse the tendency, the degradation will follow very quickly.

How else one can purify the emotional memory from the contents accumulated there?

Every emotion, it means every movement of sensitivity which has lost its trace in the memory of emotions is composed of three components: **the emotion, tension and spirit** which accompanied the emotion, or of two components: **the emotion and spirit.** Because of this tension, **emotions generally are submitted to the body.** Generally, they belong to the natural order of a man, and they do not react (or react weekly) to such practices like prayer, confession or other similar supernatural acts. **Because of this, the expression of the emotion (and parallel removal of the tension), which is present in them belongs to a man.** But the liberation from the spirit accompanying them belongs to God (under some conditions), if somebody will express to God this emotion and tension. All ascetic methods relying on the stifling of emotions can finish by the breaking of the physical structure of the body. It is a common mistake in the asceticism. The same happens with the emotions which "get over-prayed", they stay in the emotional memory as before. As I have written before, one can liberate them by the active purifications.

And as in the beginning of the therapy one should strictly respect a certain order, **first one should take care of the will, then of the emotions.** On the succeeding stage such strict order exists: **first one should liberate the emotion from the tension, then one should wait when God will liberate the emotions from the spirit which was present in them.**

And if somebody expressed their emotions to God, but noticed that some of them deeply reside in their memory and they don't want to remove themselves – the first step in the expression will be the **reinforcement of this expression.** For this purpose, one should construct a dummy of a person at which this anger is accumulated and express this anger and at the same knock this dummy **by a stick, bar, or hose, expressing (shouting) this accumulated anger. This exercise will reinforce maximally this act.** The breaks between the expressions should be longer (up to 4-6 weeks) and one should control any jumps in the blood pressure, which usually occur 4 -7 days after such expression.

Once more one should go through the whole history of life and express such fortified anger in 4 relations: at others, at oneself, at devil and at God. All this is done **to liberate the emotions from the tensions which are also parallelly transferred to the body.** One should not do this exercise on the earlier stages of the therapy, because the schizophrenia is psychosis and this exercise additionally liberates this psychotic element. The ill person without the experience and with the psychotic element not liberated to a large extent cannot take control over this appearing psychosis.

There are also many past emotions **where the pictures are, but they exist without any tensions.** In such emotions only the spirit is present which dominated in those days in the life of the ill person. The presence of this spirit makes the picture stay in the emotional memory and does not move to the archive (because of the spirit) or has not eroded. This **causes the split in the spirituality.** The spirituality can't progress, as this spirit present in the pictures influencing the will demands to be fed, for example by watching the television, unnecessary talks and other similar acts.

To eliminate this state one should use the method known from psychology: recalling of these images and expressing them to God in the form of a free talking about them. One should again recall a certain period from the life (for example 1 year), and tell about it in detail, expressing the emotions to God: anxiety, longings, desires, shame, defeat, humility, spiritual or mental weakness, barriers impossible to overcome at that time. **One should tell God about all these states, trying to recall and express the emotions from this period by describing them.**

The point is to once again **recall the situations and through them recall the spirit which was present in them,** and which has the bridgeheads in the emotional memory due to these not released situations. This exercise should last about 1 hour and the break between the exercises should be 10 -21 days, depending on the intensity of the emotions.

This expression will make the spirit of the old reality appear, and by recalling and expressing these situations to God it will be liberate itself in a great part. **The spiritual duality will disappear**, the will is no longer distracted by the world, the sensual part does not demand to be fed.

The old concentration will come back and all the spiritual blockades will disappear. The person will live among sensual events which accompany the normal life, but none of them will attract their completely liberated will.

One can pose a question: how long such a way to the simple union may last?

One can estimate that it may take about 10 – 20 years. There are some factors that determine this.

God is a person and when He will create the relation to a man is His individual decision. In addition, there is an effort of a man to create such a relation.

But there is also an additional factor – the response of the human body to the connections with the emotional memory. If somebody struggled through the illness (or the ill emotionality), for example for 10 years – the reverse way will take him ½ or ⅔ of this period. This results from the physiology. The body is not able to undertake quicker changes. And this is a real barrier in the healing.

In the spirituality making the first step and undertaking the spiritual way is already liberating, because it turns the sight to the future.

The scheme of active purifications presented in this book is described with the assumption of the longest cycles. The contemplative prayers lead (and it should be so), and the active purifications overcome the crises which have appeared. The ill person was waiting for the crises to appear. An advantage of this method is that everything results as if naturally from the preceding state. With such long cycles, the ill person understands better themselves – there is no danger of spiritual chaos. This method is relatively mild and clear. The minus of this method is the possibility of "rinsing by the prayer" and "the praying up of the emotions". The first thing can cause the loss of freshness during the prayer or aversion to the prayer. This prayed and repressed emotions and feelings pose a danger that they will remain in this state. But the arrangement of the will is better in this method. Unfortunately, there are no perfect methods for this illness.

The time of the treatment of schizophrenia is long. But I know many people who are treated with the medicines for 30 – 50 years and they have not healed. In such cases (and there are many), this 10-20 years of the spiritual way (connected with the internal discipline), eliminate the medicaments and entering again the life (but with another optics) has a different meaning.

The healing process is not the way presented in the film "A Beautiful Mind". It means the way from the bottom of the illness up to the top of the importance in the world. The film shows in a beautiful way one form of the illness, but the presented way (although the ill person went through it) is false as a proposition. It is so, because during this illness the ill person goes through total denudation – and all the hierarchy of values changes with no return. The natural hierarchy proclaimed by the world (and before by the ill person too) will not return. This hierarchy will not be of any support to the ill person in the future.

After the healing the ill person will enter the life in God, will understand it and this will be the price, the treasure, which s/he had been looking for, the homeland found after a long exile. In God he found Master and Friend, whom with a great Joy s/he will serve, whose beauty and wisdom s/he will be endowed, in whom s/he will find the image of oneself full of love and kindness.

S/he will also notice that the environment has gone its own way, which it has been moving for centuries, with its natural schemes and ways with all its false assumptions. For the former ill person they are lost without return. These assumptions in the past pushed the ill person to the margin of life and despite the natural longing, s/he should never return to them.

Schizophrenia affects good people and bad people. It means people who try to follow the theses in God and who don't want to do this. If the schizophrenic is a bad person, it is because s/he wants to be like that. If s/he were a healthy person – s/he would be the same. Such people are dominated by the devil very quickly. Their illness presents with the extraordinary savagery and brutality.

The will in this illness is weak – sometimes it does not control the reactions as during psychosis. But the general rule is such as mentioned above. But even with such will and occupied emotional memory one can try to follow the theses in God. There were some saints who suffered from schizophrenia as Saint John of God, or Polish Saint – Saint Albert Chmielowski – and many with the schizoid trait as Saint Augustine. One can be ill and be saved. The mystery of the sanctity is situated more than what is affected by the illness.

Why I wrote this book?

Because this illness was also my destiny. Before the explosion of it I was looking for the answer to many questions bothering me – and I didn't find them, even in the places which should give them. Later, I observed how the ill people, the same like me were tragically wandering for many years and were directed from psychiatrists to priests, who also were not able to help them. I observed also their parents depressed, helpless and frightened by the enormity of this illness. I observed how they have lost all heir hope.

To whom I wrote this book?

To all ill people who despite the long struggle day by day have undertaken the spiritual way received the grace of the contemplative prayers, which improved their state. But later they experienced a crisis, with which they were not able to cope – and with their great surprise plunged them in the illness again. I wrote for all ill people who want to undertake the spiritual way – with all its troubles and complications.

The basic thesis of this book is that schizophrenia can be healed, but on the spiritual way – and only under one condition – it has to be undertaken radically. Such thesis I haven't found so far as the method of healing. I observed how many things have changed in my life, how many great moments I have experienced and how the perception of life has changed comparing to the one before the illness.

I will finish with the poem by William Cowper who describes the personal way of the ill person and which can also be a motto of this book.

I was a stricken deer, that left the herd
Long since: with many an arrow deep infixed
My panting side was charged, when I withdrew,
To seek a tranquil death in distant shades.
There was I found by one who had himself
Been hurt by the archers. In his side he bore,
And in his hands and feet, the cruel scars.
With gentle force soliciting the darts,
He drew them forth, and healed, and bade me live.

CHAPTER 23

THE SCHIZOPHRENIC DEPRESSION AND ITS STAGES

In this chapter I will examine the falling into the schizophrenic depression. I will show the succeeding stages of this process. Later, I will compare these stages to the stages of the spiritual progress on the spiritual way.

A beautiful metaphor of the falling into depression is an extract from the poem by William Cowper: *The Castaway*:

Obscurest night involved the sky,
The Atlantic billows roared,
When such a destined wretch as I,
Washed headlong from on board,
Of friends, of hope, of all bereft,
His floating home for ever left.

Not long beneath the whelming brine,
Expert to swim, he lay;
Nor soon he felt his strength decline,
Or courage die away:
But waged with death a lasting strife,
Supported by despair of life.

He shouted; nor his friends had failed
To check the vessel's course,
But so the furious blast prevailed,
That, pitiless perforce,
They left their outcast mate behind,
And scudded still before the wind.

Some succour yet they could afford;
And, such as storms allow,
The cask, the coop, the floated cord,
Delayed not to bestow:
But he, they know, nor ship nor shore,
Whate'er they gave, should visit more.

Nor, cruel as it seemed, could he
Their haste himself condemn,
Aware that flight, in such a sea,
Alone could rescue them:
Yet bitter felt it still to die
Deserted, and his friends so nigh.

He long survives, who lives an hour
In ocean, self-upheld;
And so long he, with unspent power,
His destiny repelled:
And ever, as the minutes flew,
Entreated help, or cried -"Adieu!"

At length, his transient respite past,
His comrades, who before
Had heard his voice in every blast,
Could catch the sound no more:
For then, by toil subdued, he drank
The stifling wave, and then he sank.

Cowper finishes the poem with a sad conclusion:

No voice divine the storm allayed,
No light propitious shone;
When, snatched from all effectual aid,
We perished, each alone;

When is a depression a schizophrenic depression?

When **the emotional memory is overloaded, i.e. the memory concerning the emotions and feelings.** This overloading of the memory with the spiritual contents causes that the emotions and feelings do not act as before, and they do not separate the reaction from the impulse, they merge with the spirit dominating in the environment. **They start to a greater extent to influence the will, to hobble it later.**

What is **a depression** and why does it occur?

In the spirituality **the equivalent of a depression is the night.** Basing on the description of the night, one can explain the phenomenon of depression. A man disintegrated internally after the original sin must with the help of grace lead themselves to the internal unity. In this unification process, the powers of a man must be totally change.

The will must liberate itself from the influence of the lower part and from the schemes of their activity.

The cognition, because of the new purified spiritual cognition, must throw away the preceding natural schemes.

The internal senses: the memory and the imagination must be purified from the accumulated contents.

The emotions and feelings must separate themselves from the transmission of the external impulses, also those coming from the evil spirit.

The initiator of this is the will pulled by God. This pulling causes the adaptation of other powers to this differently arranged will. By the lower parts one can't unify with God, all powers **react to God's presence with the night. It is a sort of temporary trouble, during which they adapt to the new arrangement of the will**. The will and the reason are also affected by the night, because of the close contact with God, which is a sort of the shock to them too. Without the night a man is not able to leave the lowest human level, the sensual level. The adaptation of powers to the new arrangement is alas painful.

The schizophrenic depression is the process opposite to the process of the night. It is the reaction to the hobbling of the will by the evil spirit acting through emotions and feelings and causes the spiritual pain in the feeling.

The night is a stage on the way to the deeper union with God. The depression on every stage finishes with a greater disintegration and a greater hobbling of the will.

As the whole spiritual process leading to the union has its stages, the process of entering in the depression has also its stages, and **they are the reversal of the spiritual way.**

The first stage of the contemplative prayer and the contemplative part of the spiritual way is **the prayer of quiet.** During this stage God pulls the will and has born for the first time by His visible presence in the spiritual heart of a man. **The prayer of quiet extracts from the natural life, from its schemes.** Until it happens, nobody suspects that such possibility of another way exists, this another way is marked by the nature. This is the way initiated by God, by His grace and the way, which leads to Him.

The beginning of the schizophrenic depression is well illustrated by the metaphor of Cowper of fall overboard. Something makes a person separate themselves from their natural schemes, which are natural schemes dominating in the environment. The original injury and a very tender emotionality cause that the memory concerning the emotions is charged and emotions and feelings do not react freely any more, they do not react as they were before. **This touch of emotions and feelings results in different reactions** and it is subjectively perceived as a separation from other people, especially from the people at the same age. It is an astounding phenomenon where suddenly with the emotions and feelings touched by the spirit one can start to perceive the world differently, as if it has changed. The moon shines differently, the sun does not give the shine as before, the dog barks as if it transmitted some kind of a mysterious message, the trees have lost their branches, and the clouds are darker than before. The world perceived before suddenly remained only in the memories. And a person tries to restore this world by force. But even the places visited when a person was happy cannot be recalled. A 20-year-old man **starts to live with their past,** when s/he had the aim in life, when s/he achieved personal successes. As if something had radically changed in their life. Because of the accumulated tensions in their memory, **s/he lives with their past**, or s/he runs away to the future, s/he dreams about the life between the romantic heroes and thinks about their great acts.

And sometimes s/he **escapes to ridicule,** s/he makes a jester of oneself. Generally, s/he is thrown out from the emotional life of their generation, **s/he isolates oneself.** Their life starts to be different from their peers.

Thus, this change in the emotionality and sentimentality results in leaving the world, and it is the equivalent of the extraction from the world during the first contemplative prayers.

The second stage of the spiritual way is **the spiritual intoxication.** God touches the spiritual heart to satiate it with His tender love in such a way that a person will not look for any feelings beside Him. It is the spiritual phenomenon similar to the first love, where the degree of satiation directed to the natural sphere will never repeat itself again. **The task of this period in the spirituality is to separate a person from the natural love, to satiate this love.**

In the schizophrenic depression on this stage one can experience a feeling associated with the desire. Where does it come from and also where does a greater sexual tension in this period come from?

It comes from the overloaded emotional memory and the tensions in the emotions which want to be released. There is some dependence between the emotions and feeling. These two spheres overlap to a certain degree. The greater emotional tension causes a greater tension in the sentimentality and in the sexual sphere. The simplest but wrong release of this tension leads to the sexuality. It is wrong, because it does not remove it. The people who have noticed that they have the tension in the emotional sphere should introduce the active purifications and it is the way to get rid of these tensions. One should not use sexuality for this purpose, which would be the easiest, but it does not eliminate such tensions.

The **third step of the spiritual way is the simple union,** the union of the will. The will is for the first time liberated from the influence of the past emotions and from the sphere of the external world.

In the schizophrenic depression the reversal of this phenomenon takes place which is **the hobbling of the will,** where the will is prisoned by the emotions. The description of this long process can be found in the *Diary* of the Polish poet Jan Lechoń (1899-1956).

1.09.1949 The night was bad. I woke up with the feeling that I am choking – I realise that I am living in a constant fear ...

The fear is the result of the progressing disintegration and the presence of the evil spirit in the emotional memory.

5.09.1949 Bad writing. I have to be careful and not to lose the dramatic plot of the chapter in the analysis. It is very difficult for me to keep the proportions between the characteristic of the episode character and her role in the action.

The poet is conscious of the progressing disintegration. During the disintegration the details start to dominate and come to the fore.

6.09.1949 ...for the first time When I am writing, I don't remember different elements, of different realities. I don't remember how one can buy the tickets in the Paris Metro, how cloak-rooms in the restaurants looked...

The forgetting is the proof that the emotional memory is overloaded.

10.09.1949 Very bad writing. I couldn't restore the yesterday's tone.

Because of the overloaded memory there is no emotional continuity. Emotionality of one day cannot be repeated the next day.

16.09.1949 Today I was persecuted by the stupidly malicious thoughts about a very close person.

The appearance of obsessions which a person cannot throw away (and normally one can do this by the act of the will) is a proof that the will becomes hobbled and the emotional memory starts to be occupied by the evil spirit.

17.09.1949 There is a point in the Park Avenue, when you look up from which you can only see the heaven and no other perspective. It makes impression of the way to nowhere similar to the sight on the Van Dyck square in Bruges. Only there the sense of death relates to the past, but here you can feel the announcement of it, as if the future annihilation or nothingness.

The first characteristic pessimistic thoughts which will be completed on 11 June 1953 by the loss of hope which is **the most characteristic symptom of the hobbling of the will.**

27.09.1949 For some days I have had again such disorder inside and I don't know if it is mental or physical.

6.10.1949 Again the day spent on nothing. Nerves and many small things....But when my balance teeters, only the imagination works and it presents me random things according to its own mysterious pattern. It is sometimes the greatest enemy of the will.

The will is hobbled, disintegrated, as if cut into the pieces. The imagination is not the enemy, but by its hyperactivity it tries to compensate the hobbling.

8.10.1949. Today the first real failure in writing. A few hours by the table without any result, without the possibility to focus thoughts between the worst hesitations and losing the hope that anything can come out of this.

8.10.1949 Probably now I should write poems, because I feel some kind of illogicality, for which the novel is not the best form. This night I was speaking to myself in lyrics...

The dialogue to oneself or somebody is the dialogue with the evil spirit. The spirit is situated in the emotional memory and very often occupies the future ill person.

11.10.1949 Is it possible that I would not rest from this unimaginable duality, which tears me apart, which sense I don't understand, and which relates to everything in me: my thoughts, my feelings, my senses?

3.11.1949 The total failure. No associations between sentences. No melody, everything is doubtful, all words are without strength, colourless.

4.11.1949 The same emptiness in my head and indecision.

8.11.1949 Again such emptiness in myself...

The union of the will is preceded by the emptiness, it also accompanies the hobbling of the will. During the hobbling the emptiness is the result of separation from the environment and the entrance to the sphere of the evil spirit and this spirit present in the emotional memory isolates the future ill person.

13,11.1949 Nearly all my close friends seem to be different to me than some months ago.

This is the most characteristic symptom of the beginning of the hobbling of the will. People change, leave to another not defined space (even if they live nearby), some relations finish only because of this new perception. Of course such new changed perception additionally limited by the spirit isolates the future ill person.

15.11.1949 Great changes in my style of writing. I know that it means something, because I know that there are changes inside me which are absolutely breakthrough.

19.01.1950 My thoughts were dispersed a lot.

25,01.1950 All day the struggle between the will to write and the fear that this would not go on.

The lapses in concentration are the next result of the hobbling of the will.

12.02.1950 Morning and evening by the desk...and between the returning attacks of anger.

14,02.1950 ...internally, I am troubled and lost...

Greater and greater consciousness of the own internal disorder.

20.03.1950 Today again the great tiredness and terrible emptiness in my head and in my feelings.

28.05.1950 I have the feeling of almost physical intervention of the foreign wills in my life. Some feelings, acts, relations contradictory to what I wanted are independent of my will. I seem to be asleep and in this dream the new reality inside and around me is created.

13.07.1950 I am short of the French words. In brain there is either "calcium" or big nerves.

The sudden loss of the memory and a great tension are one of the most characteristic traits of this period.

12.09.1950 Some hours by the desk without any result. I couldn't get through different pictures...

The pictures in the overloaded emotional memory start to live their own spiritual life.

20. 08.1950 I tried to return to the narrative tone, which would introduce me to the action again and to permit me to finish this chapter. Unfortunately! I am full of my own complications...

Progressing disintegration causes the complications in the cognition.

1.09.1950 Again I see my despair and helplessness and lack of ways. It is very hard to me.

The evil spirit limiting the spiritual cognition tries to close all possible ways of exit from the situation.

30.11.1950 ...something went wrong with my sensitivity, some sort of stupefaction – I am reading and there are no affections, no impressions.

7.07.1951 The constant lack of Polish words, of invention. Both in writing and speaking, I am forgetting different things and I must note everything down.

The problems with the articulation of thoughts are the next symptom of this period and the result of the overloaded emotional memory.

13.08.1951 I have terrible emptiness in my head and I force myself to write a few sentences daily.

21.08.1950 I have the feeling of total internal emptiness, but also of hope that something new can be created, or something will be created in me.

5.08.1952 For the first time since I arrived here I feel tired not with the heat, but with New York and America. To rest in an unknown country, between strange, indifferent people, not to feel like in the centre of the world, but to be with myself all the time.

For the first time the "perforation of the system" is visible. The spirit dominating in the environment starts to overload the ill person, while before it was neutral. The structure of the centre of emotions starts to break spiritually, it is the structure which previously protected from the external influences.

In October 1952 the emptiness and lapses of concentration appear again, but the "perforation of the system" will cause growing tiredness.

20.01.1953 One page about America. Despite the tiredness...

23.01.1953 I wrote one page despite the tiredness.

27.03. 1953 In the evening I struggled with the real tiredness...

10.03.1953 Three pages. I think that this is a triumph, because today I was tired, I don't know why...

11.03.1953 Three pages: the triumph over the tiredness...

12.03.1953 ...and later crazy tiredness.

15.03.1953 Three pages, despite the tiredness...
21.03.1953 I don't remember such tiredness as I felt yesterday...
24.03.1953 In the morning I was very tired...
27.03.1953 But I was so tired...

One of the most important symptoms of the hobbled will and additionally of the "perforation of the system" is **the appearance of permanent tiredness**. It is the reversal of the spiritual lightness which appears with the union of the will, because of its liberation from the influence of memory concerning the emotions and feeling.

22.05.1953 I didn't do anything. I am walking like an idiot, I don't know which way to go.

The natural will which follows the thesis "I want" is hobbled.

11.06.1953 Today two stanzas or all the poem, which is called Chełmoński or the Homeland. Not planned, written in five minutes, who knows whether it is any good.

One can say that this poem is very good because it shows **the most important factor of the troubled will: the loss of hope on the basic level** (it means without breaking of the imagination which will happen after 3 years).
The last two lines in free translation are:

I know what I need – I miss my homeland,
Which has never been and is not on the map.

Something definitively finishes and will never come back. The consciousness of this for the first time reached so deeply, and it will be a background for the future life. **It is a turning point** of falling in the depression.
The hobbling of the will is a process. It does not occur as violently as the invasion of the spirit to the spiritual heart. In the example of the poet mentioned above, it lasts almost 4 years. Lechoń was

50-54 years old, he took the medicines, he prayed which made the process slow down. In the case of a young person such hobbling lasts 6-12 months, but the states are exactly the same as the states described above. One can recognize the hobbling only because of them. **One can recognize that it happened by the changes which take place the next time.**

The person with the hobbled will is deprived of defence. S/he will not block the knocks of the spirit by the will nor by the emotions which have stopped to react, nor by the hobbled feeling which doesn't react properly.

In the spirituality on this stage **the simple union, the union of the will takes place.** The characteristic trait of it is the liberation of the will from the influence of the emotions and feeling. The will is free for the first time, liberated from the domination of the lower part, liberated from the influence of the spiritual environment. As a result of the spiritual development, **the emotions and the feeling will not transmit the stimulus coming from outside,** from the world. The external world stops to hurt – as it did till now. It will go its own way or rather it will stay at one place – with its schemes for centuries. God will separate from the world and attach a man who tries to turn to Him to Himself.

In the troubled will it will be exactly opposite. **The overloaded memory prisons the will so much that it is not able to liberate itself from the hobbling.** For the first time the thoughts that there is no exit from this situation and everything is determined appear. The quasi concentration of the emotions and feelings takes place. They get stiff, they will not react to the external impulses. Because of this **the ill person will not amortise the knocks from outside that s/he receives.** A person is merged with the environment, the hobbled will is not able to liberate itself from this state. The devil will use it **to give the series of brutal knocks which reach the centre of the soul.** These knocks will go to the deepest layers of the soul. **The process of destroying the future ill person will accelerate in a terrible way.**

The moment of the union of the will is clear and one can feel it visibly. As I have already written, the image of Christ who enters by the closed door is a good illustration of it.

In the hobbling of the will this moment is expressed with **the first deeper reflection about the impossibility of exit from this state which looks like some kind of a trap.** After that, (it lasts about 2-3 months), the nature of the devil's knocks changes. The devil starts to knock with a great precision and these knocks reaching the depth of the soul. The devil destroys the future ill person very quickly, because he deprived them of the possibility of defence.

The union of the will is preceded by **the spiritual emptiness,** which one should experience. The hobbling of the will is announced by the loss of memory which makes **the reason defect.**

The unitive way after the union of the will starts with **the wound of love** made by God. The soul perceives this touch made by God as wounded. The aim of this wound is to deeper pull the soul to God. God wounds and goes away. In this way He pulls to Himself. The wounded person starts to look for God with greater intensity.

At this stage in the depression **the flash of great sentimentality appears.** And the next stage of the depression starts. The feeling as if it wanted to extract itself from the hobbling and to pull the hobbled will and liberate it from this hobbling. Of course, it is not possible.

Very often it is an old feeling which now appeared suddenly with a great, new power. And because of this explosion a person is totally dominated. In the hospitals one can meet people dominated by this feeling and talking about it. One can meet also the object of such feeling, a person embarrassed and irritated by it, showing that s/he did not want such a huge feeling.

The example of such feeling after the hobbling of the will is described by Lermontov in the poem *Demon.*

I love you with no earthly passion,
such love that you can never find:
with rapture, in the towering fashion
of an immortal heart and mind.
On my sad soul, from world's first aeon,

deeply your image was impressed;
ever before me it progressed
through wastes of timeless empyrean.
My thoughts had long been stirred and racked
by just one name of passing sweetness:
my days in paradise has lacked
just your perfection for completeness.

A host of souls who owe me duty
I'll bring, I'll throw them at your feet;
magically for you, my beauty,
handmaids will labour, deft and fleet;
for you from the eastern star I'll ravish
a golden crown; I'll take for you
from flowers the midnight dew, and lavish
upon your crown that selfsame dew;
I'll bring a sunset ray; ecstatic,
I'll clasp it, belt-like, round your waist,
with breath of healing aromatic
the airs around you will be laced;
all day the strains of heavenly playing
will lull your hearing with their tune;
I'll build you halls with an inlaying
of turquoise, rooms with amber strewn;
I'll sound the bottom of the ocean,
high up above the clouds ill climb,
all, all, that's earthly, my devotion
will give you – love me!...

Mikhail Lermontov poem *Demon* from *Narrative Poems of lexander Pushkin and Mikhail Lermontov*, translation by Charles Johnston

During the spiritual way some time after such a deep wound the ecstasy occurs. I described it in chapter 21. The ecstasy is experienced by the concentrated soul. During the ecstasy the structure is not damaged because the ecstasy touches only a person who is internally concentrated and purified. The ecstasy after a certain time leads to the night, physical powers go out, one can see the element of darkness, psychotic, demoniacal, providential described before as stages of the new higher level of spirituality.

There is a moment in the depression when this non-fulfilled feeling (because it can't be fulfilled) causes a great tension leading to the breaking of the physical and mental structure. The future ill person who wanted to fulfil their enormous feeling **becomes indifferent,** enters in **a sort of stupefaction.** S/he moves to another spiritual space as if falling one step down. But simultaneously s/he liberates from this feeling. As a result of the destruction of the structure, their body does not react any more to the training stimulus as before.

Between the period of the hobbling of the will and the invasion of the spirit to the spiritual heart, a new group of symptoms appears. In the life of Lechoń this period lasted from June 1953 to April 1956.

13.06.1953 ...today I had such a terrible day that I hadn't had for years. I am cut out from the world, locked in myself, although I react normally. But this normality is a mechanism, a consciousness about how I should behave as if the instinct died in me. Writing, it seemed to me during some days, can be a sort of return to myself. Until today I haven't reached a point of dark despair thanks to writing.

17.06.1953 A fatal day of total neurasthenia, I don't enjoy anything and myself the least.

19.06.1953 I wrote the last five verses out of the darkest solitude and despair.

The evil spirit together with the hobbling of the will deprived of the defence, now he wants to quickly destroy the man. The nature of the attacks changes. Dark long series of insolent knocks from different sides appear leading to the destruction.

20.08.1953 Two pages – what I wanted, but not how I wanted it.
22.08.1953 Two pages, too long sentences, too many digressions.
23.08.1953 Too many unnecessary words on the two pages written today. When I examined them in the evening I was frightened that I didn't notice this garrulity in the morning.

Too many words prove the psychotic element. The spirit breaks the next level in the man and this always causes a psychosis.

15.09.1953 ...the thoughts overlap one another. ...finally all was too pompous, too definitive.
16.09.1953 My writing was bad. All foggily, all beside. The preceding pages seemed too garrulous, too trivial when I was reading them today.

The psychotic element results in the cognitive complications.

8.11.1953 I was stopping all the time, my thoughts were running away, I could barely pull out my voice. I felt the emptiness in my mind and terrible tiredness.
9.11.1953 I can't remember when I had such a stage fright as before this speech.
25.11.1953 The same as yesterday, this tiredness not with the work but with the repulsion to what I have to do.
5.12.1953 The mind is totally empty.
10.12.1953 I went to bad tired with the talking which I cannot bear any more.
14.12.1953 My speech (on the radio) could cheat other people, but not me. It was a twaddle, not a speech...I was repeating the same all the time...
6.12.1953 Recently, I talked too much and my mind is empty.
17.01.1954 Bigger and bigger problems with the memory.
22,01.1954 I bought a too bright tie, too vulgar shoes, clothes.

A greater internal disorder translated to the external appearance.

18.03.1954 ...I couldn't sleep almost all night.
19.03.1954 The second night I couldn't sleep and I feel terrible.
28.03.1954 I have had terrible nights for one week.

The sleeplessness is the symptom of extremely overloaded emotional memory.

6.04.1954 Wild tiredness after two sleepless nights despite taking double Luminal. Terrible solitude.
9.04.1954 ...Tiredness for the rest of the day, anger at oneself and others.
11.04.1954 Unwillingness to do anything.
1.05.1954 On a day like today, when I don't want to do anything and I don't like anything.
14.04.1954 ...how I lost myself in the details.

Hobbling, paralysis of the will. Cognitive disintegration.

15.05.1954 A sudden attack of fury at oneself and all the world, because of unedited volumes of my poetry and unfinished poems.

Insatiability, non-fulfilment are the states opposite to the states after the union of the will.

10.06.1954 I understood that I have emptiness, or as if emptiness in my head, or my heart, or my imagination.
29.06.1954 ...my thoughts were elsewhere and I didn't know where.
20.07.1954 The day so bad that I don't remember for a long time. Dark pessimism, repulsion to the work, mad irritation at everybody I don't know why. A crazy feeling of the wasted life.
27.07.1954 The most horrible in this tiredness is the feeling that only now I can see the reality and it is terrible. I am so empty and so depressed that I am not able to have my own reality which would return and change that reality.

It is the beginning of the tearing of the centre of emotions. The devil tries to enter with his own harassing consciousness, of course to cause pain and destroy a man. He does it in the spiritual way, using the disposition for contemplation, because this is a spiritual cognition hugely false, coming from the devil.

28.07.1954 I wrote two pages about Tuwim (Polish poet J.T.), looking for the words with a great effort. But also with some surprises, it means that something is inside me. But I don't know totally how to take it out from inside and not to tremble because of the tiredness, because of the emptiness in my mind which is also the emptiness of my soul.

When he enters, the evil spirit makes it impossible to take out the cognition previously fulfilled in the other spirit.

6.08.1954 Today such advice was given to me that I was not able to calm down for several hours.

4.11.1954 Sudden impoliteness from somebody who did not look like to someone who would do this. One should force oneself to keep strong, but it will not help a lot.

The characteristic trait of this period is that the evil spirit attacks from every side by the frontal insolent attacks made by people as if arranged, influencing them by their not correctly arranged wills and attacking by them the future ill person. The resistance falls down rapidly, a relatively weak spiritual knock triggers greater and greater consequences.

26.03.1955 What a hideous day, again the change of the weather and nerves are trembling because of this. Besides, Libra, my dear, beloved, the tenderest and now insensitive Libra, always invisible. All the time it seemed to me that Rudolf and Mimi (in La Boheme by Puccini) are me and Libra.

2.04.1955 With me and Libra it is over. One little person and in many opinions such a "normal" deprived me of the illusions.

4.04.1955 Dear Libra! I did not want, I really did not want it and I feel very bad without You.

14.04.1955 It is You little Libra who made me stop believing that I will write anything in my life and all seems to me to be small, boring and not worth of the effort.

18.05.1955 Libra my dear, my lovely who doesn't know, You can't know how bad I feel without You and who You are to me. Tell me what I should do that you will start to think about me as before.

18.05.1955 Libra is my favourite flower, favourite smell, favourite colour, this is not my love, but something that I like the most in the world.

In this period (after the hobbling of the will) **the explosion of the great feeling** takes place. This explosion which wanted to be extracted from the hobbling, but this attempt of extraction after some time makes one going down. As I have written, it happens often in this period.

16.07.1955 I have a feeling that the world stood at one place and I look at it without any feeling.

It is the total blockade of emotions and feelings.

4.09.1955 My fuddle for some months. Something has fallen down internally in me which is not myself.

6.09.1955 Few sentences, all of them worthless. I think that simply I don't know how to write. That I have nothing inside me, that I have told everything. And it is very bad with me, inside, in my soul, in the terrible empty soul.

11,09.1955 My mind is empty like a barn before the harvests.

18.09.1955 All my thoughts are so old banalities, many time repeated by me and no new composition of the words appears in my mind.

The total intellectual stupefaction takes place. Now **the internal powers will go away.**

27.09.1955 I only have examined 10 pages and my powers went out. Something happened with me. I am missing something inside, but no doctor discovered it till now.

3.01.1956 I didn't do anything after that, and for the first time for some weeks I am tired physically not with work, but because of nerves.

Going away of the internal powers takes place very often during the night of spirit. Also the powers go away before the consummated union which is the last union with God. The internal powers simply go away, and after some time they come back. It is very difficult, because any attempts at changing this state do not help. The man is totally defenceless when it occurs. In the illness **this state is practically the last characteristic state before the invasion of the evil spirit to the spiritual heart.**

I have known personally a person who had the schizophrenic depression, and whose powers went out. The psychologist to whom this person talked did not diagnosed this condition correctly and did not refer this ill person immediately to the hospital. After 3 weeks this person committed suicide, because hardly anyone is able to recover from this condition with their own forces. I would like to pay attention of all clinical psychologists to this frequent dangerous condition.

Now the evil spirit leads to **the invasion to the spiritual heart.** The "awaking" from the old life happens. This awaking has the tragic dimension, because the presence of the spirit causes a great pain, from which it is no possible to liberate oneself. This presence is very painful and the reality (or rather a part of it shown by the spirit) is very painful too.

Awaking in the ecstasy is connected with the properties of the soul to exit from itself and because of it with the new spiritual cognition. After the invasion of the spirit the physical structure is torn. There is new, incisive cognition (which proves its spiritual character). The invasion practically causes (after a short time) the breaking of the limbic system. So, there is clarity without the ill emotions and feeling which limited the cognition before.

Descriptions of this extraordinary struggle from this period of the invasion of the spirit to the spiritual heart can be found also in the "Diary" of Jan Lechoń from1956.

23.02.1956 In each of us, which is banal, some people are situated. They are brothers between them or close relatives. In me alas, only two people are situated who have nothing common and they are in the constant war with themselves.

6.03.1956 My thoughts were entangling and all seemed mysterious and complicated. And naturally one doesn't know from where it comes and how to avoid it.

8.03.1956 I wrote one page and I was short of words and I was not able to exit from the blind alley as many times before. I am nearly sure that I was turning around these thoughts which I was writing in this article.

25.03.1956 For some days I have felt like on the boxer's ring – when I get up I am knocked down. I keep strong but every thing that I catch is burning and spearing. For some days I have the inflow of hostility, no lenience, although outside I am playing the naive friendliness.

7.04.1956 Today a great trouble not a problem, it is rather misery. Unexpectedly, against all forecasts of the experts. I felt everything opposite to the forecasts of all these experts, to all this misery now the feeling of something beyond the reason is added, the consciousness that the presentiments and omens are more important than the logic and reality. God, good God please don't leave me!

One can suppose that the invasion of the spirit took place on 7 April. The next day will confirm this tragic condition as the lack of hope and dark periods get longer and longer. The evil spirit harasses in a terrible way which is difficult to stand. **This pain will tear the centre of emotions** and it will be the next step of the depression.

8.04.1956 So bad that it seems it cannot be worse. As Cocteau writes about Marie Bell who played Fedra that she doesn't know where to place the soul – me the same – I don't know either. Everything that my thought touches, there is something I don't want to think about it.

9.04.1956 The trouble from yesterday is a little less important, simply because yesterday was too dreadful. But a new similar one came and there is no end to it.

11.04.1956 I feel like I didn't write anything and I will never write anything in the future. And as if I wasn't myself.

12.04.1956 Running away from the sorrow, later the statement that we do not direct our life, that there is no justice and no mercy and no reward for the virtue...For some days my life seems to be "a tale told by an idiot"– gloomy and lousy.

14.04.1956 Very difficult. So difficult that I feel like a tragic hero face to face with the fate. And I am surprised that it is me...

16.04.1956 Yesterday it was so terrible that today it should be better, although I know that nothing has changed.

19.04.1956 ...the wild tiredness – I didn't do anything.

22.04.1956 On the outside there is peace, self-control, even humour. I know what I should do and what I should feel, but inside there is revolt, madness, and this is what I really feel.

23.04.1956 Horrible night and all the day was woozy.

25.04.1956 Bad thoughts and only a little desensitized by the work.

28.04.1956 I go to bed tired and anxious.

3.05.1956 What was yesterday, was one week ago, and two weeks ago. Only I am so tired that I didn't suffer.

5.05.1956 I am still far away from myself and I am afraid to go nearer – I am so hurt.

9.05.1956 Nightmarish night and the day was not better. I tried to write something at least as a medicament to my horrible nervous breakdown I was not able to write even two lines and what I have written till now looked like without melody and sense.

15.05.1956 The radio programme was not good or actually I was not good in it. Later all the day running away from myself. In the evening terrible sorrow.

16.05.1956 All the dramas in life one can endure, as one can believe that one can change something in them by own will. If the thought comes that the fate makes a fool of ourselves the tragedy starts, and there is no place for Christian God, because there is no mercy. And in this time only an honour, the stone face which one should show to the people and to gods – without hope, reward, respect, with only one problem – not to present oneself under one's own fate, under the terrible misery.

17.05.1956 I have a feeling that I woke up from the dream of almost all my life that since my childhood when I was crying during the nights because of the thought that "we shall die." I had not experienced such pessimism which no life forces could handle.

This is the next characteristic moment in the schizophrenic depression – **the tearing of the centre of emotions**. The barrier of emotions and feelings through which the ill person perceived the world is eliminated. The world is fully perceived as real, but in this case this perception is caused by painful invasion of the spirit to the spiritual heart. Perception by through the spirit, only a part of the reality is spiritually perceived – only the negative one. Such perception does not give any hope. The devil causes pain and he closed the full perception and the full perspective of the ill person, and he damaged the physical structure. **Through this enormous pain, he wants to totally destroy the man.**

18.05.1956 The day lost. Sadness, tiredness. Very bad.

19.05.1956 Again the day of crazy sorrow and new complications.

21.05.1956 Only one stanza of the poem, which came to my mind or rather to my troubled heart. And after this, endless despair and humility.

22.05.1956 And such mental waves went through me as if somebody hypnotised me from outside. First very bad, then fine.

24.05.1956 A very bad day, I was not able to do anything.

25.05.1956 Today such big worry that I cannot bear it, nor understand it, nor express it. I behave as if nothing had happened and momentary I catch myself on this illusion that everything is like before. But it is not, and nothing is the same like after the death of another person.

26.05.1956 All the time the same sorrow on the bottom and only one can simulate (worse and worse) that it is otherwise.

27.05.1956 But today it was the worst day for some years, for many years. I went to pieces and I told many people (about my problem), because I was not able to stop it.

28.05.1956 As today is better, because yesterday was one of the worst days of my life. And I am surprised that today I had some hours of forgetting.

The forgetting is the reason for the whole system of perception to defect. This is also a typical state of this stage, once the painful consciousness changes to some kind of dementia, where the reason doesn't react and doesn't perceive and so on.

29.05.1956 Nothing new. A pole of the tough sorrow in me. And hardly am I able to go among people because it is so painful to smile and not to tell what I should tell – and I should shout about what is now inside me.

30.05.1956 I cannot express what I have been through today. Not in my life but inside myself. I came back home late and it seemed to me that all was imagined, that I create the problems myself, which are not in my life. But I know that it is simply the tiredness. But I know that it is only the child's illusion which came to allow me rest for a moment. One can always find in the intelligence, in the will, in the heart something that will help us in the struggle against the life and against people. But in the struggle against oneself there is only prayer.

8.06.1956 Suicidal death: the jump from the high floor of the hotel in New York.

These descriptions after the invasion of the evil spirit are very valuable. They show how the evil spirit acts later. And how he breaks the imagination after the invasion. The imagination in the opinion of the medieval mystiques is the lower part of the soul and is associated with the sensuality which is the highest part of the human body. Because of this, **the devil is able to break it only in the end.**

The breaking of the imagination is associated with a cruel harassment depriving a man of any hope. Psychiatrists define this state as **anxiety** which does not really express this terrible suffering during this state.

The most common division of the stages of the spiritual way is the division based on the Carmelite spirituality. From the first contemplative prayers – **the prayer of quiet,** the satiation of the sphere of the sentiment is **the spiritual intoxication.** Later there is a **simple union (the union of the will),** then **the ecstatic union,** and in the end **the consummated union** with the image of the Holy Trinity.

One can meet many cases of schizophrenic depression where falling into depression occurs according to the specific spiritual key. The successive stages are: **hobbling of the emotions, insatiability of the sphere of the sentiment, hobbling of the will, invasion of the spirit to the spiritual heart together with the breaking of the centre of emotions.** All these stages have their characteristic symptoms.

What conclusions can be drawn on the basis of the described above comparison of the spiritual way to the falling into schizophrenic depression?

The way of the person falling into depression is the reversal of the spiritual way of the person with the disposition for contemplation. Such person has the spiritual levels which can be offered to God or the evil spirit tries to occupy them.

The people with the disposition for contemplation need more time to develop their spiritual abilities. One should not force them to lead the active life, as one can do with the people predisposed for the active life. **The activism destroys the spirituality** and it can lead to the depression. **It not a fault of such people but the fault of inadequate spiritual way forced on them, which makes the spiritual development impossible or kills their spiritual life.** The possessed from Gerasa was the product of his environment. **Alas, the theses which now prevail about the lack of the spiritual influence of the environment on the outset of the illness are totally wrong.**

The new spiritual way marked by Christ, which draws away from the worn-out patterns dominating in the natural life and from the "prophets" who articulate them, leads to the complete self-fulfilment and the union with God. It completes what these natural patterns lack and which is an inherent quality of a man who is composed of the body and the immortal soul.

CHAPTER 24

BIBLIOGRAPHY

Quotations taken from The Holy Bible, New International Version®
NIV® Copyright © 1973 1978 1984 2011by Biblica, Inc. TM Used
by permission. All righs reserved worldwide

William Cowper *Hymns XXXVII Temptation* The complete poetical works of William Cowper University of Michigan

Chapter 1
Mihai Eminescu poem *Of the hundreds of tall ships* translated by
Roy MacGregor-Hastie Poems Dacia Publishing House Cluj –
Napoca 1980
Francis Scott Fitzgerald *The Great Gatsby* Cambridge University
Press 1991
Eugene O'Neil *Long Day's Journey Into the Night* Complete Plays
© The library of America 1984

Chapter 3
Goethe poem *A little violet stood upon the meadow* translated from
German to English by Sharon Krebs © 2015 by Sharon Krebs –
source lieder.net website used by permission
Eugene O'Neil *Long day's journey into the night* Complete Plays ©
The library of America 1984
Shelley *Prometheus Unbound* The Complete Poetical Works of Percy Bysshe Shelley Edited by Thomas Hutchinson London 1927

Chapter 4
Jules Lefèvre-Deumier *Le passé* translation Janusz Tomasik

Chapter 6

Vincent Van Gogh – The Letters source – Van Gogh Museum Amsterdam From letter 244 – To Theo van Gogh. The Hague, Thursday, 6 July 1882

Chapter 7

The sentence of *Diary* of John Lechoń, translated by Janusz Tomasik

Chapter 8

Excepts from Richars of St. Victor: The Twelve Patriarchs, The Mystical Ark, Book Three of the Trinity. Translation and Introduction By Grover Zin, © 1969 by Paulist Press New York/Mahwah,NJ Used by permission of Paulist Press.

Shelley *Prometheus Unbound* preface The Complete Poetical Works of Percy Bysshe Shelley Edited by Thomas Hutchinson London 1927

Vincent Van Gogh – The Letters source – Van Gogh Museum Amsterdam From letter 419 – To Theo van Gogh. Nuenen, on or about Friday, 4 January 1884

J.W.Goethe *Faust* translation Walter Kaufmann Anchor Books Doubleday & Company INC. New York 1961

Chapter 15

William Cowper poem *On the Reed* The complete poetical works of William Cowper University of Michigan

Chapter 19

Saint John of the Cross *A Spiritual Canticle of the Soul* translated by David Lewis Prior of St. Luke's Wincanton 1909

Chapter 21

Saint John of the Cross *A Spiritual Canticle of the Soul* translated by David Lewis Prior of St. Luke's Wincanton 1909

Adam Mickiewicz *Selected poems* edited by Clark Mills The Noonday Press New York 1957

Juliusz Słowacki poem *King-Ghost* fragments translated by Janusz Tomasik

Chapter 22

William Cowper *The Task – Book III The Garden* (fragments) The poetical works of William Cowper London, Edinburgh, New York 1855

Chapter 23

William Cowper poem *The Castaway* The poetical works of William Cowper London, Edinburgh, New York 1855

Jan Lechoń *Diary* 1949-1956 fragment translated by Janusz Tomasik

Jan Lechoń poem *Chełmoński or Homeland* translation by Janusz Tomasik

Mikhail Lermontov poem *Demon* from *Narrative Poems of Alexander Pushkin and Mikhail Lermontov*, translation by Charles Johnston Translation, copyright © 1979 1980 1981 1982 1983 by Charles Johnston

Used by permission of Random House, an imprint and division of Penguin Randon House LLC. All rigrts reserved.